Grigory I. Tunkin and Rüdiger Wolfrum (eds.)

International Law and Municipal Law

Veröffentlichungen des Instituts für
Internationales Recht an der Universität Kiel

Herausgegeben von

Jost Delbrück · Wilhelm A. Kewenig · Rüdiger Wolfrum

103

International Law and Municipal Law

Proceedings
of the
German-Soviet Colloquy on International Law
at the
Institut für Internationales Recht
an der Universität Kiel
4 to 8 May 1987

Edited by

Grigory I. Tunkin and Rüdiger Wolfrum

Assistant Editor:

J. Enno Harders

Duncker & Humblot / Berlin

Gedruckt mit Unterstützung der Fritz Thyssen Stiftung, Köln

CIP-Titelaufnahme der Deutschen Bibliothek

International law and municipal law: proceedings of the German-Soviet Colloquy on Internat. Law at the Inst. für Internat. Recht an d. Univ. Kiel, 4 to 8 May 1987 / ed. by Grigory I. Tunkin and Rüdiger Wolfrum. Assistant ed.: J. Enno Harders. - Berlin: Duncker u. Humblot, 1988
(Veröffentlichungen des Instituts für Internationales Recht an der Universität Kiel; 103)
ISBN 3-428-06426-7
NE: Tunkin, Grigorij Ivanovič [Hrsg.]; German-Soviet Colloquy on International Law <1987, Kiel>; Institut für Internationales Recht <Kiel>; Veröffentlichungen des Instituts ...

Satz und Druck: Vollbehr u. Strobel, Kiel
Printed in Germany

ISBN 3-428-06426-7

Preface

Scholars of public international law both from the Union of Soviet Socialist Republics and the Federal Republic of Germany convened for the third time to hold a colloquy on public international law. After 1982 in Heidelberg and 1984 in Moscow, 21 participants met in May 1987 at the Institute of International Law of the Christian-Albrechts-Universität at Kiel for another German-Soviet Colloquy on International Law, specifically discussing the interrelation of "International Law and Municipal Law".

The forum provided for an intensive dialogue and discussion of ideas and opinions concerning the reach of international law into municipal law. Although differences of thought remained, which were partly due to the subject matters discussed, *e. g.*, the Council for Mutual Economic Assistance and the European Communities, respectively, there has been more common ground covered by the Colloquy than most of the participants may have anticipated. As the Proceedings reveal, this was especially the case in regard to the deliberations on the significance of United Nations resolutions. Again, nuances in perception of self-executing norms of international law generally, and regarding human rights specifically, emerged — nuances, however, which resulted from differences of the two constitutional systems under review and pertinent application of international law by their domestic courts. On the Colloquy's major task though, the topic of incorporation of various rules of international law into municipal law, there was wide agreement.

Our colleague *Theodor Schweisfurth*, Heidelberg, greatly contributed to the German-Soviet Colloquy on International Law, its coming into being, and its development on a permanent basis.

In this process, it appeared of consequence to the *Editors* to dedicate this third Colloquy to one single subject area and finally to have the Proceedings jointly published. It is trusted that the publication will provide another stepping-stone for a continued series of the German-Soviet Colloquy on International Law and that it may enhance one of its major aims, the furtherance of international understanding.

The funding of the Colloquy by the *Deutsche Forschungsgemeinschaft* and the *Fritz Thyssen Stiftung* as well as for the publication of the Proceedings by the *Fritz Thyssen Stiftung* is gratefully acknowledged.

Moscow/Kiel, in March 1988

Grigory I. Tunkin   Rüdiger Wolfrum

Contents

Abbreviations

ADD	=	Addendum to UN document
AJIL	=	American Journal of International Law
al. / alt.	=	alternative
AöR	=	Archiv des öffentlichen Rechts
Art. (s.)	=	Article(s)
BGB	=	Bürgerliches Gesetzbuch (Civil Code of the Federal Republic of Germany)
BGH	=	Bundesgerichtshof (Federal Supreme Court — on Civil / Criminal Matters — of the Federal Republic of Germany)
BGHZ	=	Entscheidungen des Bundesgerichtshofes in Zivilsachen (Reports of the Federal Supreme Court, Civil Matters, of the Federal Republic of Germany)
BGHSt	=	Entscheidungen des Bundesgerichtshofes in Strafsachen (Reports of the Federal Supreme Court, Criminal Matters, of the Federal Republic of Germany)
BVerfG	=	Bundesverfassungsgericht (Federal Constitutional Court of the Federal Republic of Germany)
BVerfGE	=	Entscheidungen des Bundsverfassungsgerichts (Reports of the Federal Constitutional Court of the Federal Republic of Germany)
CMEA	=	Council for Mutual Economic Assistance
CMLRev.	=	Common Market Law Review
COMECON	=	Council for Mutual Economic Assistance
comp.	=	compiler
CPSU	=	Communist Party of the Soviet Union
Doc.	=	Document
EC	=	European Community/European Communities: -European Economic Community, -European Coal and Steel Community, -European Atomic Energy Community
ECHR	=	European Convention on Human Rights
ECR	=	Reports of the Court of Justice of the European Communities
ECJ	=	Court of Justice of the European Communites
ECSC	=	European Coal and Steel Community
ed(s.)	=	editor(s)
EEC	=	European Economic Community
EEZ	=	Exclusive Economic Zone
EP	=	European Parliament
EPC	=	European Political Co-operation
EPIL	=	Encyclopedia of Public International Law, *Rudolf Bernhardt* (ed.), Instalments 1—10, Amsterdam / New York / Oxford 1981—1987
et al.	=	et alii

etc.	=	et cetera
EURATOM	=	European Atomic Energy Community
EWG	=	Europäische Wirtschaftsgemeinschaft (European Economic Community)
FAO	=	Food and Agriculture Organization of the United Nations
GA	=	General Assembly of the United Nations
GAOR	=	General Assembly Official Records (of the United Nations)
GATT	=	General Agreement on Tariffs and Trade
G.C.D.	=	General Conditions for Delivery of the Council for Mutual Economic Assistance
GG	=	Grundgesetz (Basic Law of the Federal Republic of Germany)
GYIL	=	German Yearbook of International Law
ibid.	=	ibidem
ICAO	=	International Civil Aviation Organization
I.C.J.	=	International Court of Justice
I.C.J. Reports	=	Reports of Judgments, Advisory Opinions and Orders of the International Court of Justice
id.	=	idem
ILO	=	International Labour Organisation
IMF	=	International Monetary Fund
ILA	=	International Law Association
ILM	=	International Legal Materials
Inst.	=	Instalment
ITU	=	International Telecommunication Union
JöR	=	Jahrbuch des öffentlichen Rechts
lit.	=	littera
NATO	=	North Atlantic Treaty Organization
No.	=	Number
NYIL	=	Netherlands Yearbook of International Law
OECD	=	Organisation for Economic Co-operation and Development
OEEC	=	Organization for European Economic Co-operation
ÖZöRV	=	Österreichische Zeitschrift für öffentliches Recht und Völkerrecht
para.	=	paragraph
PCIJ	=	Permanent Court of International Justice
RdC	=	Académie de Droit International, Recueil des Cours
RIW	=	Recht der internationalen Wirtschaft
RSFSR	=	Rossijskaja Sovetskaja Federativnaja Socialističeskaja Respublik (Russian Soviet Federated Socialist Republic)
SALT II	=	Strategic Arms Limitation Talks, 1979
SEA	=	Single European Act of the EC, 1987
sent.	=	sentence
seq.	=	sequentes
SU of the RSFSR	=	Sobranie uzakoneij i rasporiazhenij RSFSR (Collected Legislation of the RSFSR)
transl.	=	translator

UN	=	United Nations
UN Doc.	=	United Nations document
UNCTAD	=	United Nations Conference on Trade and Development
UNESCO	=	United Nations Educational, Scientific and Cultural Organisation
UNICEF	=	United Nations Children's Fund
Vedomosti SSSR	=	Vedomosti Verchovnogo Soveta Sojuza Sovetskich Socialističeskich Respublik (News Bulletin of the Supreme Soviet of the Union of Soviet Socialist Republics)
vol.	=	Volume(s)
WHO	=	World Health Organization
ZRP	=	Zeitschrift für Rechtspolitik

Application of Customary International Law to Municipal Law

By Gennady M. Danilenko*

Ladies and Gentlemen, dear Colleagues:

I am the first speaker and it is my pleasant duty to express, on behalf of all Soviet participants, the gratitude for the hospitality of our hosts in this beautiful city of Kiel. I hope that this Colloquy and the envisaged publication of the papers will be a success.

My assignment is to discuss the application of customary international law to municipal law. I will not dwell on various theories on the nature of the relation between international and municipal law. Rather, I intend to *focus on conditions* in which rules of customary law are given effect in the municipal sphere.

In preparing my paper I thought that I might most usefully deal with this topic by commenting on two related issues. First, I will make some general remarks on methods of implementation of customary international law. Then, I intend to deal briefly with some problems that might arise in this connection in view of the specific nature of customary law.

Although international customary law is supposed, strictly speaking, to regulate relations only between States, in many instances it cannot be realized unless its normative content is adequately implemented in municipal law. In particular, domestic implementation require customary rules aimed at establishing a certain pattern of relations involving subjects of national law.

Application of international customary law to municipal law depends directly on the applicability of custom at international level. International customary law is incorporated or transformed into municipal law only in cases where the relations of a given State with other subjects of international law are not regulated by existing treaty rules. For instance, prior to 1986 the USSR was not a party to the Vienna Convention on the Law of Treaties[1]. Correspondingly, the provisions of the 1978 Decree on

* Dr., Senior Researcher at the Institute of State and Law of the Academy of Sciences of the USSR.

[1] UN Doc. A/CONF. 39/27 Rev. I (1970).

the Procedure for the Conclusion, Execution, and Denunciation of International Agreements of the USSR[2], to the effect that the USSR concludes and applies international treaties "in accordance with the generally recognized principles and rules of international law" before, and after, the entry of the Vienna Convention into force, implied only a reference to international customary law. As soon as the USSR had joined the Vienna Convention[3] its relations with many other signatories of this instrument began to be regulated by the rules of *treaty law*. Consequently, references to the "rules of international law" in the said Statute, specifically, pertinent to the procedure of observing the treaties, (Art. 19), and sanctions in cases of a material breach of a treaty by other parties (Art. 23), amount to references to rules of *treaty law*, in so far as they concern the participating countries.

Under the existing international law, the definition of the ways and means of compliance with international obligations lies completely within the competence of States. In practice, States use varying methods of implementing rules of international law in their municipal law. The choice of specific methods depends on many factors. Important among these are peculiarities of domestic legal systems and internal organizational structures of various States. The object of legal regulation and the specific content of relevant customary rules also play an important role.

I. Methods of implementing international customary law

Implementation of international customary law to municipal law presupposes that the latter contains certain regulations obliging subjects of municipal law to observe the provisions arising out of existing international customary law. Depending on the legal techniques used implementation of international customary law in municipal law can be either direct or indirect. Direct application of international custom, based on what as a rule is called incorporation, presupposes references in municipal law to such customary law. Within the framework of this method, rules of international customary law can directly apply to subjects of domestic law by proclaiming all existing international customary law to be part of the law of the land. Incorparation may also confine itself to sanctioning the application of individual rules of customary law in relations involving subjects of domestic law. Indirect application of international custom is associated with the adoption of special

[2] *See* Code of the Laws of the USSR (in Russian), vol. 9, 12; translated in: *William E. Butler*, comp., transl., Collected Legislation of the Union of Soviet Socialist Republics and the Constituent Republics, Union of Soviet Socialist Republics, vol. 3, Dobbs Ferry, New York 1981, V-1, 2—6.

[3] *See* Vedomosti SSSR (News Bulletin of the Supreme Soviet of the USSR) (1986), no. 16, item 263.

national laws reflecting the provisions of existing international customary law. This method, based on a more active role of the law-maker, who adapts international customary law obligations to the conditions of a specific national legal system, is usually called transformation.

In countries with Anglo-Saxon legal systems incorporation of all international customary law into domestic law is provided for by unwritten constitutional principles, supported by established judicial practice. Great Britain adheres to the principle formulated a long time ago by *Blackstone* and recognizing international customary law as part of the law of the land.[4] The United States practice is based on the principle underlying the often-quoted statement in the *Paquete Habana* Case where the court declared that international law was part of American law and, thus, the courts had to resort to "customs and usages of civilized nations" in situations where "there is no treaty and no controlling executive or legislative act or judicial decision"[5]. In some countries general incorporation of international customary law into municipal law is stipulated for in constitutional acts. For example, the Constitution of Austria lays down that "the generally recognized rules of international law are valid as integral parts of Austrian federal law"[6]. The Constitution of the German Democratic Republic says that "the generally recognized rules of international law serving peace and peaceful international cooperation are binding upon the State and every citizen"[7]. Under the Constitution of the Federal Republic of Germany "the general rules of public international law shall be an integral part of Federal law"[8].

Against the background of the incorporation method, used in the constitutions of a number of countries, it is interesting to consider the significance of Art. 29 of the 1977 Soviet Constitution which reads that the USSR's relations with other States are based on fulfilment in good faith of obligations arising not only from the international treaties

---

[4] *William Blackstone*, Commentaries on the Law of England, vol. 4, Oxford 1749, 20. For a brief review on the practice of British courts *see* also *Ian Brownlie*, Principles of Public International Law, 3rd ed., Oxford 1979, 45 *et seq.*

[5] For more details on the significance of this decision and subsequent American practice *see Jack M. Goldklang*, Back on Board the Paquete Habana: Resolving the Conflict Between Statutes and Customary International Law, in: Virginia Journal of International Law 25 (1984), 143—151 (145 *et seq.*).

[6] Art. 6 of the Constitution of the Republic of Austria. For more details *see Ludwig Jordan*, Bemerkungen zu Artikel 9 der österreichischen Bundesverfassung, in: Zeitschrift für öffentliches Recht 7 (1928), 453—459; *Ignaz Seidl-Hohenveldern*, Relation of International Law to Internal Law in Austria, in: American Journal of International Law (AJIL) 49 (1955), 451—476.

[7] Art. 8 of the Constitution of the German Democratic Republic.

[8] Art. 25 of the Constitution of the Federal Republic of Germany (*see* Documentation, 192). For more details *see Bruno Simma*, Droit international coutumier et droit interne selon la Loi fondamentale, in: *Michael Bothe / Raul E. Vinuesa* (eds.), International Law and Municipal Law: German-Argentinian Constitutional Law Colloquium, Berlin 1982, 117—128.

signed by the USSR, but also from "the generally recognized principles and rules of international law". The first question that arises in the process of interpreting Art. 29 concerns the definition of the notion of "generally recognized principles and rules of international law". For many Soviet lawyers the concept of "generally recognized principles and rules of international law" signifies in the broadest social and political meaning the totality of treaty and customary rules recognized by all existing groups of States — socialist, western, and developing. At the same time the concept of "generally recognized principles and rules of international law" may have a narrower, more special meaning. In some contexts it may be used to denote primarily the generally recognized customary rules. For this reason, Soviet specialists believe that speaking of "the generally recognized principles and rules of international law", Art. 29 of the 1977 Constitution of the USSR means first and foremost the generally recognized customary rules. In his analysis of Art. 29 *Igor I. Lukashuk* says that "the generally recognized principles and rules of international law are largely of a customary nature, i. e., they exist in the form of international custom"[9]. *V. G. Butkevich* points out in respect of Art. 29 that the Constitution of the USSR draws a distinction between "customary law and treaty law"[10].

A more complicated question is whether Art. 29 of the USSR Constitution can be regarded as a general reference incorporating international custom into Soviet law. As to this point doubts arise in the first place because Art. 29 is included in Chapter 4 of the Constitution which lays down the principles of Soviet foreign policy. An additional argument is that, in laying down the principle of fulfillment in good faith of obligations arising from the generally recognized principles and rules of international law, Art. 29 starts with the words "the USSR's relations with other States are based on observance" of this and other principles. And, finally, Art. 29 does not straight-forwardly state that Soviet law in one way or another incorporates the generally recognized principles and rules of international law.

No wonder that the prevailing view in Soviet doctrine is that general reference to the rules of international law in general, and to international customary law in particular, is unknown to Soviet law.[11] Only some

---

[9] *Igor I. Lukashuk*, Customary Norms in Contemporary International Law (in Russian), in: Soviet Yearbook of Internationl Law 1978, 86—100 (98).

[10] *V. G. Butkevich*, Application of the Rules of International Custom in State Courts (in Russian), (Vestnik of the University of Kiev), International Relations and International Law 15 (1982), 41.

[11] *See R. A. Muellerson*, The Relationship Between International and Municipal Law (in Russian), Moscow 1982, 75; *see* also *id.*, The Constitution of the USSR and the Relationship between International and National Law (in Russian), Moscow 1980; *G. V. Ignatenko*, Interaction and Internal and International Law (in Russian), Sverdlovsk 1981.

authors are more or less inclined to regard the provisions of Art. 29 as having legal significance for the application of the rules of international custom by Soviet courts. Specifically, *Butkevich*, who has done a study into legal regulation of the application of international custom by Soviet courts, writes with a special reference to Art. 29 that "drawing a distinction between customary and treaty law the Constitution requires that the prescriptions of both be equally observed"[12].

It seems that the arguments against the feasibility of viewing Art. 29 of the USSR Constitution as a norm incorporating international customary law into Soviet municipal law, or enabling the Soviet courts to apply the rules of international custom, are strong enough. It is indisputable that this Article aims to lay down the principles of the USSR's relations with other States. It says nothing about the operation of international custom on Soviet territory. At the same time, it must be borne in mind, that the fixation in the fundamental law of the USSR of the principle of observance in good faith of obligations arising from the generally recognized principles and rules of international law implies, that observance of the relevant principles of international law is binding on all public agencies: not only those concerned with foreign relations, but also all other competent authorities. In this connection there is every ground to claim that Art. 29 lays an important legal basis for consistent observance of the rules of international customary law by all bodies of the Soviet State, including it in the framework of internal relations.

Notwithstanding their overall significance, constitutional provisions for general incorporation of international customary law into municipal law cannot serve as an adequate method in all cases. Experience indicates that general references alone to international law in municipal law pose a series of practical problems for the law enforcement agencies caused by at least two factors. The first is, that by virtue of their peculiarities the rules of international customary law cannot be used in most cases for direct regulation of relations which involve subjects of domestic law. The rules of international customary law normally provide only a general framework for the actions of international law subjects. As the Chamber of the International Court of Justice put it, custom "can of its nature provide only a few basic legal principles which lay down guidelines to be followed"[13]. In view of this factor, the implementation of international custom, if any, usually requires specification and adaptation of relevant normative prescriptions. Using American terminology concerning international treaties, it may be said that, as a general rule, international customary law is not self-executing.[14]

[12] *Butkevich* (note 10).
[13] I.C.J. Reports 1984, 290.
[14] This point of view enjoys broad support, especially in the United States'

Nothing can be changed in this respect by the provisions occurring in individual constitutions to the effect that general international customary law directly creates rights and duties for the subjects of domestic law.[15] There is no doubt, the actual non-self-executing of international customary law is a major reason for its exceptionally rare direct application by the courts in the majority of States, including those whose constitutions proclaim the principle of custom's direct action. The second of the afore mentioned factors is, that it is difficult to ascertain the existence and meaning of the rules of international customary law. When the legislator requires the law enforcement agencies to apply general customary law only in a general form, the judges, arbiters, and other officials accustomed to deal largely or exclusively with domestic law are not always in a position to determine the applicable law in a specific sphere of relations. The effect of these factors can be, to a certain extent, balanced by the method of special references. In this case, the law-maker, at least, indicates the specific sphere of relations where, in his opinion, rules of international customary law can be found to regulate relations involving subjects of national law.

The method of special references is widely used in many countries, including the USSR. Under Soviet laws international customary law can be incorporated through references to the "rules of international law". Such references are contained, for instance, in the already mentioned Arts. 19 and 23 of the Statute on the Procedure for the Conclusion, Execution, and Denunciation of International Agreements of the USSR and Art. I of the Statute on Foreign Diplomatic and Consular Missions on Soviet Territory[16]. References to the "generally recognized rules of international law" can be found in a number of statutes. The Soviet lawmaker also provides for direct references to international customary law. For example, Art. 3 of the USSR Consular Rules[17] stipulates that the activities of Soviet consular authorities shall be governed, *inter alia*, by "international customs"[18].

---

courts. See for an analysis of some court decisions in *Howard S. Schrader*, Custom and General Principles as Sources of International Law in American Federal Courts, in: Columbia Law Review 82 (1982), 751—783 (757, 758). The attempts of some authors to prove the contrary seem not convincing, *see* *Steven M. Schneebaum*, The enforceability of Customary Norms of Public International Law, in: Brooklyn Journal of International Law 8 (1982), 289—307.

[15] The Constitution of the Federal Republic of Germany may serve as a good example. Art. 25 states that general international law "directly creates rights and duties for the inhabitants of the Federal territory", (*see* Documentation, 192).

[16] See Code of USSR Laws (note 2), 42, and *Butler* (note 2), V—1, Statute on Diplomatic and Consular Representations of Foreign States on the Territory of the USSR, 2—11 (7, 8).

[17] See Code of the USSR Laws (note 2), 24, and *Butler* (note 16), Consular Statute of the USSR, 2—21 (2).

[18] Analysis of Soviet legislature shows that occasional allegations in the Western doctrine to the effect that the Soviet legal system is "hostile" to inter-

At the same time, from the point of view of internal law enforcement procedure, problems relevant to the identification and application of customary rules that arise within the framework of the incorporation method can only be entirely avoided through the use of transformation techniques. Depending on the object of regulation and the content of existing rules of international customary law, transformation may be the only effective means of implementing the norms of international customary law at municipal level. The transformation method has gained most extensive ground in countries with developed systems of domestic legislation on foreign relations, including the Soviet Union. The USSR has adopted a series of legislative acts which adapt or transform provisions of international customary law into Soviet law. Thus, the Statute on Foreign Diplomatic and Consular Missions on Soviet Territory has transformed into Soviet law not only treaty law, but also existing customary diplomatic and consular law.

Completing this brief analysis of the incorporation and transformation methods, it is ought to be pointed out that the differences are largely based on varying institutional approaches to the legal solution of problems related to the determination of the existence and scope of applicable international customary law. When the incorporation method is used it is up to the courts, arbitration tribunals, and other judicial bodies to determine the existence and scope of the rules of international customary law and to apply them to a specific situation. In the case of the transformation method the decision on applicable rules of international customary law is made at highest legislative levels where a relevant transforming act is adopted. When the courts or other judicial agencies face a certain problem they do not have to ascertain international practices, they apply the relevant rules of municipal law reflecting the underlying original norms of international law. It should be stressed, however, that the indicated differences do not necessarily mean that incorporation and transformation may be in contrast as regards the centralized or decentralized resolution of respective problems. In the

national custom are baseless. *Antonio Cassese*, for example, claims that the provision of Art. 29 of the 1977 Constitution of the USSR on the fulfilment in good faith of obligations arising from the generally recognized principles and rules of international law, which he regards as incorporation of international custom, constitutes "a departure from the Soviet tradition of ignoring international custom"; *Antonio Cassese*, Modern Constitutions and International Law, Recueil des Cours 192 (1985/III), 331—476 (378). In reality, however, the traditions of Soviet legislature testify to the contrary. As far back as 1921 *Vladimir I. Lenin* for instance, signed a statute on the ship's crew in the merchant fleet of the Russian Federation. Art. 5 of the Statute reads that "the ship master shall observe international custom" (*see* SU of the RSFSR, 1921, no. 67, item 514). The Statute on General and Particular Averages, adopted the same year, provided that they "shall be settled in accordance with the generally accepted customs of merchant shipping" (see *loc. cit.*, no. 70, item 567).

case of incorporation technique the final decisions on applicable international law are also made at the highest legislative, judicial, or executive levels. For example, by provision of Art. 2 para. 8 of the Constitution of the United States, which grants to Congress the power to define "offences against the law of nations", Congress may always define the applicable rules of international customary law by a special act. The respective interpretation of Congress shall be binding on all judicial bodies.[19] In the Federal Republic of Germany disputes concerning the domestic applicability of general rules of international law are resolved by the Constitutional Court.[20]

It is also important that in decision-making on problems relevant to applicable rules of international customary law and their contents, the courts, arbitration tribunals, and other law enforcement agencies of many countries which use the incorporation method follow, as a rule, the views of central authorities responsible for foreign relations. In the USA, for instance, the courts usually follow "the views of the State Department"[21]. In Austria the final decision on the applicable rules of international customary law also rests with the administration.[22]

II. The development of customary international law and methods of implementation: Some problems

Peculiarities of custom as a source of international law create a number of problems in the process of its implementation into municipal law, irrespective of the method of implementation used. In particular, the change of international custom, possible due to the impact of new practices of States, gives rise to problems as regards discrepancies between the rules applied in municipal law and the changing rules of customary law.

Critics of the transformation method usually claim that its application leads to situations in which legislative acts reflecting customary law, at a certain stage of its development, cease to be consistent with the generally recognized rules as international conditions change. It is doubtful that inconsistencies between "fixed" legislation and "flexible" international custom are inevitable in all spheres, especially in view of

---

[19] *See* on this point *Schrader* (note 14).

[20] *See* Art. 100 para. 2 of the Consitution of the Federal Republic of Germany, (*see* Documentation, 195).

[21] *Lori Fisler Damrosch*, Application of Customary International Law by U.S. Domestic Tribunals, in: Proceedings of the 76th Annual Meeting of the American Society of International Law 1982, 251—255 (253). *See* also *Phillip R. Trimble*, Revisionist View of Customary International Law, in: UCLA Law Review 33 (1986), 665—732 (688).

[22] *See Seidl-Hohenveldern* (note 6), 456

the fact that internal legislation is one of the main forms of State practice constituting new customary rules.[23] New legislation can lead to changes in international customary law and subsequently could be regarded as reflection of international customary law. Thus, the latest legislation on exclusive economic zones has drastically changed the content of international customary law. It is impossible to determine precisely when this practice acquired the nature of a compulsory legal rule, but there are grounds for asserting that at least after the judgment of the International Court of Justice in the *Case Concerning the Continental Shelf* (1982)[24] the adopted laws may be regarded as reflection of existing international law.[25]

On the face of it, the incorporation method seems to cause no problems of inconsistency between internal practices and international rules as both current and future international law are incorporated into municipal law. A more detailed analysis of the practice of countries oriented to the incorporation method indicates that this method does not rule out discrepancies between internal practices and international standards. This is caused, in the first place, by extensive limitations to which the incorporation doctrine is subjected in practice. Specifically, extensive use is made of the principle which precludes the application of international customary law in cases where there exist internal acts irrespective of their inconsistency with the rules of international customary law. For example, British courts apply international custom only if it does not run counter to Parliamentary acts.[26] The American tradition has been that a later domestic act supersedes the incorporated custom while a new rule of international customary law in no way affects the existing legislation. A recent attempt to introduce another approach has been a failure. The American Law Institute included in its Restatement of Foreign Relations Law of the United States a clause, to the effect, that a new norm of international customary law supersedes any inconsistent pre-existing provision in the law of the United States, but the

---

[23] This is widely recognized, specifically, in the judgments of the International Court of Justice. *See*, for example, I.C.J. Reports 1951, 134—135; I.C.J. Reports 1969, 32—33; and I.C.J. Reports 1982, 92.

[24] In its judgment the Court stated that the concept of the exclusive economic zone "may be regarded as part of modern international law". I.C.J. Reports 1982, 74.

[25] If one followed this line of argument then the USSR Edict "On the Economic Zone of the USSR" of 1984 [Vedomosti SSSR 1984, no. 9, item 137; *translated* in: *William E. Butler*, comp., transl., ed., The USSR, Eastern Europe and the Development of the Law of the Sea, vol. 1, London / Rome / New York 1986, F. 2, 3—14 (3)], for example, may be regarded as reflection of existing customary rules in spite of the fact that its Preambel refers only to the provisions of the UN Convention on the Law of the Sea [UN Doc. A/CONF. 62/122 (1982)], which is not yet in force.

[26] *Brownlie* (note 4), 45.

suggested amendment met strong criticisms from American lawyers and was later changed.[27]

Problems of inconsistency between internal law and the rules of existing international customary law, in case of incorporation, may also be determined by other factors. The application of international customary law as integral part of the law of a land may result in such an interpretation of its content that it would significantly depart from its true meaning. In this context the principle of *stare decisis*, operative in the Anglo-Saxon systems of law, plays an essential role. In rendering a judgement based on international customary law, the British courts, for example, are bound by prior judicial decisions,[28] notwithstanding the fact that the relevant rules could have changed since they were last addressed by the said courts. The American courts are also bound by existing precedent, even though the international customary law may have changed. In this connection, *H. Schrader* points out that "American international law can depart from internationally recognized standards"[29]. Experience indicates that actual inconsistencies between internal legislation and international customary law may and do take place in the States whose constitutions proclaim priority of international customary law over municipal law. For instance, under the Constitution of the Federal Republic of Germany general rules of international law "shall take precedence over the laws"[30]. The Greek Constitution lays down that "the generally accepted rules of international law shall prevail over contrary provisions of law"[31].

However, constitutional provisions of this kind could not in itself guarantee the actual observance of international obligations even in cases where they are supported by internal procedures for conflict *resolution*. For example, the Constitution of the Federal Republic of Germany lays down that decisions on disputes concerning applicable rules of international customary law shall be made by the Constitutional Court.[32] It is obvious, however, that the judgment of the Constitutional Court with respect to the existence and scope of application of an international rule, is meaningful only within the framework of West German municipal law. Other members of the international community may have

[27] For more details *see Goldklang* (note 5); *Trimble* (note 21), 674, 687, 678.

[28] *See Brownlie* (note 4), 45.

[29] *Schrader* (note 14), 761.

[30] Art. 25 of the Constitution of the Federal Republic of Germany, (*see* Documentation, 192).

[31] Art. 28 of the Constitution of the Republic of Greece. For more details *see* *A. A. Fatouros*, International Law in the New Greek Constitution, in: AJIL 70 (1976), 492—506.

[32] Art. 100 para. 2 of the Basic Law of the Federal Republic of Germany, (*see* Documentation, 195).

their own point of view on problems pertinent to existing customary law and the obligations thereof for the Federal Republic of Germany. They may argue that notwithstanding the operation of the internal constitutional procedure, certain existing West German laws or practices may continue to be in conflict with the generally recognized principles of international law.

III. Conclusion

The analysis of the theory and practice of implementing international customary law at municipal level shows that the use of one or another type of implementation techniques does not in itself guarantee effective fulfillment of international obligations by States. Experience indicates that positive results depend not only on the legal techniques used, but also on a number of political factors related to the attitude of a given State towards existing international law and relevant international obligations.

Incorporation of Customary International Law into Municipal Law

By Walter Rudolf*

I. Relationship between international law and municipal law

The relationship between international law and municipal law has nowhere been discussed more intensively, more persistently, and more profoundly than in Germany. Eighty-eight years ago, in 1899, *Heinrich Triepel* published the first monograph being a fundamental approach to this problem. A dualist conception of international and municipal law was thereby established and soon a controversial discussion was started with the participation of, above all, German, Austrian, and Italian jurists. In the same year the nowadays almost forgotten paper by *Wilhelm Kaufmann*, who argued for monism based on natural law, was published.[1]

Triepel's dualist conception was further developed in 1905 by *Dionisio Anzilotti* who became some father of a moderate dualism as it was lateron also supported by *Gustav Adolf Walz*, *Herbert Kraus*, and by myself.[2] This doctrine proceeds from a separation between international and municipal law as both legal orders differ from their source, their subject of regulation, their addressees, and their structure as law of co-ordination or as imperative law of subordination. However, the connection between international law and transformed international law applied as municipal law has not been demolished. To give a picture, we do not find two circles tangent to each other, as *Triepel* mentioned, but we deal with two intersecting circles. One circle stands for international

---

* Dr. iur., Professor of Law, Faculty of Law and Economics, Johannes-Gutenberg-University Mainz, Under-Secretary of State of the Ministry of Justice of the Land Rheinland-Pfalz, Mainz.

[1] *Heinrich Triepel*, Völkerrecht und Landesrecht, Leipzig 1899; *see* also *id.*, Les rapports entre le droit interne et le droit international, in: Recueil des Cours de l'Académie de Droit International (RdC) 1 (1923), 77—121; *Wilhelm Kaufmann*, Die Rechtskraft des Internationalen Rechts und das Verhältnis der Staatsgesetzgebungen und der Staatsorgane zu demselben, Stuttgart 1899.

[2] *Dionisio Anzilotti*, Il diritto internazionale nei giuridici interni, Bologna 1905; *Gustav Adolf Walz*, Völkerrecht und Staatliches Recht, Untersuchungen über die Einwirkungen des Völkerrechts auf das innerstaatliche Recht, Stuttgart 1933; *see* also *id.*, Les rapports du droit international et du droit interne, RdC 61 (1937 III), 375—456; *Herbert Kraus*, Die auswärtige Stellung der Bundesrepublik Deutschland nach dem Bonner Grundgesetz, Göttingen 1950; *see* also *id.*, Der Deutsche Richter und das Völkerrecht, in: *S. Constantopoulos / Hans Wehberg* (eds.), Festschrift für *Rudolf Laun* zu seinem siebzigsten Geburtstag, Hamburg 1953, 223—238; *Walter Rudolf*, Völkerrecht und deutsches Recht, Tübingen 1967.

law, the other for municipal law. The plane covered by both circles represents international law as applied municipally, being the remainder of international law and at the same time part of municipal law.[3]

The monist theory reached its climax in *Hans Kelsen*'s construction of legal logic. Monism was, above all, further developed by *Alfred Verdross* who supported a moderate monist conception with the primacy of international law. Thus, both international and municipal law together are the very elements of one homogeneous legal order with international law being superior to municipal law. As State practice confirms the opposite, *Verdross* saves the unity of his legal world picture by stating a provisional finding only which has to be legally observed at any rate. Moderate monism with the primacy of international law found its proponents everywhere, with quite different arguments. Here in Kiel the primacy of international law was supported by *Eberhard Menzel*, for example.[4]

The theoretical controversy between monists and dualists calmed down largely. Attention was preferably directed to the method of application of rules of international law in municipal law, which often, however, only meant a continuation of the theoretical controversy in a rather practical field. This was the case because the dualists supported the conception of the necessity to transform international law into municipal law, while the monists were in favour of an automatic or explicit adoption. Soon, however, the idea was supported that the theoretical dispute was of no significance at all to the enforcement of international law, since the application of rules of international law within municipal law in any case required a national act of application.[5] In the mid-sixties a commission of the German Society of International Law, directed by *Karl Josef Partsch*, came to the conclusion that the *Vollzugslehre* (doctrine of enforcement) as a variant of the moderate theory of adaptation should be preferred to the strict theory of transformation. In my opinion a moderate theory of transformation should be given preference over the doctrine of enforcement.[6] *Partsch* objects that, regard-

---

[3] *Triepel* (note 1), 111; *Rudolf* (note 2), 141 *et seq.*

[4] *Hans Kelsen*, Das Problem der Souveränität und die Theorie des Völkerrechts, Beitrag zu einer reinen Rechtslehre, 2nd ed. Tübingen 1928, 111 *et seq.*; *see* also *id.*, Les rapports de système entre le droit interne et le droit international public, RdC 14 (1926 IV), 227—331; *Alfred Verdross*, Die Einheit des rechtlichen Weltbildes auf der Grundlage der Völkerrechtsverfassung, Tübingen 1923; *Eberhard Menzel*, Völkerrecht, München/Berlin 1962, 53.

[5] *Heinz Wagner*, Monismus und Dualismus: eine methodenkritische Betrachtung zum Theorienstaat, in: Archiv des öffentlichen Rechts (AöR) 89 (1964), 212—241.

[6] *Karl Josef Partsch*, Die Anwendung des Völkerrechts im innerstaatlichen Recht, Überprüfung der Transformationslehre, in: Berichte der Deutschen Gesellschaft für Völkerrecht 6 (1964), 13—155; *Rudolf* (note 2), 171.

ing the effect, a moderate transformation hardly differs from the theory of enforcement.

But whatever the theoretical positions may be, nobody claims anymore that international law as superior law shall override municipal law. The only controversial point is whether international law can directly be applied municipally on the basis of a national order of application — this is the position of, above all, *Partsch* and *Hermann Mosler*; or whether there is a need for a transformation into municipal law without disrupting the connection with international law — an idea followed by *Karl Doehring* and also by myself, for instance, and as I presume, now as before, by the German Courts.[7] After all, practical consequences resulting from the different opinions do hardly exist. By virtue of a moderate theory of transformation transformed international law can be easily placed into the hierarchy of national norms. This operation cannot be so easily achieved by the doctrine of enforcement, but, nevertheless, it is finally accomplished, too. Besides, for the incorporation of general customary international law into municipal law, this question has explicitly been settled by the Basic Law in the Federal Republic of Germany.

II. Customary international law as a law of co-ordination

Customary international law is indispensable for international relations. Each State maintaining international relations must necessarily also apply customary international law, because international relations cannot completely be regulated by treaties under international law. In order to keep up international relations, all sources of law mentioned in Article (Art.) 38 para. 1 of the Statute of the International Court of Justice are of importance as norm categories to be applied by this Court. The only way to escape the application of customary international law for a State is to exclude itself from international relations as Japan did until 1854. Nowadays, this is almost impossible because of the interdependence between the States.

According to Art. 38 para. 1 *lit.* b, customary international law is an international custom as evidence of a general practice accepted as law. A practice can only exist if it lasts for a longer period of time. This does

[7] *Partsch* (note 6), 22; *Hermann Mosler*, Das Völkerrecht in der Praxis der deutschen Gerichte, Karlsruhe 1957; *see* also *id.*, L'application du droit international public par les tribunaux nationaux, RdC 91 (1957 I), 619—709; *Karl Doehring*, Die allgemeinen Regeln des völkerrechtlichen Fremdenrechts und das deutsche Verfassungsrecht, Köln/Berlin 1963, 35 *et seq.*; *see* also *id.*, Staatsrecht der Bundesrepublik Deutschland, Unter besonderer Berücksichtigung der Rechtsvergleichung und des Völkerrechts, 3rd ed. Frankfurt am Main 1984, 79; *Rudolf* (note 2), 164 *et seq.*

not mean, however, that it must last for decades, as it has been pointed out by the International Court of Justice in the *North Sea Continental Shelf* Cases[8] for the existence of the continental shelf according to customary international law. Practice must be accompanied by a subjective element. It must be carried out in such a way, as to be of evidence for the belief that this practice is considered obligatory and required by the existence of a rule of law to do so. Whether a general practice is evident, one can only find out through an analysis of the prevailing conduct of the States. Nevertheless, it is more difficult to prove whether a practice is accepted as law. There are no logically incontestable objective criteria for the acceptance of a particular practice as law. That is, why the doctrine that the States act in a certain way because they believe they are under the obligation to do so, an opinion supported by some Western writers but also by *Tunkin*,[9] offers a practicable way out of the dilemma. However, this operation is only capable of providing an assumption for the existence of a rule of customary international law, but it cannot furnish irrefutable proof.

In my today's report, I cannot enter into the meta-juridical question concerning the reason for the validity of customary international law. It is sufficient to state that customary international law must be based on the consent of the participating subjects of international law. The doctrine originating from *Hugo Grotius* of *pactum tacitum*, of tacit consent, is capable of explaining the origin, the existence, the change, and the disappearance of customary international law.[10]

It is to be distinguished whether a rule of customary international law is applied generally, i. e. universally, or whether it is valid only to a limited extent, regionally, or perhaps even only locally. In any case, general customary international law can only arise if its rule in question is approved of by all subjects of international law concerned. Thus, a rule cannot be considered as part of general customary international law if a State has consistently and unequivocally manifested the refusal to accept it. The objecting State would at least not be bound to such a rule, according to the practice of the International Court of Justice since the decision in the *British-Norwegian Fisheries* Case.[11] The distinction between general customary international law and customary law with limited regional scope is important for our topic, because German law provides an explicit rule of incorporation for general customary international law only.

---

[8] I.C.J. Reports 1969, 3—53 (22, 29), reprinted in: International Legal Materials 8 (1969), 340—385 (357, 363).

[9] *E. g. Georg Dahm*, Völkerrecht, vol. I, Stuttgart 1958, 32; *Grigory I. Tunkin*, Das Völkerrecht der Gegenwart, Theorie und Praxis, Berlin 1963, 86.

[10] *Hugo Grotius*, De iure belli ac pacis, libri tres, Paris 1625, Prolegomena 1.

[11] I.C.J. Reports 1951, 116—206 (131).

III. Applicability of customary international law in municipal law

Customary international law — just like any kind of international law — can be applied in two different ways. On the one hand, it is only applicable among the States themselves without having any effect on the municipal sphere. Only the States as such are bound and, however, connected therewith and also those national organs which are at the same time organs of international relations and international law. But customary international law can, in addition, establish rights and duties of the citizens within a State, in case it can actually be applied municipally.

There is no need for express regulation in the national legal system concerning the application of customary international law in relation with other subjects of international law. If a State participates in relations governed by international law, it stands to reason that this State is bound to the rules of customary international law. Since a State can only act through its organs, it is the duty of the State organs, competent under constitutional law, to comply with customary international law. These organs are at the same time organs of international relations.

This does not mean, on the other hand, that rules of customary international law, which are to be applied only in the field of relations between States, cannot be incorporated into municipal law at all. Concerning those rules of international law, applicable exclusively between States without causing legal effects within the State, the German legal system contains only regulations on the competence of some organs — like on the authority of the Federal President to represent the Federation in international relations (Art. 59 para. 1 of the *Grundgesetz* (Basic Law) of the Federal Republic of Germany). Those regulations settle competences and correspond to the traditional rules of international law.

Besides, regulations of customary international law can be incorporated into municipal law if their object is to cause municipal legal effects and if they do not require any supplementation by national law. In order to integrate a rule of customary international law into municipal law, the suitability of the rule must be given according to its contents and its purpose in order to produce municipal legal effects without the necessity of any further act of municipal or international law. The rule of customary international law is to be directly applicable within the State. It must be apt to be incorporated and the implementation is not to require the aid of any further national act of legislation: the rule of international law must be self-executing in order to be incorporated into municipal law. This is not only true for treaties under international law, but also for rules of customary international law.[12]

[12] *Doehring* (note 7), 138 *et seq.*; *Rudolf* (note 2), 257 *et seq.*

Whether and when a rule of customary international law is capable of being applied and thus capable of being incorporated is ascertained by means of interpretation. As there are no exact terms to be taken into consideration in the case of rules of customary international law contrary to treaties of international law, it is central whether the rule of customary international law would be able to address citizens and State institutions by way of municipal law, provided, that it is transformed into a rule of national law. This is, why general rules of customary international law can be incorporated, too, if they only obligate the States themselves to realize the municipal enforcement, as far as a necessary supplementation of a specific rule out of itself is possible without any further national legislation, and if its meaning and purpose allow this supplementation.[13] If a rule of customary international law is capable of being incorporated into municipal law then the German legal system asks for the distinction whether it is a general rule of customary international law or part of a regional custom. On the general rules, Art. 25 of the Basic Law provides that they shall be an integral part of Federal law and shall directly create rights and duties for the inhabitants of the Federal territory. The Federal law does not contain regulations on such rules of customary international law without general and universal character.

IV. Incorporation of customary international law according to Article 25 of the Basic Law

Let us at first examine the incorporation of customary international law according to Art. 25 of the Basic Law.

1. Generally recognized rules and general rules of international law

A look at the history of law shows that the application of rules of international law in municipal law was originally effected by means of customary law. In the Anglo-Saxon law this was reflected in the theorem "international law is part of the law of the land". In this context, it was cleared up since the decision of the English High Court in 1876 in the *Franconia* Case[14] that the rule of international law must be adapted by national law. However, contrary to English law, the adaptation in Germany did not need to be effected by an act of parliament, but it was realized somehow by customary law. In the *Franconia* Case a German court would certainly have affirmed the competence to punish the captain of the vessel for the offence committed within the national territorial sea.

[13] *Rudolf* (note 2), 258.

[14] *R.* v. *Keyn, The Franconia,* 1876, 2 Exchequer Division 63.

As the first norm of written law, Art. 4 of the Weimar Constitution of 1919 contained the regulation that the generally recognized rules of international law were in force as binding components of German law. This regulation is, in fact, attributed to a publication by *Verdross*[15], which induced the constituent legislator to determine commitments under international law constitutionally within the State and to secure the direct municipal application of general customary international law. Art. 4 of the Weimar Constitution was the model for similar regulations in the Constitutions of Austria, Esthonia, Spain, and Cuba and after the Second World War also of France and Italy as well as of Korea and of some Latin-American States, and of both Constitutions of the German Democratic Republic.[16]

After World War II the Constitutions of the *Länder* Württemberg-Baden, Hesse, Bavaria, Württemberg-Hohenzollern, Baden, Bremen and the Saarland included regulations on the incorporation of the generally recognized rules of international law into municipal law; the Hessian Constitution and the previous Constitution of the Saarland going the furthest in their formulations by incorporating "the rules of international law" as binding parts of municipal law.[17] This means that, according to the text, customary international law with limited scope of application and treaties under international law were also covered.

During the deliberations on the Basic Law in the Parliamentary Council as constituent legislator, there was accordance on a clause of incorporation to be inserted in the constitution. The aim was to express that the German people is willing to understand by international law more than only an order — the rules of which engage exclusively the States as such. The point at issue was whether only the generally *recognized* rules of international law allowing a narrow interpretation or whether,

---

[15] *Alfred Verdross*, Reichsrecht und internationales Recht, Eine Lanze für Art. 3 des Regierungsentwurfs der deutschen Verfassung, in: Deutsche Juristen-Zeitung 24 (1919), 291—293.

[16] Art. 9 Austrian Bundes-Verfassungsgesetz; Art. 4 of the Esthonian Constitution of June 15th, 1920; Art. 7 of the Spanish Constitution of December 9th, 1931; Art. 7 para. 2 of the Cuban Constitution of July 5th, 1940; Art. 14 of the Preamble of the French Constitution of October 27th, 1946; Art. 10 para. 1 of the Italian Constitution of December 22nd, 1947; Art. 7 of the Constitution of (South) Korea of July 12th, 1948; *e. g.* Art. 6 of the Preamble of the Constitution of Venezuela of July 5th, 1947; Art. 5 para. 1 of the Constitution of the German Democratic Republic of October 7th, 1949, and Art. 8 para. 1 of the Constitution of March 26th, 1968.

[17] Art. 46 of the Constitution of Württemberg-Baden of November 28th, 1946; Art. 67 of the Constitution of Hesse of December 1st, 1946; Art. 84 of the Constitution of Bavaria of December 2nd, 1946; Art. 7 of the Constitution of Württemberg-Hohenzollern of May 20th, 1947; Art. 57 para. 2 of the Constitution of Baden of May 22nd, 1947; Art. 122 of the Constitution of Bremen of October 21st, 1947; Art. 63 of the Constitution of the Saarland of December 15th, 1947.

on the contrary, the general rules of international law with a wide interpretation should become part of Federal law. Finally, the view more favourable to international law prevailed, in spite of the objections expressed by *Hermann von Mangoldt*.[18] Thus, Art. 25 of the Basic Law provides that "the general rules of public international law shall be an integral part of Federal law". Whether a rule can be qualified as being general depends on the extent to which it is applied as a legal rule. We cannot speak of a general rule if it only contains a political postulate *de lege ferenda* and if it is not an expression of a practice governed by an *opinio iuris*. There is also a lack of generality if the rule only has a regional character or if it is contested considerably. For this reason, ultimately a *general* rule always constitutes a generally *recognized* rule of international law, and also because customary international law which is not recognized, *i. e.* not governed by an *opinio iuris*, is not conceivable.

If a litigation arises and if it is doubtful whether a pertinent rule of public international law is part of Federal law the court shall obtain a decision from the *Bundesverfassungsgericht* (Federal Constitutional Court) according to Art. 100 para. 2 of the Basic Law. It is true that the latter cannot decide with compulsory effect for the *sphere of international law* whether a certain rule of public international law is to be qualified as a general rule of international law, because this competence to decide is vested in the International Court of Justice, for instance, or in an arbitration tribunal, provided, that all the other requirements are met. But the Federal Constitutional Court decides definitely on a rule being part of Federal law. If the decision turns out to be positive the rule applies as Federal law even if its qualification as general rule of international law was affirmed erroneously. If the Federal Constitutional Court denies that a rule of international law has become part of the Federal law through Art. 25, this decision means a clarification for the German legal order insofar as the rule in question is no Federal law even if an international court or an arbitration tribunal would have confirmed its status as a rule of customary international law. In both cases the Federal Constitutional Court takes its decision on the existence of a general rule of international law only incidently — possibly even in the wrong way. Considered from its practical result, the idea of this decision, representing an act of recognition or rejection on behalf of the Federal Republic of Germany, cannot be totally denied. Thus, the problem of recognition in the cases of litigation has been shifted into the sphere of judicial interpretation.

---

[18] *Werner Matz*, Entstehungsgeschichte der Artikel des Grundgesetzes, Art. 25, Jahrbuch des öffentlichen Rechts der Gegenwart (JöR) 1 (1951), 229—235 (231, 232).

2. *Manifestations of general rules of international law*

The rules of general customary international law belong to the general rules of international law. As it is well-known, treaties under international law can also contain rules of general customary international law, *i. e.* rules of customary international law can be fixed by treaty. This occurs especially in treaties codifying rules of customary international law. But legal provisions of general customary international law can just as well appear in any other treaty under international law.

It is controversial whether Art. 25 covers those rules being subject of treaties under international law, too. This question is of eminent importance as the general rules of international law have priority over laws, while a treaty under international law, incorporated into German law according to Art. 59 para. 2, can only be ranked as simple Federal law. The question concerning the rank played a role especially in connection with the European Convention for the Protection of Human Rights and Fundamental Freedoms of November 4th, 1950.[19]

In the opinion of the Federal Constitutional Court, treaties under international law have priority over customary international law, according to the provisions *lex posterior derogat legi priori* and *lex specialis derogat legi generali*.[20] *Doehring*, on the other hand, points out that for the application of general rules within municipal law treaties are not required. In case a treaty contains such general rules it is — according to that view — insofar of a declaratory nature.[21]

In my opinion, treaties under international law on the one hand, even if containing rules of general customary international law, and general customary international law on the other hand, are to be treated as different specific categories of rules in the sense of Art. 38 para. 1 of the Statute of the International Court of Justice. Already in the decision of the *North Sea Continental Shelf* Cases[22] the International Court of Justice indicated that customary international law can exist side by side with a treaty under international law. The International Court of Justice has clearly pointed out this view in its decision on the merits in the Case *Concerning Military and Paramilitary Activities in and against Nicaragua*.[23] This judgment is worthy of note with regard to the incorporation into municipal law, too.

---

[19] *Friedrich Klein*, Die Europäische Menschenrechts-Konvention und Artikel 25 des Bonner Grundgesetzes, JöR 11 (1962), 149—177.

[20] *Entscheidungen des Bundesverfassungsgerichts* (Federal Constitutional Court Reports — BVerfGE) vol. 18, 441—452 (448) [hereinafter cited as: BVerfGE 18, 441—452 (448)].

[21] *Doehring* (note 7), 130.

[22] I.C.J. Reports 1969, 39.

[23] I.C.J. Reports 1986, 14—527 (93 *et seq.*).

The contents of a treaty under international law representing general customary international law merely repeat the contents of a general regulation of customary international law already existing in this status as customary international law, being incorporated into municipal law by Art. 25 of the Basic Law and holding the higher rank. Art. 25 does not affect any law of treaty at all, but refers to the form as general customary international law only. For treaties solely Art. 59 para. 2 is relevant, even if these treaties contain rules of general customary international law. Besides that, due to the often diffuse structure of rules of customary international law, an identity between treaty and customary international law might frequently not be in existence. As far as the European Convention on Human Rights is concerned, the incorporation into German law has been effected according to Art. 59 para. 2 as the Articles of the Convention are worded in such a precise manner that, at least as a whole, the Articles can hardly be considered rules of general customary international law.

It is also contested whether "the general principles of law recognized by civilized nations" in the sense of Art. 38 para. 1 *lit.* c of the Statute of the International Court of Justice belong to the general rules of international law which are, by operation of Art. 25 of the Basic Law, part of the German legal system. In this report, however, I do not need to go into the details of this question as it has definitely to be answered in the negative. As the German legal system is one of a "civilized nation" the general principles of law of Art. 38 para. 1 *lit.* c are already part of German law at any rate.[24]

If those principles are always the same with regard to their contents they do not need to be transformed as they are immanent in the German legal order anyhow. Their incorporation would be similar to a reception. If the principles are, however, tailored to, and corresponding to, the order of international law then they are incapable of being incorporated, because they are only to be observed for the conduct of subjects of international law, that is to say, in the area of relations between the States themselves.

Following *Doehring*'s view who, indeed, considers the general principles of law as being general rules of international law covered by Art. 25 of the Basic Law, would bear as a consequence that these rules — at the same time probably rules of German private law — would be ranked higher than the remaining German laws. In my opinion, there is no reason for this assumption.[25]

---

[24] *Rudolf* (note 2), 255 *et seq.*
[25] *Doehring* (note 7), 125 *et seq.*; *Rudolf* (note 2), 257.

The opinion of a criminal division of the *Bundesgerichtshof* (Federal Court of Justice)[26] is not convincing that through Art. 25 all treaties under international law are in a higher rank than the remaining German laws, obtaining this rank through the general rule of international law: *pacta sunt servanda*. This phrase refers to the adherence to treaties under international law by the subjects of international law as such. It cannot address itself to individuals and State organs not being organs of international relations at the same time. For this reason, it is not capable of being incorporated into municipal law. The Federal Constitutional Court rightly held that the general rules exclusively have priority over the laws but not, however, treaties under international law.[27]

The number of those general rules of international law, part of municipal law and with priority over laws and directly creating rights and duties for the inhabitants of the federal territory, seems to be limited. Between 1952 and (March) 1987 the Federal Constitutional Court examined the existence of a general rule of international law in 28 cases on the merits. After having negated the existence of such a rule for 16 times, it detected one for the first time in 1977.[28]

Since then, six more cases have been decided where a general rule of international law as part of Federal law was established.[29] This means that out of 28 cases 22 were decided in the negative and no more than six positively. Thus, Art. 25 of the Basic Law is of minor practical importance. Also, according to the practice of the Austrian Supreme Constitutional Court concerning Art. 9 of the Federal Constitutional Law which contains a similar clause, the relevance of the general rules of international law for the citizen is rather little.[30]

3. *Legal consequences of Art. 25*

With Art. 25 the entire general customary international law capable of being incorporated generally gets incorporated into the legal order of the Federal Republic of Germany. There is no need for a special order of application as in Art. 59 para. 2 of the Basic Law regarding treaties under international law. The national act of application arises, to the contrary, from Art. 25 itself. This regulation of the Constitution, generally and perpetually, provides the order of legal application for general customary international law. It is this Article which constitutes the standard

---

[26] *Entscheidungen des Bundesgerichtshofs in Strafsachen* (Reports of the Federal Supreme Court on Criminal Matters — BGHSt) vol. 5, 396—407 (402).

[27] BVerfGE 6, 309—367 (362).

[28] BVerfGE 46, 342—404.

[29] BVerfGE 57, 9—28; 59, 380—387; 60, 253—305; 63, 332—339; 67, 43—64; *Beschluß* of March 31st, 1987, Az. 2 BvM 2/86.

[30] *Felix Ermacora*, Der Verfassungsgerichshof, Graz/Wien/Köln 1956, 352.

transformer of general customary international law and effects its reception into municipal law. The general rules of international law, indeed, always remain part of international law, despite their transformation into municipal law. They are even closer linked to the system of international law than treaties under international law, due to their presence in municipal law being inseparably connected with their existence in international law.[31] They have become, however, through Art. 25 Federal law, too, and they directly produce rights and duties for the inhabitants of the Federal territory, as the explanatory sentence (sent.) 2 of Art. 25 adds.

Art. 25 sent. 2 rules that the regulations of general customary international law have priority over German laws. Hence follows actually that incorporated general customary international law has priority over Federal laws and over the entire law of the *Länder*. It is controversial whether incorporated law takes a rank between the Constitution and simple Federal laws, the same rank as the Constitution, or even a rank higher than the Constitution. This question of ranking plays a role in German municipal law because its legal order is built up hierarchically: At the top there are situated unchangeable constitutional principles (Art. 79 part. 3), followed by "normal" constitutional law of the Federation. Below the Constitution the laws derived from the Constitution can be found. Unter that, executive orders of the different levels of government are situated, which again must spring from higher ranking law. Subordinate rules contradicting law of a superior rank are illegal.

The opinion held, above all, by *Menzel*,[32] that incorporated general rules of international law have priority even over the constitutional law of the Federation is the most far-reaching. The term "law" in Art. 25 is, this view accordingly, to be understood as "any legal rule" in the sense of Art. 2 of the *Einführungsgesetz zum Bürgerlichen Gesetzbuch* (Introductory Act of the Civil Code).

Based on the most various reasons, justified objections were raised against this theory.[33] It was argued that Art. 25 did not belong to those constitutional rules, being especially protected and unalterable, according to Art. 79 para. 3, and thus could be overruled by Federal law amending the Constitution. Neither could the constitutional legislator create a law of higher rank than constitutional law, because the rank of a rule was determined by the rank of the respective legislator. A rank superior to the Constitution could only be established by following the strict monist theory with the primacy of international law. The Federal Constitutional Court stated in an early decision of 1952 that Art. 25 had

[31] *Rudolf* (note 2), 262.
[32] *Menzel* (note 4), 64.
[33] *Rudolf* (note 2), 264 *et seq.*

"generally proclaimed the primacy of international law over municipal law as a constitutional principle of the German Federal Republic", naturally also governing the constitutional law of the *Länder*.[34] This statement can — on a systematic interpretation of the whole decision — only mean that general customary international law has priority over the normal laws of the Federation and the entire law of the *Länder*, the latter as a whole subordinate to Federal law, as far as the Federation's competences go (Art. 31). For this reason, the incorporated rules of general customary international law, at best, hold the rank of the Federal Constitution.

This result is also doubted, since a subsequent general rule of international law could alter constitutional law in contradiction to the provision ruling that every change of the constitution must necessarily alter the text of the Constitution (Art. 79 para. 1). Nevertheless, not only some teachers of law such as *Doehring*, *Partsch*, and myself, but competent officials of the Federal Foreign Office also hold the opinion that the general rules of international law are of constitutional rank. The majority of the legal writers, to the contrary, seems to favour an intermediate rank between the Constitution and the normal laws, a view supported by, for instance, *Bernhardt*, *Mosler*, *Scheuner*, and *Seidl-Hohenveldern*.[35] The question of rank is of importance in the case of existence of parallel German law. Provisions of Federal law concerning diplomatic immunity only have declaratory and explanatory significance in view of the higher ranking corresponding rule of general customary international law incorporated into municipal law.[35a] In the same way, the special transformation of general customary international law into constitutional law, through particular rules of municipal law referring to international law, becomes unnecessary due to the introduction of the general incorporation. These specific municipal regulations, too, keep declaratory character only.

The legal importance of Art. 25 is certainly inferior to what the Fathers of the Constitution had assumed since, apart from the question of rank, no essential legal changes have occured in view of the existing situation under customary international law through the introduction of Art. 25 and, already in 1919, through Art. 4 of the Weimar Constitution. The main value of Art. 25 consists in the expression of the political confession in favour of international law. Juridically, this is reflected in the fact that

---

[34] BVerfGE 1, 208—261 (233); *see* Art. 31 of the Basic Law: Federal law shall override the law of the *Länder*; Art. 79 para. 1 of the Basic Law (*see* Documentation, 192, 193).

[35] *Doehring* (note 7), 182 *et seq.*; *Partsch* (note 6), 70, 71; *Rudolf* (note 2), 267, 268; so *Meyer-Lindenberg* / *von Schenck*, according to *Partsch* (note 6), 61.

[35a] *E. g.* §§ 18—20 *Gerichtsverfassungsgesetz* (Constitution of Courts Act).

an interpretation of the entire German law in favour of international law is required.[36]

Finally, it has been clarified by Art. 25 that the actually existing general customary international law, provided its capacity of being incorporated, has become part of Federal law. This clarification was necessary, as in the Parliamentary Council the view was supported, among others, that the constitutional clause of international law concerned the "ethical core of international law".[37] This is not correct because Art. 25 does not cover the law common to all human beings, but the rules of general customary international law really in force, which need not necessarily belong to the ethical core of international law. At any rate, I would not consider the rule that a diplomat does not have to pay motor vehicle tax for his wife's car as part of the ethical core of international law; nevertheless, it is covered by Art. 25 as a rule of general customary international law.

V. Incorporation of particular rules of customary international law

1. Incorporation beyond Art. 25

As Art. 25 of the Basic Law incorporates the *general* rules of international law, that means, the rules of general customary international law, the question remains how the *special* rules of customary international law have to be treated. These would be covered by this Article if the term "general" were referred to the *contents* of the rule and not to the number of the subjects of international law, *i. e.* to the extent of application. The latter, however, is assumed by some authors, such as *Friedrich Klein, Heinz Guradze,* and *Hermann Meyer-Lindenberg,* but this opinion is rightly rejected by the majority since, as *Roman Herzog* convincingly demonstrated, useful marks for the distinction between general and "non-general" rules of customary international law referring to the contents of the rule do not exist.[38]

The reverse conclusion, arguing that the incorporation of rules emanating from local customs is impossible because Art. 25 incorporates general customary international law into municipal law only, must be

[36] *See* especially *Rainer Hofmann,* Zur Bedeutung von Art. 25 GG für die Praxis deutscher Behörden und Gerichte, in: *Walter Fürst / Roman Herzog / Dieter C. Umbach* (eds.) Festschrift für *Wolfgang Zeidler,* Berlin / New York 1987, vol. 2, 1885—1898.

[37] *Adolf Süsterhenn* in the Parliamentary Council; *Rudolf* (note 2), 275.

[38] *Klein* (note 19), 167; *Heinz Guradze,* Der Stand der Menschenrechte im Völkerrecht, Göttingen 1956, 173; *Hermann Meyer-Lindenberg,* Die Menschenrechte im Völkerrecht, in: Berichte der Deutschen Gesellschaft für Völkerrecht 4 (1961), 84—130 (106, 107); *Roman Herzog,* Nochmals: Verfassungsbeschwerde gegen Verletzungen der Menschenrechtskonvention?, in: Die Öffentliche Verwaltung 13 (1961), 775—778.

refused by reason of the Constitution's confession in favour of international law. An analogous application of this Article to particular customary international law though could be taken into account. However, the conclusion *a maiore ad minus*, which is possible under Austrian law with regard to Art. 9 of the Austrian Federal Constitutional Law, must be rejected in German law due to the privileging of incorporated general customary international law over national laws. It is moreover not consistent with the text and the purpose of Art. 25 to extend the rise of rank to particular customary international law.[39]

Although Art. 25 can neither be applied explicitly nor analogously to particular customary international law, the possibility of an incorporation of regionally limited customary international law will also have to be taken into consideration in the Federal Republic of Germany. A prerequisite for this is that the German legal order recognizes a legal rule transforming particular customary international law corresponding to the English legal maxim "international law is part of the law of the land".

Such a provision, indeed, is at hand. As the practice of the Supreme Court of the German *Reich* reveals,[40] a legal provision existed already before 1919, incorporating rules of general as well as those of particular customary international law into municipal law. This is, why Art. 4 of the Weimar Constitution did not bring about any amendment, just as little as Art. 9 of the Austrian Federal Constitutional Law, but — to speak with the words of *Alfred Verdross* — "only led to the codification of a principle which had already taken its shape through the practice of independent courts"[41].

This customary rule for the incorporation of customary international law existing at all times has not fully lost its importance, neither through Art. 4 of the Weimar Constitution of the German *Reich* nor through Art. 25 of the Basic Law, as these clauses of international law are only transformers of the generally recognized or, with other words, of the general customary international law. It continues being valid for the particular customary international law which is recognized within the Federal Republic of Germany and applied municipally.

This clause of customary national law, too, causes the incorporation, just like Art. 25 with reference to the general rules of international law.

---

[39] *See Walter Rudolf*, Die innerstaatliche Anwendung partikulären Völkergewohnheitsrechts, in: *René Marcic et al.* (eds.), Internationale Festschrift für *Alfred Verdross*, München / Salzburg 1971, 435—448.

[40] *Entscheidungen des Reichsgerichts in Strafsachen* (Decisions of the Supreme Court of the German *Reich* on Criminal Matters) vol. 23, 266—268 (267); *Entscheidungen des Reichsgerichts in Zivilsachen* (Decisions of the Supreme Court of the German *Reich* on Civil Matters) vol. 62, 165—168 (166).

[41] *Alfred Verdross*, Völkerrecht, 5th ed. Wien 1964, 118.

Insofar it differs in the same way as Art. 25 differs from the regulations concerning municipal application of treaties under international law, especially from Art. 59 para. 2, as the latter contains the statutory power of transformation.[42]

There is a particularity to be noticed with regard to *local* customary international law. If a local regulation through customary international law exists, there is at the same time always a corresponding parallel national regulation. There can be no case imagined where local customary international law affecting citizens and national organs could develop without parallel national (customary) law appearing. Long-lasting practices such as, for example, fishing rights in areas next to common maritime boundaries with foreign States and in historical bays or rights of passage to enclaves do not just constitute customs of international law, but reveal, at the same time, also appearances of municipal law. That is, why local customary international law does not require any incorporation into municipal law as it is always derived from parallel municipal law. Therefore, it is not covered by the customary rule of transformation of German law either.[43]

2. *Classification of incorporated particular customary international law*

Finally, the question concerning the classification of transformed particular customary international law into the hierarchy of national sources of law remains to be answered. As the customary transformer for these rules of international law belongs to unwritten Federal law, it is difficult yet to determine this transformer's rank. Possibly even more difficult is to determine the rank of particular customary international law transformed by it. This is true for any customary law, since the German hierarchy of rules is tailored to statutory law. As the point of reference for the question of rank is a formal one, namely the rank of the law-maker, and as rules of customary international law, on the other hand, can only be classified in substance, with regard to their contents, a relationship between both forms of ranking is not impossible — otherwise customary law could never displace statutory law. This relationship, however, cannot be determined in general.[44]

The rank of particular customary international law incorporated into municipal law depends on the respective political and legal value of the rule of international law concerned. It will not be possible to concede any particular rule of international law a rank superior to a simple law.

---

[42] *Rudolf* (note 39), 444.
[43] *Op. cit.*, 445, 446.
[44] *Rudolf* (note 2), 280.

If, also, the rules of particular customary international law would come before the laws, such primacy would have had to be laid down explicitly as a constitutional rule.

It might be doubtful whether the rules of particular customary international law, at least those with higher importance among them, can be granted the rank of Federal law. If so, *posterior* rules could have priority over existing Federal laws — a result which would be delicate in view of the legislative monopoly of the institutions participating in legislation. Nevertheless — taking into account the favourable position granted to international law inherent by the Basic Law and regarding the fact that such important rules of particular customary international law should be rare — the possibility of repeal in part of statutory law through *posterior* particular customary international law should be accepted in the same way as the abrogation of laws through *posterior* municipal customary law has to be considered.[45]

As the cases of incorporation of particular customary international law into municipal law should not appear very frequently, the jurist's interest remains fixed to Art. 25 of the Basic Law. But, in addition, as this rule does not very often become relevant, the incorporation of customary international law into municipal law plays a role of considerable less importance than the incorporation of treaties under international law.

[45] *Rudolf* (note 39), 447, 448.

Discussion

Wolfrum, Chairman:

It is quite difficult to try to put a structure on the discussion and I normally rather refrain from trying to do so. I would propose, however, to discuss first the questions touched upon by both speakers, namely self-executing and non-self-executing customary international law. The second point could be the scope accepted. There was a slight difference between Mr. *Danilenko* and Mr. *Rudolf*, although, basically they were on common ground.

Bernhardt:

I would like to ask whether the whole notion of "self-executing" and "non-self-executing norms" does not need more clarification and sophistication. To a certain extent, the notions are connected with the internal judicial order in the following respect: If one speaks of self-executing norms — sometimes norms are meant which can immediately be applied to concrete disputes and which permit a clear decision in a dispute before a national court. Such norms of customary international law are rare. In Germany we have had some immunity cases before the Federal Constitutional Court, the Court had to decide whether customary international law grants immunity or not. Other norms may have only an indirect influence or relevance. I can hardly imagine any norm of customary international law which is entirely incapable of being taken into consideration in certain disputes before German courts. For instance, international law may play a role in a case before a national court concerning the pollution of the environment without being the only relevant factor. Even the prohibition of the use of force could play a certain role in litigation before German courts, for instance, if a soldier is not prepared to take part in certain exercises or measures because he considers this to be contrary to international law. In general, the notion of non-self-executing and self-executing rules is to a certain extent doubtful.

Rudolf:

It is clear that I should oppose this opinion. I think that the notion is useful though. We have a lot of norms in international law which are self-executing to the effect that they are applicable internally in the

State without adding any other rule of national law. Most of these norms are also part of customary international law which can be applied in the national legal order — as you already mentioned, for example, all norms of State immunity. It may happen that the same rule, based on customary or treaty law, may be self-executing in the municipal law of one State and non-self-executing in another. Imagine, for instance, Article 6 of the European Human Rights Convention. In Germany it is self-executing, but in Austria some additional norms were necessary to make the execution of this provision possible. It depends on the legal system whether a norm is seen as a self-executing or non-self-executing order. I think, if some additional national rules are required, one cannot speak of self-executing. The term self-executing does not mean self-executing in a way being, at any rate, part of the national law. Even a self-executing norm must be transformed, must be incorporated, there must be a State act to apply it to the national legal system. There is, for instance, the rule that piracy is not allowed. But a German or a Soviet court cannot apply this norm in the interior legal order. Merely saying that piracy is not allowed is not sufficient to punish a person. One must have additional national criminal provisions stating the punishment will be one year, or six years, or something like that. Those additional rules are indispensable. A lot of international norms influence municipal law but, in fact, they do not exercise any real influence, because it is necessary to have some additional norms of the interior legal order. I just mentioned this problem during the break to Mr. *Mosler:* There is the German Cheques Act. This Act originally was not a municipal German law, but an international treaty. It was self-executing and one could apply this treaty as if it were German law. Meanwhile, I think, most of the German lawyers rather do not know that it was a treaty; it seems that it has lost its international scope and has now become a German law. It is internally applied because it was self-executing.

Wolfrum, Chairman:

Before I give the floor to Mr. *Simma*, I would like to call upon Mr. *Bernhardt* who just wanted to exercise his right of reply.

Bernhardt:

I want to avoid a misunderstanding. The whole question of self-executing and non-self-executing is only of interest in States where in principle international law forms part of the law of the land. You can use these notions also in different contexts, but this is hardly advisable. If international customary norms are in principle applicable in internal law, then even those norms which are considered to be non-self-executing can be relevant under certain conditions. Thank you.

Simma:

I would like to agree very much with Mr. *Bernhardt* when he expressed his conviction that we are in need of further sophistication and clarification of the notion of the "self-executing character" of an international rule. I think, that, maybe under the influence of European Community Law, most German lawyers have a view of self-executing rules as being rules which create rights and duties immediately for private persons, rules which can be pursued before national courts. As you know, that is the notion of direct applicability as it has been developed in European Community Law. But if we see, for example, what the Federal Constitutional Court has said in the *Philippine Embassy* Case, we find that it develops there a differentiation which I think is very important. The Court held that direct applicability can also mean that a rule of customary law is applied by a national organ as part of the objective law of the land. I guess that what Mr. *Bernhardt* had in mind and also what you, (*Mr. Rudolf*), had in mind is more in conformity with the second view, with the larger notion of direct applicability or of self-executing character. Now, if this is the case, I would very much like to disagree with what you have said about Article 25 Basic Law. If I understood you correctly, you said that customary law must be, like treaties, self-executing in order to be incorporated into domestic law. I would say that, as far as the wording of Article 25 is concerned, you do not find any support for this view. To give you just one example (on which, I think, Professor *Bleckmann* disagrees with me): A German court would have to decide on its own on whether a certain territorial entity, like Southern Rhodesia or a Bantustan, is a State for the purpose of State immunity and so on. Faced with such a question, a German court would not be bound — that is another point I would like to make in your direction — to follow any executive orders or directives (like the respective Orders in Council in case of English courts), but it would have to decide itself whether the entity under consideration is a State or not. It would then apply basic customary rules on the pre-requisites of statehood. I think that all of you will doubt that the famous *Drei-Elemente-Theorie* is self-executing! Such a view would just not make any sense. The situation would be similar in a case where, for instance, a German court would have to decide whether a foreign expropriation is contrary to international law or not, like in the *Chilean Copper* Case, or the *Bremen Tobacco* Case. I think you would hesitate to say that the good old *Hull* formula, according to which prompt, effective, and adequate compensation has to be granted (if this formula ever existed as a rule of law), is a rule which is self-executing in a strict sense, but it certainly would have to be applied by the German courts.

With regard to Mr. *Danilenko*'s thesis, I would like to ask him whether direct application in the broader sense is really as rare as he implied, when he said that there are only very few rules of customary law which are capable of being directly applied, and that the principle is the non-self-executing character of customary law. I would like to point out that we are watching a growing tendency in jurisprudence, and a growing readiness of courts, to accept certain rules of international law as customary rules applicable by these courts. Let me just point out that we have American court decisions, accordingly torture is a violation of customary law, like the famous *Filartiga* Case. Then we have the *Rodriguez* Cases, according to which arbitrary detention is a violation of customary law. We have the German Constitutional Court's ruling pursuant to which the basic norms on the treatment of aliens are of customary character. We have a whole number of cases on expropriation, on State immunity to the same effect. So, I think, that the tendency goes towards and not away from direct applicability of international customary law. With regard to what you have further said — that even in case of application of the incorporation technique, in the last resort the decision on the content of a rule of customary law is made on the highest executive level — you gave examples from various countries, among them Austria. Let me start with Austria. There was indeed a law in Austria providing in cases of doubt to a court the right, not the duty, to ask for an advice by the Foreign Ministry. But I would like to point out that this law has been abrogated several years ago, because the view was taken — and I think rightly so — that this law was in violation of the constitutional separation of powers between the judiciary and the executive. With regard to the Federal Republic the same is true. There exists, for instance, a note which the German Foreign Ministry has sent out to all diplomatic missions saying that these embassies should watch out with regard to State immunity cases because the German executive has absolutely no influence on the courts. Then the note goes on to sketch what German courts had said on State immunity and again point out that there is nothing the Executive can do about this. So we do not have in the Federal Republic the possibilities which the US Executive obviously had at its disposal in the famous case of *Jackson* v. *People's Republic of China*. So, there is a clear and total independence of German courts from the Executive. Thank you.

Let me close by a short remark which has to do with the organisation of our meeting. I think that I have never attended a conference at which on every table we have found flowers. I think this should not only be taken as a compliment to the ladies in our room but also as a sign of hope, because we can see that flowers of very different colours — even flowers with different shades of red — can coexist on a rather narrow space. Thank you.

Bothe:

I would like to argue along the lines of Mr. *Bernhardt* and Mr. *Simma*. The notion of "self-executing" may give a false impression, namely that there is one kind of international legal norm which has to be respected by the relevant actors in the internal sphere of States, and another kind of norms about which the internal actor can just forget, which do not concern the national judge. This is, to say the least, an over-simplification. On the other hand, it is certainly true, and Mr. *Rudolf* has mentioned a number of examples where it is obvious, that one norm of international law is not like the other. The difference in content between the norms logically leads to different results where these norms are applied, especially in the internal sphere of States. We can, for example, differentiate between promotional obligations and strict obligations, or between obligations as to a result, and obligations as to a certain conduct. This difference of content or of regulatory style is also known in municipal law. There are different kinds of norms in constitutional law, on the one hand fundamental rights which are directly applicable, on the other, constitutional principles which are only directives for the political organs and cannot be applied directly, without additional implementing legislation. But under certain conditions, when there is an appropriate case, the latter principles, too, are indeed applied by the courts. The same holds true for international law. This means that the real effect of a norm depends on the case. Also, norms which are not self-executing may be applied by the municipal judge if there is an appropriate case for doing so.

I would like to give you a few examples in order to make clear what I mean. Take the law of reprisals. This seems to be a clear-cut interstate question, a rule which is not fit for direct intra-state application. But when it comes to a question of whether the termination of a contract by the government constitutes an illegal taking of property or a lawful act, it may well be relevant to ask whether such termination of a contract can be characterized as a reprisal against the State of which the other party to the contract is the national. Such problems are in particular raised by the practice of embargoes, which is a current question. In this situation, courts may well be called upon to pronounce themselves on the question whether a reprisal is justified under international law or not.

Coming to the question of criminal law, it is of course true what Mr. *Rudolf* said. One cannot base a criminal condemnation on the fact alone that the alleged perpetrator did something forbidden under international law. Additional national laws providing for a criminal sanction are needed. But take for instance the question of war crimes. War criminals are punished on the basis of national norms, for example concerning murder and torture. The question of whether an intentional killing constitutes a war crime or a legitimate act of war (which may not be punished) has to be answered by reference to the international law relating to the conduct of hostilities. These rules are clearly inter-state norms which normally are not capable of internal application. But they have an impact on the application of national criminal law, as the case may be.

To get away from the laws of war, I will give you a last example. Certain administrative decisions are to be taken on the basis of a balancing of values, such as the protection of the environment, or of human health, and other economic or administrative considerations. We have such norms in building or planning codes, in particular. My example is taken from the regulation of waste disposal, a case that happened recently. The question was whether, by the establishment of a waste disposal site, a site would be destroyed which was protected under the Cultural Heritage Convention. This decision on the establishment of a waste disposal site is one of these administrative measures where certain values have to be pondered against one another, according to the German Waste Disposal Statute. It is in my view quite clear that international law has to play a role in defining and determining the weight of such values. The Cultural Heritage Convention certainly defines the obligations of States in a way which carefully avoids to make these obligations self-executive. Nevertheless, the administrative agencies concerned and any court reviewing the action of these agencies cannot ignore the fact that there is some degree of international obligation to protect these sites, although the law gives to the agency a broad margin of appreciation. Administrative decisions which simply discards the argument that the Cultural Heritage Convention has to be taken into account would in my view be illegal under German law.

Danilenko:

I have three interrelated questions: The first is, how do you define a self-executing norm? The second, is there a possibility from the point of view of any internal law, for instance, Austrian or German, of giving a legal definition of self-executing norms? The third, does it make sense in practice for law enforcement agencies? How would such definition influence the practice?

Tunkin:

I believe, we probably embarked on the single problem relating to the two reports, a problem which is in my mind not of major importance — self-executing or non-self-executing norms. I agree with the previous speakers that in international law in general, and in customary law in particular, there are norms which may be called self-executing as Mr. *Rudolf* previously explained, and those which require certain supplementary norms of national law. But what I would like to add to that is, that, in my view, much depends on the municipal law of a specific State.

Then, Mr. *Chairman*, I would like to say a few words on the concept of customary international law. It seems that there is much confusion nowadays in this field. What is customary international law? Let us take the decision of the International Court of Justice on the *Nicaragua/United States* Case. What is meant there by customary international law? First, it is not treaty law and, further, those are general norms of international law. I entirely agree with Mr. *Rudolf* that customary norms may be general, or regional, or even bi-lateral. You will remember that the International Court of Justice has itself accepted that there may be bi-lateral customary norms. In my view, it is very unfortunate that there is confusion about customary international law and general international law, namely that customary international law only is general international law. In the present situation I have written about that in my books. The treaty norms may be also norms of general international law as, for instance, the principles of the Charter of the United Nations. In my view, there are norms of general international law which for some States are treaty norms and for the others are customary norms. The concept that general international law is only customary international law may lead, for example, to a conclusion that the rule of prohibition of the use of force and the threat of force is not a rule of general international law, because it is a rule of the UN Charter which is a treaty. General international law is partly customary law, partly treaty law.

Then the problem of relations between international law and municipal law: I entirely agree that general international law does not prescribe either, that norms of this law must be part of municipal law of each State, or to the contrary. There is no such rule of general international law. Therefore, it all depends on the municipal law which may consider norms of international law as part of this law or not. Of course, international law is obligatory to all the States, and in this sense it has a supremacy over internal law. Still there is the problem, as you know, whether this primacy of international law is automatic or non-automatic.

Rudolf:

I think, I should first answer the principal three questions posed. May I answer the second question first. What is a self-executing norm? Is there a legal definition of self-executing? What is the practice in this field? There is no legal definition of what is "self-executing" because the term self-executing is an invention of lawyers, of professors, and it is nowhere laid down as a legal definition. What is a self-executing norm must be decided by municipal law — insofar we totally agree, Mr. *Tunkin*. International law only addresses to the States, and the States have to act in order to execute this international legal norm. It is possible that the legal rule is applicable in the internal legal order. This, however, is a decision of the municipal legal system. The municipal legal order decides whether a rule of international law can be applied in the internal sphere of the State. This is a question to be decided by the courts or by the administrative authorities, if the answer is positive you can apply this legal norm. If the municipal law cannot apply this rule without any additional norms, the State is obliged to create these additional norms. I cannot agree with Mr. *Bothe* that it is a second class norm if it is not self-executing. It is not a second class, but it is necessary for the State to provide additional norms in order to execute the rule of international law — if it is not applicable because of the wording, in the case of a treaty, or because it is not consistent enough to be applied without any additional legal norm in the municipal order. As a consequence, municipal law decides what is self-executing and what is not self-executing. I think we do agree. We also agree on the other point that treaties and general law may exist side by side.

Tunkin:

Of course it is right that in the case of specific norms the municipal law is required to implement the norms of international laws; the State is bound to do that, but how it will do that — it may be administrative norms, it may be other norms, it depends on the State. Of course, if we take treaties, there are many provisions directly obligating States to enact certain laws, for instance, the Convention on Air Piracy contains provisions that States must enact legislation to that effect.

Oppermann:

Mr. *Chairman*, after the important statement of Mr. *Tunkin*, I think we can now go beyond the question of direct applicability. I have one or two questions, especially to Mr. *Danilenko*. But I want to say first, that I felt very much enriched and inspired by these two important speeches we heard this morning. Mr. *Tunkin*, your remark that we have a general international law constituted by general treaty law on the one hand, and general customary law on the other hand, is quite understandable. I have no difficulty in following this idea. But nevertheless, I think the differentiation between treaty law and customary law remains an important one, even if you have this common general law.

Furthermore, I am very interested in understanding the scope of customary law in accordance with the Soviet doctrine. Therefore, I would like to ask you, Mr. *Danilenko*, to develop a little bit upon the ideas you gave us in your speech. What is the scope of customary international law in accordance with the Soviet doctrine? In particular, how big, in your opinion, is the corpus of general customary international law, mutually recognized by different political systems of States, between the Socialist world and others, for instance? Is there much common ground? Could you perhaps cite one or two examples of customary rules which are really common?

We have, of course, the Charter of the United Nations, as you said, Mr. *Tunkin*. In the *Nicaragua* Case, the International Court of Justice has stated that fundamental rules of this Charter belong equally to customary international law. It is very interesting that the General Assembly of the UN went even further when it proclaimed that the Constitution of the Republic of South Africa violates the Charter of the United Nations and is not valid. How is this possible? Is there a direct applicability of fundamental rules of general customary international law which may override even the sovereign internal will of the existing State? I am not commenting on the internal situation of the Republic of South Africa, but here you find the idea that fundamental rules of customary international law can override the sovereignty of States also in internal affairs. You are very near to the famous notion of *ius cogens*. Would the Soviet doctrine of general customary international law include any rule with the character of *ius cogens*? The International Law Commission has recently introduced similar ideas in discussing the notion of "international crimes".

You mentioned at the end of your statement that, for the cause of general customary international law, political factors are very important. Here again I would like to know what you mean by this phrase. Political factors are important in the sense — if I understood you correctly — that a certain rule of general customary international law may go further, or, perhaps, may not go so far, following the political impact behind it. What are they like, these political factors?

Another short remark: The two speakers mentioned the procedure of our German Constitutional Court following Article 100, second chapter of the Constitution, where the Court has a right to find out whether a certain general rule of international customary law exists or not. You said quite correctly, Mr. *Danilenko*, and Mr. *Rudolf* was of the same opinion that even if the Federal Constitutional Court says that a certain rule exists or not, this is binding only inside the German legal system. This is true, but I want to mention that the German Court is extremely careful not to state only the German point of view. In every major case of this kind, which is put before it, it takes an expert opinion from the Heidelberg Institute of Public International Law, comparing thoroughly all existing tendencies of international law to be found throughout the world. Only on the basis of this extensive comparison the Court reaches its decision. If I understand correctly, it has followed the Heidelberg opinion here. This, of course, is not an absolute argument in the sense that the judgment has world-wide validity, but I think we are on pretty firm ground of comparative international law up to this point.

Danilenko:

As regards the scope of international customary law in general, this is a more general problem and we, as I understood, do not discuss it here. Nevertheless, I would like to state that of course from the point of view of Soviet lawyers, there are a number of general rules of international customary law which are recognized by all States. There is no difficulty in following this line of argument. I can cite a number of examples, for instance, in the area of the law of the sea. The International Court of Justice, for example, has stated that the notion of the exclusive economic zone (EEZ) can be regarded as part of modern international law, at this juncture. Although the 1982 Law of the Sea Convention is not yet in force, a number of its principles are already customary international law. The Soviet Union has a decree on the economic zone of the USSR. It was adopted on the understanding that the practice of States is developing in the direction of recognition of the EEZ. There are also a number of rules of international customary law in the area of the law of outer space that the Soviet Union recognized and even stated on a number of occasions, that it does recognize their existence. It is the official Soviet point of view that a number of principles of the Outer Space Treaty can be regarded as principles of international customary law and as also binding States which are not parties to that treaty.

If we follow the line of argument of the International Court of Justice in the *Nicaragua/US* Case then we have to recognize that a number of principles enshrined in the UN Charter, including the principle forbidding the use of force in international relations, can also be considered as principles of international customary law. Those principles are also relevant for internal relations when the relevant cases arise in the internal sphere. As regards the political factors, I only wanted to point out the fact that the technique in itself does not guarantee the actual observance of international customary law. Technique may vary. I think, however, that much depends on the attitude of a given State to international law in general. That is, what I meant by political factors.

Mr. *Simma* mentioned the trend to apply international customary law more widely in domestic courts. I would not be so sure. There are really a number of cases involving international customary law in the American practice at this moment. But other States do not follow this line and, for instance, in the Federal Republic of Germany, as Mr. *Rudolf* has stated, it is a rarity when courts apply international customary law directly. In the Soviet practice it is also the case.

Rudolf:

I did not say that in our domestic courts international law is not applied. I only stated that there are only a few norms of general customary international law which are recognized as norms of customary international law by the Federal Constitutional Court. As these decisions are not always published it may happen that in the lower courts there are some cases, maybe not as often as in the United States, but there are cases, extradition cases for example, where international law is applied by these courts. But when these rules of international law are applied there is no doubt that they are part of international law. The Federal Constitutional Court is only asked if there is any doubt whether there exists a norm of international law incorporated by Article 25 of the Federal Constitution, or not. So, I did not mention the problem whether international law is applied in our courts at all. I solely said there are only a few rules of international law recognized as general norms of international law by the Federal Constitutional Court. These norms are surely applied by the lower courts, that is clear.

Well, Mr. *Oppermann* said, that usually our Federal Constitutional Court asks the Max-Planck-Institute in Heidelberg whether there exists a norm of customary international law. Nevertheless, you should not get the impression that in reality not the Constitutional Court decides what is a norm of customary international law, but the Max-Planck-Institute is the decisive organ to decide upon this. The problem is, indeed, the same as in all States. Every State can only decide upon its internal jurisdiction. But, asking if this decision is correct in the view of international law, you have to compare this decision with those of courts in other States. To find a norm of customary law it is, indeed, unavoidable to observe the judicature in several other States, too. When the German Constitutional Court decides that a certain rule is part of general customary international law it may happen that, for instance, a court in the Soviet Union, in the United States, or in the United Kingdom, too, is of the opinion that a certain practice constitutes a custom. It may be that in the international field the professor compares all this and comes to the conclusion: Yes, there is a norm of general customary international law.

May I add some remarks to Mr. *Bothe*. He says that international law is also applied by national courts in an indirect way. This is evident but even in the cases of war crimes, the national criminal statute is the original source to be applied by the courts. It is the same with the

Soviet penal code, with the German penal code, and with the United States' penal code. Indeed, in interpreting a rule of the national code you may have a look at what is to be considered true in the international field. One of the most important meanings of Article 25 of our Federal Constitution, in my opinion, is the obligation to regard international law and to interpret the whole national law in favour of international norms. But that is neither a problem of self-executing, nor a problem of non-self-executing rules, nor of your cases on State immunity. There are no cases on self-executing on the one side, and on non-self-executing on the other; I even say that a German court would not dare to state that a South-African Homeland's agent enjoys personal immunity, because this would be against the competence of a German court. A German court cannot make international policy in Germany. You have to decide a specific case, and if a State is not recognized by the Federal Republic of Germany it would be contrary to law if a German court would vest such an agent with personal immunity.

Simma:

Let me just remind you of the case of the *Rhodesian Banknotes* — pending, I think, before Frankfurt and Munich courts. In this case a printing firm in Munich concluded a contract with the *Ian Smith* authorities concerning the printing of banknotes for the newly proclaimed State of Southern Rhodesia. The case was not decided because a settlement was reached between the parties. But, I think, as far as I read the decision of the court of the first instance, the courts did say that according to *Georg Jellinek*'s theories — and all the old stuff which we have studied at the universities on the elements of statehood — Southern Rhodesia seemed to be a pretty good case of a State. So I doubt whether you are right in saying that a German court cannot make policy. I would rather think that in any application of international law a court would make policy to some degree. I think that we cannot distinguish between the computer-like application of the law and policy-making.

Rudolf:

Probably this decision of the Munich court was rendered at a time before you, as a professor in Munich, were able to train and influence the judges when they have been students at the university. It happens that lower courts take wrong decisions. This is not astonishing.

Simma:

May I make just one further remark. We certainly have the case where German courts have said, for instance, that recognition of confiscations of foreign property abroad would be against the *ordre public* of the Federal Republic. In these cases the notion of the *ordre public* is really "filled out" by reference to public international law. I think that here we have a clear case of courts engaged in making policy and I think that, to a certain extent, it is a task of courts to make policy of that kind — to maintain certain rules of international law.

Mosler:

In a leading case the first stage of which occurred in Frankfurt 20 years ago, the question was whether Her Majesty's Government of the United Kingdom was still to be recognized as sovereign power in Rhodesia which had declared its independence. Rhodesian banknotes printed in Germany were seized at the moment when the man with the luggage entered the plane. It was dramatic, perhaps more interesting from a dramatic point of view than from the aspect of international law. Your second example refers, as I think, to the *Chilean Copper* cases. My view in these cases has been that there was no international obligation based on unwritten rules of the public order of the international legal community, that the internal law of Chile could not be applied in Germany or in any other country because it was held to violate principles of international law regarding foreign property. It was open to the *forum* State to act this way or the other; in our cases it was left to the courts. They could make legal policy in this margin.

But this is not what I was going to say. Excuse me, Mr. Chairman, I first wanted to reply to the intervention of Mr. *Simma*. I wish to come back to some points of non-self-executing and self-executing norms, which have not yet been raised. Of course, everyone is in agreement that States have to fulfil their international obligations, including customary law and the general principles of law. There is also agreement that all States have domestic jurisdiction to give effect to international obligations as they think it appropriate. But then two problems arise — one of policy and one of legal technique. It is clear that the policy in the Federal Republic of Germany and of many other European States is directed towards a closer and narrower co-operation between States, and even to supra-national forms, which we will discuss after tomorrow. If I understand your situation in the Soviet Union correctly, it is more the traditional view to keep the two legal orders separate in theory and practice, but the principal point of departure is the same.

Much has been said about self-execution and non-self-execution. Mr. *Tunkin*, you spoke of the eventual need of implementing international law, not only of treaty law but also of customary law. I think the main point in applying customary law is to clarify the precise contents. We all know the difference between principle and rule, and also that principles are legally binding but are not as concrete as rules. Unwritten principles and rules are by definition such clear limits as treaties. If you have, for instance, a commercial treaty granting nationals of the other party a certain status in one's own country, then there must be a domestic implementation. But, if one has to apply a general principle or international customary law, a more precise specification is required. I do not deny that implementation could be useful, but very often implementation does not exist, although the principle is binding. Let us take the example of immunity which already has been taken up. The principle *ne impediatur legatio* is binding but the status of diplomatic personnel needs certain technical rules. Mr. *Bernhardt* referred to civil contracts undertaken by diplomats. Exemption from indirect taxes can only be realized by specific rules. If a court has to decide such a case, it must find the applicable rule. For example, the question arose whether it was an interference with the immunity of the foreign State to change the land register of the premises of a foreign mission. These are things which should be implemented by law; if not, in Germany it is the judge who decides.

Then to your point, Mr. *Tunkin*, regarding universal law and customary law: You think that the principles of the United Nations — whatever they may be, only Article 2 or more — are applicable also to non-member nations. On what basis? Because it is general international law; but what kind of general international law?

Tunkin:

Switzerland declared that it accepted being bound by it.

Mosler:

I share your view that they are binding, but the question remains whether they are general international law or world-wide treaty law, which also expresses a general opinion and practice.

Furthermore, the *Nicaragua* Case has been mentioned two or three times. I do not want to take a position to the principal questions of the merits of the dispute, but I would like to remember one special point which weakens this Case as an example in our discussion. It was not so much a question of the obligation to observe the substantive law of the United Nations' Charter: It was a question of a United States' reservation to the Optional Clause. Everyone knows the famous *Vandenberg* Clause which had been respected by the Court. Whether it was right or not, this is another question. My view was, that it was right to respect it. But then the Court examined the same question under the heading of customary law. The problem is whether the non-application of the Charter as a treaty can not also exclude the corresponding principles of customary law. My question to you or to the other Soviet colleagues is the following: Does here not another problem come into the picture, the problem of *ius cogens*? I do not think that customary law has a higher rank than treaty law and if you are able to make treaties as you want, with the exception of provisions against *ius cogens*, then I think the same rule is also valid as far as customary law is concerned. You can exclude by a treaty, or a special *Compromis* submitted to an international court, customary law which does not belong to *ius cogens*. I believe in *ius cogens*, whatever the contents may be.

Tunkin:

So I do not.

Mosler:

Yes, I know. But don't you think that customary law, in this respect, is on the same level as treaty law and that *ius cogens* is still binding?

Tunkin:

All international law is binding. Some people say there is binding international law and some say there is no binding international law: All rules of international law are binding, but norms of *ius cogens* are those norms from which States cannot derogate by their mutual consent, by their treaties. That is the only difference, but a very important one.

*Usenko:**

It is my opinion that the problem of the definition of "self-executing" and "non-self-executing" norms gain in importance as the relationship between international and municipal law intensifies. There are cases when even in States that have declared international law to be part of the law of the land, courts have declined to apply rules of international law, because they hold that these norms were not self-executing. Clear statement in municipal law of various States on this point would greatly promote the effectiveness of international law. Thank you.

Lukashuk:

Just a few remarks. First of all I want to stress that it seems to be a very fruitful thought by Mr. *Bernhardt*. He was speaking about the application of general rules of customary international law by judges. Maybe we cannot call it application, they still take these rules into consideration, partly, in some way, and this seems to me very impor-

* *Editors'* note: The contribution was made in German and has been translated subsequently.

tant for the judges. Then there is another problem, self-executing rules. Mr. *Simma* and Mr. *Usenko* were speaking about different notions of self-executing rules. Maybe I am wrong, Mr. *Rudolf*, but it seems to me that you have the only notion of self-executing rules, the notion in the spirit of the European Economic Community. You mean rules which are directly applicable. So it seems to me there are two main notions. One because of the wording, it is in the US and in the Soviet Union the same. It means rules which could be applicable after the transformation, because of their wording, and another notion is that of the rules which are directly applicable. When we make a proper distinction on this point it would be much easier for us to understand the problem.

Coming to the last question: I would agree with Mr. *Simma* so that there is a tendency to closer interaction between international and municipal law, and we can do nothing to prevent this tendency. Especially judges will have more problems with these interactions. We, as lawyers, speak about rules on the problem, constitutional rules, and so on, but it seems to me it is not as easy as we think. Because it is not enough to propose another rule, constitutional, or on other questions; judges are not happy in those cases when they meet with international law and somehow they try to get around international law. So, the whole juridical system must be reorganized in order to be ready for interaction, more active interaction with international law. It is no problem that we need another law and so on, no, but the whole education of judges must be reorganized. We want to be prepared to decide such problems. Thank you.

Wolfrum, Chairman:

May I lead the discussion back to the interventions made by you, Mr. *Tunkin*, your ideas being taken up by Mr. *Oppermann*, and after that by Mr. *Mosler*. I fully agree that, with respect to treaty as well as customary law, some kind of "general international law" or "universal international law" exists, which forms a specific layer of law. However, I still would like to have the question answered you raised: How does this "universal international law" come into existence? This is not a matter of *ius cogens*, although, equally the question of binding third parties — to use a phrase of treaty law — is at stake. Which subjects of international law, States or international organizations, are the creators of such law; what are its essentials? As far as I am concerned, law can be derived either by means of interpreting existing provisions of international law — finding the common denominator — or by means of providing for general principles. In the latter case, such "universal international law" will be developed primarily in the framework of international organizations.

Oppermann:

Let me say just one phrase. I would like to try to help in answering this very fundamental question. Aren't we back to the famous *conscience publique* of the *Martens* Clause on which *Rudolf von Laun* tried to build up the whole structure of international public law?

Tunkin:

In my view, we have to start at the very beginning and, namely, how the rules of international law are created. You know that there are different theories, which do consider that rules of international law are created by some natural or sociological phenomena. In my view, and the practice confirms this view, the only possibility of creating norms of international law is the co-ordination of the wills of States. If we proceed from this assumption then we must accept that the foundation or the creation of the norms of international law, either customary or treaty norms, is the same — the co-ordination of the wills of States. That would explain many things. The interaction between a customary and a treaty way of creating norms of international law takes an important part in this process of creating new rules of *ius cogens*.

The Relevance of Resolutions and Declarations of International Organizations for Municipal Law

By Philip Kunig*

I. Introduction

Let me begin by quoting the final sentences of our Polish colleague *Krzysztof Skubiszewski*'s contribution on international legislation to *Rudolf Bernhardt*'s Encyclopedia of Public International Law: "With the exception of the European Communities, the beginnings of law-making through international organisations are definitely modest, and there are no signs of any change in this regard. The process is note-worthy, however, for it stands the closest to genuine legislation in international law."[1] — "Modest" but "important", "note-worthy" but "no signs of any change". It seems to be adequate, when dealing with a topic deserving such divergent attributes, that one aims at those areas which seem to have some practical importance; *en passant* I shall cast a glance also to the more theoretical legal problems concerned.

The municipal legal order of each State has to be the point of departure if one tries to analyse the legal relevance of acts of an international organisation.[2] Even if there may be types of organisations[3] — some of them being "subjects" of international law[4] — and basic patterns of how to react to acts of an organisation on the inner-state level, a limitation of the topic is necessary in order to avoid generalizations. Therefore I

---

* Dr. iur., Professor of Law at the University of Heidelberg.

[1] *Krzysztof Skubiszewski*, International Legislation, in: *Rudolf Bernhardt* (ed.), Encyclopedia of Public International Law (EPIL), Inst. 5, Amsterdam / New York / Oxford 1983, 97—104 (103). General questions of codification in international law as the classical form of "international legislation" are considered by *Anatol Petrowitsch Mowtschan*, Kodifizierung und Weiterentwicklung des Völkerrechts, Berlin 1974.

[2] The interrelationship between international and national law is generally summarized by *Siegfried Magiera*, Völkerrecht und staatliches Recht, in: *Eberhard Menzel / Knut Ipsen*, Völkerrecht, 2nd ed., München 1979, 49—73, and by *Igor Lukashuk / Walter Poeggel*, Wechselverhältnis zwischen Völkerrecht und innerstaatlichem Recht, in: Deutsche Außenpolitik 27 (1982), 73—86.

[3] *See Rudolf L. Bindschedler*, International Organisations, General Aspects, in: EPIL 5 (1983), 119—140, and *Henry G. Schermers*, International Organizations, Resolutions, in: *op. cit.*, 159—162.

[4] *Bardo Faßbender*, Die Völkerrechtssubjektivität internationaler Organisationen, in: Österreichische Zeitschrift für öffentliches Recht und Völkerrecht (ÖZöRV) 37 (1986), 17—49.

take the liberty to put emphasis as follows. Firstly, the constitutional order of the Federal Republic of Germany will be the major example, in accordance with the customs and traditions of these colloquies. I shall add comparative remarks only if it seems appropriate to do so. Secondly, I concentrate on governmental, not non-governmental, organisations. Thirdly, I leave aside the European Communities as well as other supranational organisations. However, I will merely touch upon Article (Art.) 24 of the Basic Law of the Federal Republic of Germany which enables the Federation to transfer sovereign rights to intergovernmental institutions. Art. 80 *lit.* a of the Basic Law is to be mentioned briefly, providing for the determination of a state of tension by virtue of a decision taken by an international organisation within the framework of a military alliance.

I have been asked by the *spiritus rectores* of the colloquium to talk about resolutions and declarations of international organisations — all sorts of unilateral acts therefore, but not about treaties concluded by an international organisation. Unilateral acts are to be considered if they are formal acts, not mere "action", for example, the factual admission of a liberation movement to an organisation, which may constitute or imply recognition and thereby influence legal development as well as national decision-making. I further speak of decisions, primarily for the sake of simplicity and according to Art. 18 of the United Nations (UN) Charter, which even calls a "resolution" a "decision".

The width of this field automatically implies that non-binding norms will be in the foreground, binding norms set by international organisations being a rare example. Decisions of an international organisation may conform with the specific legal requirements established by its respective founding charter, or they may fall "ultra vires".[5] In the following, only decisions are looked at which cause no doubts in this respect.

Decisions may concern individual questions by their wording already. They may also try to formulate standards of general international, or national political, or legal behaviour. They may address themselves to States only and they may be adequate for direct municipal application. I apply the term "self-executing" here without having the idea to raise the terminological discussion of this morning's session again, understanding the term in the sense given to it by *Igor Lukashuk*.[6] Most resolutions leave it to the addressees themselves by which means they follow the normative demand established by the resolution: The result is what

[5] For the United Nations *see Jochen Abraham Frowein*, United Nations, in: EPIL 5 (1983), 272—281 (278).

[6] *See generally* in our context *Peter Rösgen*, Rechtssetzungsakte der Vereinten Nationen und ihrer Sonderorganisationen. Bestandsaufnahme und Vollzug in der Bundesrepublik Deutschland, Diss. Bonn 1985, 208—231.

counts, not the way by which a desired result is arrived at. We shall see how the status of a self-executing act may contribute to municipal relevance, however.

Decisions may concern the internal or the external level of an international organisation. Here we are confronted with the external level and thereupon with the relationship of the organisation to Member-States, not to third States. Though it could be tempting to evaluate the relevance of particularly the policy of regional organisations to non Member-States, a question similar to the one posed by *Christian Tomuschat* in a report on third party effects of international treaties in 1987:[7] Is, for example, the policy of the Organisation of African Unity, materializing in a number of resolutions concerning strictly inner-African matters, of legal relevance to extra-continental States?

I sum up provisionally: I shall talk about governmental, non-centralized organisations, about formal unilateral decision-making of these organisations, and the significance of such decisions to Member-States — irrespective of intra-organisational legal validity, irrespective of the substantial structure of the decision.

The task is to deal with the "relevance" of such decisions. By this, legal relevance is meant in its broadest sence, always *legal* relevance not mere political relevance. Only political relevance must be noted if, for example, a national trade union in a conflict on wage increase refers to recommendations of the International Labour Organisation (ILO). The level of political relevance is also concerned if one looks at follow-up mechanisms like the ILO-system's control and report procedures, and the permanent trialogue of governments, multi-national corporations, and national associations established by the ILO.[8] Legal relevance is relevance to the legal order. This, I understand in a broad sense, thereby not only including decisions of international organisations which, on the national level, end up as binding law.

I do not restrict myself to decisions which are internationally binding. It is true, of course, as merely all former investigations into this problem equivocally state, that non-binding decisions and resolutions not necessarily have to be transformed into national law. However, it should be interesting to find out whether they are explicitly transformed or dealt with as if transformed. I hope to be more precise on this point later on.

[7] *Christian Tomuschat*, Völkerrechtlicher Vertrag und Drittstaaten, (paper presented at the 21st meeting of the *Deutsche Gesellschaft für Völkerrecht*), Tübingen, April 8th to 11th, 1987 in: 29 (1987) Berichte der Deutschen Gesellschaft für Völkerrecht, forthcoming.

[8] For a description of the mechanisms mentioned in the text *see* Internationales Arbeitsamt, Der Einfluß der Übereinkommen und Empfehlungen der Internationalen Arbeitsorganisation, Geneva 1977.

I may quote again a colleague in this context. Mrs. *Martina Haedrich* of the German Democratic Republic rightly stated that it is not a primary task to decide whether resolutions of international organisations are a "real" source of international law or not. It is much more fascinating, she said, to analyse the effect of resolutions on the process of the creation and development of law.[9] Mrs. *Haedrich* by this referred to the development of international law. I generalize and say: The same is true for municipal law as influenced by international organisations.

Because of this broad definition of what legal relevance amounts to, I do not feel obliged to give another analysis of the already classic academic debate of what is the international legal value of resolutions of the General Assembly of the UN — a controversy which in all its ramifications could not even be easily summarized.[10] My personal opinion as to this point is, that resolutions and declarations, decisions, under whatever name or flag they may sail, only win a binding character in relation to one of the classical sources of international law, or if they reflect a consensus.

The phenomenon of international organizations' behaviour which I described belongs to an area outside the transformation of treaty law or universal customary law. If a resolution or declaration would itself constitute an agreement, or would, as a sort of authentic interpretation, participate in the normative value of an agreement, or if it would contribute to the development of customary law — as it may happen especially with declarations of the UN General Assembly — the principles of treaty transformation would have to be applied. This is the case if a declaration shall be internationally binding according to the theory of formless or pure consensus. Then it may have to be considered as a general principle of international law covered also by Art. 25 of the Basic Law.

II. The relevance of decisions of international organisations to municipal law — General remarks

Coming to the sphere of municipal law one has to note that constitutions normally do not explicitly deal with the internal relevance of decisions

[9] *Martina Haedrich*, Die Wirkung von Resolutionen der UN Vollversammlung auf den völkerrechtlichen Rechtsbildungsprozeß, in: Neue Justiz 1986, 441—444 (441).

[10] Out of the flood of writing see *Rahmatullah Khan*, The Legal Status of the Resolutions of the UN General Assembly, in: Indian Journal of International Law 19 (1979), 552—559; *Bruno Simma*, Zur völkerrechtlichen Bedeutung von Resolutionen der UN-Generalversammlung, in: *Rudolf Bernhardt* / *Jost Delbrück* / *Ingo von Münch* / *Walter Rudolf* (eds.), 5. Deutsch-polnisches Juristen-Kolloquium, Band 2: Die Bedeutung der Resolutionen der Generalversammlung der Vereinten Nationen, Baden-Baden 1981, 45—76.

of international organisations. Furthermore, there is no general accepted rule of international law obliging a state to implement decisions of international organisations nor in particular those of the General Assembly. Such a principle theoretically could evolve into customary law, but this is unlikely enough. One should not try to bring it about merely by proclaiming such principle.

A basic decision of the Basic Law of the Federal Republic of Germany is important at this point. Art. 24, shortly mentioned above, enables the Federation to transfer sovereign rights to inter-governmental institutions and to join a system of collective security. The provision envisages all kinds of international organisations, universal or regional ones, with a general or limited area of competence whatsoever. Until now the Federal Republic never has transferred sovereign rights to international organisations of a classic type, particularly not to the UN nor to the North Atlantic Treaty Organisation. Other than in the Netherlands, the Constitution of which in its Art. 67 para. 2 deals with acts of international organisations more or less the same way as with international agreements (giving them internal applicability after due publication), the law of classic organisations cannot flow directly into municipal law.

The individual, therefore, is concerned by decisions of an international organisation only if an additional normative command can be identified in municipal law: "impermeability" of a classic international organisation. At least one of the branches of state organisation, seen from the perspective of a "balance" or "separation of power"-system, has to react to the international normative demand. A clash between international and municipal law therefore is possible as it is the basic philosophy of Art. 27 of the Vienna Convention on Treaties.[11] Such a clash, however, may occur provided that a decision of an international organisation itself constitutes binding law as it is possible with decisions of the Security Council of the UN. One marginal exception outside the field of supra-national organisations is to be mentioned here: the International Organisation of Civil Aviation's competences concerning flights over the high seas, where self-executing secondary rules may be directly applicable in municipal law if covered by explicit parliamentary consent.[12]

It may happen that a resolution directly influences the behaviour of a private corporation, a multinational enterprise especially,[13] but this again

---

[11] *Krzysztof Skubiszewski*, Resolutions of International Organisations and Municipal Law, in: Polish Yearbook of International Law 2 (1968/69), 80—108 (87).

[12] *See Schermers* (note 3), 161, and — for details — *Rösgen* (note 6), 63—89.

[13] In our context *see Helmut Krüger*, Internationale Verhaltenskodizes für multinationale Unternehmen, Mitteilungen der Bundesstelle für Außenhandelsinformation, Beiträge zu den Nachrichten für den Außenhandel, Mai 1985, 1—10.

is a political effect, which assumes legal implications only if a state organ reacts to these standards: for example, (i) the executive, when deciding upon a state bank guarantee, or (ii) the judiciary, when qualifying a private export treaty, or (iii) the legislature, if municipal law connects the approval of export business with the compliance with international standards. I will come back to these examples in detail. Without such a link of transfer there is no direct legal commitment of private entities. This is after all a consequence of the monopoly of powers of the State as an axiomatic feature of municipal law accepted by international law.

One curious exception has to be noted as far as the World Health Organisation's (WHO) Code on the Marketing of Breast Milk Substitutes of 1981 is concerned:[14] In 1984 one of the world's largest food corporations, the Swiss Nestlé Corporation in a contract accepted the obligation to comply with the Code. This contract was concluded between Nestlé and the international Nestlé Boycott Committee, a private association, which in return promised to finish its boycott of Nestlé products,[15] — an unusual case, in which the resolution of an international organisation was made part of a private law contract.

III. The relevance of decisions of an international organisation to legislation

A decision of an international organisation may be transformed into national law by legislation. The State as a subject of international law is obliged to bring this procedure into being only if the decision is internationally binding and existing municipal law is not sufficient to fulfil the international obligation — a rare case, as noted above. In any case, the structure and category of enactment is of interest: Is the ratifying act concerning the admission to an organisation sufficient? Is a parliamentary decision necessary?

What is in this context the function of a parliamentary act giving consent to the entry of the State into an international organisation? Such an act has a double nature. It completes the requirements for the entry into force of membership, constitutionally required according to Art. 59 para. 2 of the Basic Law but not always respected in practice: There were no parliamentary acts giving consent to membership in the Inter-

[14] For details see *Kathryn Sikkink*, Codes of conduct for transnational corporations: the case of the WHO/UNICEF code, in: International Organisation 40 (1986), 815—840.

[15] "Joint agreement, International Nestlé Boycott Comittee and Nestlé" of January 25th, 1984, signed by *Karl August*, executive vice president of Nestlé, S. A., and *William L. Thompson*, stated clerk of the Presbyterian Church, representing the International Nestlé Boycott Committee.

national Labour Organisation (ILO) or the Food and Agriculture Organisation (FAO), for example. In addition to this function, such an act transforms self-executing charter law but not secondary rules, whether binding or not. Again there may be one exception, which is in scholarly dispute though, that is, the modification of founding charters of international organisations by a decision of the organisation itself. According to some authors, such decisions are transformed in advance, at least if they are cogent for the development of the organisation in question[16] — developments which in advance may be covered by the act giving consent to the accession. This question materially belongs to the field of transformation of primary norms and is primarily one of theoretical interest, because state practice tends to transform modifications of a treaty by an organisation's decision individually, and does not consider it already generally transformed.

Concerning WHO regulations, however, instead of special transformation, the Federal Republic chose the way of general transformation, publishing all relevant regulations in the gazette. Parliament enabled the administration to react to modifications in the same way.[17]

Legislative acts of many States directly respond to acts of international organisations by taking them as a model,[18] *i. e.*, so-called "parallel legislation". A number of States, development countries in particular, made the 1948 General Assembly Declaration on Human Rights part of their national law by parallel formulations or by reference. The United States formed their economic law also parallel to parts of the Organisation for Economic Co-operation and Development's (OECD) Guidelines for Multinational Enterprises of 1976.[19] Several Latin American and Central American states promulgated a labour law legislation according to recommendations of the ILO, so did France and Sweden in the special field of the protection of workers.

Besides parallel legislation, there are other forms of legislative reaction to decisions of international organisations such as direct reference or just alterations, creating legal conditions, which make it possible to comply with an international norm internally. So, the Foreign Trade Ordinance of the Federal Republic of Germany reacted to Resolution 418 of the UN's Security Council. Similar changes of enactments occurred in the United Kingdom, Greece, and Austria. Another example for direct but soft implementation of a decision of an international organisation is

[16] *See Rösgen* (note 6), 281—312.

[17] *Id.*, 30—45.

[18] *Christoph Schreuer*, Die innerstaatliche Anwendung von internationalem "soft law" aus rechtsvergleichender Sicht, in: ÖZöRV 34 (1983/84), 243—260 (248—251).

[19] International Legal Materials (ILM) 15 (1976), 967. *Cf.* U.S. Foreign Corrupt Practices Act of 1977, in: ILM 17 (1978), 214.

provided by an act which came into force on January 1st, 1987, a modification of an older German Plant Protection Act, now referring directly to the International Code of Conduct on the Distribution and Use of Pesticides.[20] Approval of international trade with pesticides is now bound to a consideration of (not: compliance with) this resolution of the FAO.

Limits to these sorts of references are definitely set by the requirements of national constitutional law, because under the Basic Law the decision of an international organisation never can function as a restriction to individual basic rights (as sometimes is intended by resolutions of organisations belonging to the UN's family, like the UN's Educational, Scientific and Cultural Organisation's activities concerning mass media[21]).

One may, however, not underestimate this area, which does not completely belong to the field of "politics of law". The international origin of national law is not only a matter of the birth of a norm, but also of its childhood, particularly the first instances of its interpretation. Since the interpretation of norms is heavily influenced by the sense given to a term or word during legislation or consultation in the legislative bodies, the relevant processes at the international level may gain importance also for the interpretation in a national court. The same is true for follow-up interpretation of parallel or similar norms which are inspired by the organisation or are reflected by other national orders. So, here we have a process of *vice versa* exchange which may develop further and which in a closer way is to be noted already in the context of the Western European Human Rights protection system.[22] Key-terms like "health", "opinion", "profession", for example, are to be discussed in observance of the international organisation's decision. A similar process can be found in the practice of the Court of Justice of the European Communities, which earlier this year decided on the question of purity criteria of beer by applying WHO and FAO recommendations.[23]

Federal legislature in Germany deals not only with decisions of international bodies by formal legal procedures, but also by way of so-called simple parliamentary decisions. In 1977 the Bundestag formulated its "hope" and "expectation" that German corporations would orientate their general policy at the Code of Conduct of the European Communities concerning South African, and in an annex to that statement was

[20] FAO Doc. C 85/25, September 1985; *see* also *Eckard Rehbinder*, Das neue Pflanzenschutzgesetz, in: Natur und Recht 9 (1987), 68—71.

[21] *See Brun-Otto Bryde*, Internationale Verhaltensregeln für Private — völkerrechtliche und verfassungsrechtliche Aspekte, Frankfurt am Main 1981, 61—65.

[22] *Andreas A. Khol*, Internationale Gesetzgebung und staatliche Rechtsanwendung, in: *René Marcic et al.* (eds.), Internationale Festschrift für *Alfred Verdross*, München/Salzburg 1971, 167—195.

[23] European Court of Justice, in: Neue Juristische Wochenschrift 40 (1987), 1133—1136.

this Code brought to the attention of the public.[24] That was not an act of legislation, but an act with eminent political significance which may indirectly cause legal relevance to the executive and / or the judiciary — the two branches of State action we have to consider now.

IV. The relevance of decisions of an international organisation to the administration and to the judiciary

What municipal relevance has a decision of an international organisation, if the legislative power does not react at all, or if existing national law is silent or unclear on a problem mentioned or regulated by an organisation? Can there be relevance to municipal law without any legislative activity concerning the resolution? It would not be correct to assume that such relevance is generally excluded because of the fact that a constitution is silent on this point. A constitution only dealing with the international relevance of norms which belong to a classical source of international law cannot be the fundament for an *argumentum e contrario*. Arts. 24, 25, and 59 para. 2 of the Basic Law are constitutional entrances by which a norm of international law may step into the municipal order, but they are no strict barrier to infiltration of norms of a non-constitutional quality. This is a phenomenon which the drafters of the Constitution did not (and could not) intend to regulate in the negative.

The question is generally also not regulated in the negative, because of the constitutional requirements as to the stability of law or certainty as to law.[25] It is moreover not regulated in the affirmative, because there may be a constitutional principle of amiability as to international law.[26] There is no such principle regarding resolutions of international organisations, on which one could rely in a case of doubt. Therefore it is necessary to look at the problem both from the perspective of the administration and of the judiciary. Can they make use of acts of international organisations if there is no special or general transformation, or incorporation of these acts by legislation? The point of departure is that the two branches of state organs shall be bound by law and justice under the Constitution, as it is stated in Art. 20 para. 3 of the Basic Law. Are there circumstances in existence under which a decision of an international organisation acquires the status of belonging to "law and justice" outside identifiable legislative reactions?

Here one has to differentiate between administration and judiciary.

---

[24] *Deutscher Bundestag*, Achte Wahlperiode, Drucksache 8/1104, 27. Oktober 1977.

[25] *See Philip Kunig*, Das Rechtsstaatsprinzip. Überlegungen zu seiner Bedeutung für das Verfassungsrecht der Bundesrepublik Deutschland, Tübingen 1986, 390—415.

[26] *See* references at *Ondolf Rojahn*, in: *Ingo von Münch* (ed.), Grundgesetz-Kommentar, Band 2 (Art. 21 — Art. 69), 2nd ed. München 1983, 99—100, 135.

1. *Different types of administration*

Fundamental to German law is the difference between an interventionist type of administration and a beneficiary type.[27] Does the administrative act involve a burden or does it result in a benefit? The amount of what is reserved to a clear legislative decision is different according to the type of administration. Administrative action resulting in an intervention in the citizen's right to freedom or interfering with the citizen's property requires a legal justification set by legislation. Beneficiary administration, whereby the citizen benefits, is permissable without such justification. An intervention in this sense is to be assumed if the administration forbids a certain action or obliges the citizen to act in a given way. The decision of an international organisation alone can never be a justification for such an obligation. Mere publication[28] or mentioning of a decision in the context of administrative guidelines is not sufficient. This is a consequence of the so-called "proviso of legality" as a fundamental principle under the rule of law.[29] Thus, it would be impossible to prevent a German corporation from business talks with a South African state firm about the delivery of submarines by reference to resolutions of the UN General Assembly. It would also be illegal to try to oblige a citizen not to go on board of a South African aircraft, since a basis for such an administrative behaviour cannot be found in statutory law. It should be emphasized that this outline of the separation between the two central types of administration is cursory. It describes ideal types in order to show a fundamental difference. In practice the situation is more complex. This has consequences for the relevance of decisions of an international organisation to the administration. Sometimes the German legal order considers the granting of a legal position as a restitution of a general freedom provided by the individual basic rights. If such an allowance is not granted it has to be dealt with as an interventionist act. This precisely is the legal structure of grants under the Foreign Trade and Payments Act, which could come easily into conflict with certain decisions of the UN if the Security Council should arrive at binding decisions. Foreign trade, as is stated by section 1 of the Foreign Trade and Payments Act, is "free", that means, a legal justification for not granting economic aid for a certain form of foreign trade has to be found. Since foreign trade is part of a constitutionally protected area (it belongs to the freedom of property and business as

---

[27] *See Ingo von Münch*, Verwaltung und Verwaltungsrecht im demokratischen und sozialen Rechtsstaat, in: *Hans-Uwe Erichsen / Wolfgang Martens* (eds.), Allgemeines Verwaltungsrecht, 7th ed. Berlin/New York 1986, 21—26.

[28] Publication is a necessary but not a sufficient condition of transformation, *cf. Bundesverwaltungsgericht* (Federal Administrative Court), in: Neue Zeitschrift für Verwaltungsrecht 5 (1986), 830—831.

[29] *See Kunig* (note 25), 316—329.

basic individual rights), intervention here requires a formal legal provision. Beneficiary administration under these circumstances has thus to be handled like interventionist administration. Therefore, a decision by an organisation cannot function as the sole legal ground for the refusal of an export licence. It could help, however, to interprete those norms which provide such a basis.

A refusal is permissable, for example, according to section 5 of the Foreign Trade and Payments Act, "in order to fulfil obligations laid down in international agreements, to which the competent bodies have expressed their consent in the form of a Federal act". Evidently, this refers to the language of Art. 59 para. 2 of the Basic Law. This excludes the refusal of an export allowance by the sole reason to comply with the decision of an international organisation. Section 5 refers to binding international agreements not to unilateral decisions of an organisation, even if they may be binding. Another view would conflict with the requirement of the Constitution that it is Parliament which has to decide about "essential" matters.[30] This question was in dispute as far as the former Rhodesian embargo of the Security Council is concerned,[31] later on also concerning the South Africa Resolution 418.

More vaguely formulated than section 5 is section 7 of the same Act. A refusal is permissable according to section 7 in order to prevent inconveniences to the peaceful co-operation between nations and to avoid a disturbance of the foreign relations of the Federal Republic — fairly unclear terms which need interpretation. Such uncertain legal terms, in principle, are permissable from a constitutional legal perspective because they are under control of the judiciary, and again their interpretation has to take into account underlying individual basic rights. Here it seems to be possible that resolutions, especially of the UN, may serve as a sort of indirect tool on the control of foreign trade. If the administration arrives at the result that non-compliance with a certain resolution would heavily disturb the foreign relations of the Federal Republic and if a refusal of an export allowance therefore seems to be necessary, section 7 in connection with the resolution may be decisive on a matter of municipal law. The competences of the legislature remain untouched, since the legislature itself provided for a wide scope of executive action. This gives leverage, the norm does not oblige the executive to implement resolutions, but it renders it possible to a certain extent.

---

[30] *Id.* at 321—322.

[31] *See Dedo von Schenck*, Das Problem der Beteiligung der Bundesrepublik Deutschland an Sanktionen der Vereinten Nationen, besonders im Falle Rhodesiens, in: Zeitschrift für ausländisches öffentliches Recht und Völkerrecht 29 (1969), 257—315.

A kind of administration of the beneficiary type which is not equatable to interventionist administration, but also does not constitute beneficiary administration of a pure type, is the field of the control of arms' trade. An allowance to export arms and other goods of military importance is not held to be a restitution of a pre-given individual freedom by law. In accordance with the Constitution and inspired by Art. 26 of the Basic Law, section 6 para. 1 of the Arms Control Act clearly states that nobody has a right to get State aid to export arms to a foreign country. On the other hand, the Act contains certain preconditions under which a refusal is mandatory, and others, under which it is permissable. Here again decisions of an international organisation may gain importance. The administrative decision-maker may rely on them if non-compliance with the resolution "would inflict the interests of the Federal Republic in good political relations with other countries." Here, one may note an even more reluctant wording giving more discretion to the deciding authority, but again the authority is not obliged to follow any international decision, the decision being only part of an overall analysis of political costs.

If there is evidence that, as a consequence of the aid, the military goods in questions would be used to infringe international peace, or to commit an aggressional act in particular, the refusal of the allowance is mandatory (section 6 para. 3). Here one may ask the question, whether a determination by the UN's Security Council of the existence of a threat to peace, breach of peace, or act of aggression under Art. 39 of the Charter binds the deciding national authority on a sort of preliminary question. Probably one will have to accept the basic factual evidence as confirmed by the Security Council and the criteria of its decision, but not necessarily the decision itself, if there should be evidence that the Security Council's decision is influenced, for example, by bias or application of unacceptable standards.

Up to now I talked about decisions of an international organisation as a tool by which uncertain terms of national laws may be handled. Another field of implementation could be the area of administrative discretion. By this I mean all those administrative decisions which are characterized by two or more alternatives of action which are permissible all the same. Is the selection of one alternative influenced by decisions of international organisations? The answer has to be in the affirmative because, generally, every aspect of law and politics is a legitimate concern for discretional decision and a lawful element of decision-making. It has to be weighed against other concerns. Therefore it is not of mandatory but of facultative significance again. Other than in the field of foreign trade or arms' control, in discretional matters, decisions of an international organisation, in practice, will find no fruitful area of application. The only well-known example concerns arms' control decisions at the beginning of the 1970s and 1980s, when it was held that compliance with international disarmament policy should be qualified as vital to the interests of the Federal Republic and therefore constitutes a concern of weight-balancing in discretional decision-making. This reduced relevance is understandable if one looks at the parallel area of contents of international treaties as a concern in discretional decisions. Here the only area of importance is the law concerning foreign nationals, especially the right of domicile. The Federal Administrative Court ascribed even to treaties a limited relevance here, since national laws exhausted merely all relevant problems.[32]

I come back to the area of administration not pre-structured by any acts of the legislature. This is a field where decisions of international organisations can be of high importance. The best example is the approval of public guarantees in order to support export business.[33] Such guarantees are given to German export firms and banks involved in export business as security covering typical risks of international business. They occur in different forms depending on the legal nature of the counterpart, be it a foreign state, or the subdivision of a state, or a private corporation. In sharp opposition to general foreign trade law, the exporter has no claim or cause of action, and in opposition to arms' control law, no criteria, not even vaguely formulated criteria, are given by the law.

The approving of the guarantee must be qualified as an act of administration (similar to general public subsidy law). It lies in the competence of a multi-ministerial committee under the chairmanship of the Minister of Economics. After the committee's general approval, a civil law contract between a private insurance company and the exporter is concluded. Other corporations are participating on the public side. Between the federation and the insurance originates in addition another contractual relationship, a rather complicated legal structure.

What are the criteria for the administrative act, the acceptance of the surety? Since 1983, guidelines exist concerning the taking-over of export security guarantees. By legal nature they are administrative guidelines (not statutory law), but they are published in the Gazette. Relevant to the decision according to the guidelines, is, first of all, an assessment of the economic risk: — is it justifiable? —, a point of no further interest here; and secondly, the question whether the foreign

---

[32] For details *see Albrecht Randelzhofer*, Der Einfluß des Völker- und Europarechts auf das deutsche Ausländerrecht, Berlin/New York 1980.

[33] *See Friederike Pentzlin*, Der universelle ordre public im Wirtschaftsrecht als ein Ordnungsprinzip des innerstaatlichen Rechts, München 1985, 113—115, with further references.

engagement is "worthy" of public support. This decisive term is defined only in the negative, *i. e.*, "not worthy" is an operation or transaction if it is in conflict with important interests of the Federal Republic. A vague balancing of interests is required, though no material criteria are given by law nor even by inner-administrative rules. Can this gap be filled by resolutions? In practice, the above-mentioned committee works on the basis of country reports, covering merely every country in the world and being permanently modified and updated: Factual criteria are collected, normative ones not given by law. Decisions of international organisations up to now seem to play no prominent role in this context, with the exception of the South Africa Code of Conduct for Multinational Enterprises sponsored by the European Communities.[34] Even if this Code is one of an integrative organisation a few sentences may be dedicated to it, since the Code is not a decision based on supra-national competence. The codes of other organisations could be of equal relevance.

That the Code is respected as an element of decision-making is not a direct consequence of the above-mentioned guidelines, but results from a government decision of 1977. It requires the exporter's "declaration" that he is willing to accept the Code, will act in accordance with it, and affirms its general political philosophy. What this declaration really legally means is not clear yet. There are few follow-up mechanisms to secure compliance and it is doubtful whether withdrawal of the guarantee as a result of non-compliance would stand a test in court if the exporter would risk litigation. A number of questions comes to mind.[35] Is it in accordance with her international legal obligations that the Federal Republic implements the Code in such a complicated way which is difficult to control? Certainly yes, since the Code is on the softer side even of "soft law".[36] Is it permissable under German law to demand such a declaration of compliance from the exporter which is more than an urgent request but a sort of compulsion? Most probably yes again, because there are no clear legal consequences if the Code would not be honoured. This is not a problem in practice, as German firms generally respect the Code. Thirdly: Is it in accordance with constitutional law that an essential criterion for a decision of extreme economic importance

---

[34] Bulletin Nr. 9/1977 of the European Communities, 51, modified version in Bull. Nr. 11/1985, 160.

[35] For details *see Hans-Joachim von Bülow*, Schwierigkeiten mit dem Südafrika-Kodex, in: Recht der internationalen Wirtschaft (RIW) 25 (1979), 600—603; *Kay Hailbronner*, Rechtswirkungen des EG-Südafrikakodex, in: RIW 28 (1982), 111—117.

[36] An interesting Austrian view to the phenomenon of "soft law" in our context is given by *Clemens Jabloner / Wolf Okresek*, Theoretische und praktische Anmerkungen zu Phänomenen des "soft law", in: ÖZöRV 34 (1983), 217—241; *see* also *Schreuer* (note 18).

is nowhere materially regulated, except in a vague clause referring to "interests" outside the scope of legislative action? Most probably not.

We here see again the limited relevance of resolutions of international organisations to the administration. An upgrading of the value of resolutions quickly meets legal barriers; to step over them requires legislative action. It would be desirable if such legislative action was taken.

2. *The judiciary*

There are in this area no directly relevant decisions of the courts in the Federal Republic (a lot of them in other countries[37]), but one can try to shed some light on the matter if one considers it in its broader context. Is it conceivable that norms and standards of extra-national origin find their way into the reasoning of national courts? This again, one can only imagine if the demand to apply these standards is already included in general norms which need interpretation. I concentrate now on civil law, where we have several so-called general clauses or blanket clauses. I leave aside section 134 of the German Civil Code, according to which a contract is void if it violates a legal prohibition. Such a prohibition can only be one of national law. But is it possible to enrich the term "good manners", *bonos mores*, in sections 138, 826 *Bürgerliches Gesetzbuch* (Civil Code — BGB) by decisions of international organisations? A collision with good manners renders a contract void and if it is connected with a malevolent injury damages are to be paid. Also "good faith" as a general obligation in legal relations (section 242 BGB) and the term *ordre public* (section 30 *Einführungsgesetz zum* — Introductory Statute to the — BGB) as a basic feature of conflicts of laws[38] may be opened to international standards, set by organisations. The same is true finally for section 1 of the Unfair Competition Act according to which "good manners" again are a criterion for judgment on national and transboundary antitrust law. Here for example, the 1986 OECD Recommendation Concerning Restrictive Business Practices Afflicting International Trade[39] and the Set of Multilaterally Agreed Equitable Prin-

---

[37] A profound study is *Christoph Schreuer*, Die Behandlung internationaler Organakte durch staatliche Gerichte, Berlin 1977. *See* also *Edwin D. Dickinson*, International Political Questions in the National Courts, American Journal of International Law 19 (1925), 157—163; *Elihu Lauterpacht*, Implementation of Decisions of International Organizations through National Courts, in: *Stephen M. Schwebel* (ed.), The Effectivenes of International Decisions, Leyden/Dobbs Ferry, N.Y. 1971, 57—65; *Louis Henkin*, Resolutions of International Organisations in American Courts, in: *Frits Kalshoven / Pieter Jan Kuyper / Johan G. Lammers* (eds.), Essays on the Development of the International Legal Order, Alphen aan den Rijn/Rockville 1980, 199—211.

[38] *See Norbert Horn*, Die Entwicklung des internationalen Wirtschaftsrechts durch Verhaltensrichtlinien, in: Rabels Zeitschrift 44 (1980), 423—454.

[39] ILM 25 (1986), 1629—1632 (appendix 1633—1635).

ciples and Rules for the Control of Restrictive Business Practices of the General Assembly[40] may become relevant, since this set specifies certain axiomatic rules.

In 1927 already, the *Reichsgericht* held void a contract which was in conflict with import restrictions under the law of India concerning cocaine. The contract, according to the *Reichsgericht*, was contrary to *boni mores* in the sense of section 138 BGB.[41] The *Bundesgerichtshof*, in 1960, came to an equal conclusion concerning a contract of sale not in accordance with the United States Embargo Regulations,[42] and in 1972, concerning a contract of transport which violated Nigerian law on the protection of cultural property of national importance. In this latter judgment the court explicitly referred to relevant UNESCO resolutions and not only to Nigerian law.[43]

The courts have not qualified the general clauses of civil law as entrance norms for the benefit of foreign values and standards. They referred primarily to the national legal order but understood it as influenced from outside. So the courts kept room to deviate again from foreign norms if such should prove not as being identically oriented but as aiming into a different direction. The command to be applied, which is found in the general clauses, is perceived as requiring an evalution of national interests and being in the prerogative of the legislative power as well. This technique may be compared to how courts sometimes argue in the field of conflicts of law if a unification treaty has not yet entered into force: They apply it as a reflection of general standards and neglect the aspect of entry into force — a point of very recent discussion in Germany.[44] All this is of importance also for decisions of international organisations in general, for there is no principal difference between foreign national law and an organisational decision in this respect. Decisions of an international organisation here function in a quasi-objective way, they are more a sort of eludicating fact than a norm. As *Henry G. Schermers* put it: "Non-application of the Namibia decree of the United Nations would violate international public policy and would therefore be contrary to the national public policy as well."[45] However, "could", I personally would say not "would", "would" only if — as it may often be the case — an analysis of the given foreign policy leads

---

[40] ILM 19 (1980), 813; *cf. Wolfgang Fikentscher / Wolfgang Straub*, Der RBP-Kodex der Vereinten Nationen; Weltkartellrichtlinien (I), in: Gewerblicher Rechtsschutz und Urheberrecht, Internationaler Teil 11 (1982), 637—646.

[41] Juristische Wochenschrift 56 (1927), 2288—2289.

[42] *Entscheidungen des Bundesgerichtshofes in Zivilsachen* (Reports of the Federal Supreme Court on Civil Matters) [hereinafter cited as: BGHZ] 34, 169—178.

[43] BGHZ 59, 83—87.

[44] *See* text (note 7).

[45] *Henry G. Schermers*, The Namibia Decree in National Courts, The International and Comparative Law Quarterly 26 (1977), 81—96 (96).

to the conclusion that compliance with international standards is a general prevailing fact of this policy. A judge is not in the position under the constitution to follow his own foreign policy.

Which criteria enable a court to find out whether national and international goals as determined by an international organisation are identical in the sense described above? *Karl M. Meessen* correctly stated that approval of the Federal Republic of a decision in question is one important aspect, another one is the test whether the decision really formulates common values in opposition to a vague formal compromise,[46] also if the organisation is competent under its charter law to deal with the problem or if it clearly acted *ultra vires*, as the FAO sometimes tended to do in recent years. Not every organisation with a limited technical mandate (for example: concerning environmental standards of rivers) may pass relevant international documents on general questions of peace and disarmament. The substance, not the number of resolutions, nor the loudness of political articulation is important. Besides, the international documents must conform to national constitutional values and further principles of the internal legal order.[47] This constitutionally necessary retention of the judiciary may be termed with the keyword "political questions doctrine" or "judicial restraint". The judges may use decisions of international organisations if they, by doing so, follow the trail of the executive power which has a prerogative to decide upon foreign policy alternatives.[48]

V. Conclusions

I arrive at some conclusions. Out of the flood of resolutions, decisions, and recommendations of classic international organisations only those can be of relevance to an internal legal order which address themselves to matters of internal policies, this term being used as including behaviour with external implications in the competence of state organs. Decisions can be relevant to the legislative power, even if they lack a clear normative structure. They need such a structure to be used by administration or judiciary. Seen from the perspective of national orders, a command to apply is necessary which must be found in a norm of national law. Not explicit approval is required, but any norm is sufficient which can be understood as referring to international norms. On the

---

[46] *Karl Matthias Meessen*, Internationale Verhaltenskodizes und Sittenwidrigkeitsklauseln, in: Neue Juristische Wochenschrift 34 (1981), 1131—1132.

[47] *Kay Hailbronner*, Völkerrechtliche und staatsrechtliche Überlegungen zu Verhaltenskodizes für transnationale Unternehmen, in: *Ingo v. Münch* (ed.), Festschrift für *Hans-Jürgen Schlochauer*, Berlin/New York 1981, 329—362 (361).

[48] *Cf. Entscheidungen des Bundesverfassungsgerichts* (Reports of the Federal Constitutional Court) 68, 1—111 (83—89). *Generally Hans D. Treviranus*, Außenpolitik im demokratischen Rechtsstaat, Tübingen 1966.

other side, joining an organisation and its subsequent approval by the competent national authorities does not constitute an implementation of secondary rules. Exceptions to this are decisions modifying the charter of an organisation being secondary rules by procedure only, but primary rules in effect.

The question whether the decision of an international organisation is internationally binding is generally not decisive on its relevance to municipal law. It is a question of international law. The strict line between binding law and non-binding norms (which on the international level is basic[49]) is not in the foreground if one looks at the relevance of decisions to municipal law. Binding character, internationally, does not suspend from constitutional requirements outside the scope of transfer of sovereign rights to an international organisation, the latter of which is in the domain of supra-national organisations.

Decisions may inspire national legislation. Parallel legislation as well as direct reference occur. Internationally inspired municipal law is to be interpreted by taking note of the international origin of a norm and its international development.

Administrative action which involves a burden to the individual requires a formal legal basis, which cannot be replaced by an international organisation's decision. A decision may be of use, however, for the interpretation of uncertain norms referring to general interests. The same is true if administrative action resulting in mere benefits is dependent on such general norms.

If no national norms at all govern a sphere of administration (which in the Federal Republic of Germany is the case in the field of public guarantees to economic activities in a foreign country), decisions of an organisation may serve as a guideline. It would be difficult, at least in German law, to revalue international decisions in this context because basic rights of the individual to a remarkable extent require formal legislation concerning essential questions. Here is a field, however, where resolutions in the future may play a more important role.

The judiciary may use decisions in the context of interpretation of general clauses of law, but only if these decisions are in conformity with national norms and values, and if certain other criteria are met.

So the internal living space for decisions of an international organisation is limited. It is limited by requirements of constitutional law, formalizing the transfer of sovereignty to a foreign authority and up-

[49] *Wilhelm Wengler*, Rechtstheoretische und rechtssoziologische Betrachtungen zur Unterscheidung zwischen völkerrechtlich verbindlichen und völkerrechtlich unverbindlichen Äußerungen völkerrechtlicher Organe, in: ÖZöRV 33 (1982), 173—198.

holding the prerogative of the legislature to decide on essential matters. Consequently, the fortune of decisions of an international organisation depends mainly on the legislature which may implement them, in whole or in part, individually or generally, or not at all. If legislature does not react, there are certain loopholes only by which decisions can arrive at national decision-makers.

The general reluctance of municipal law to recognize acts of international organisations is a reflection of the still given axiomatic notion of sovereignty, in spite of all the epilogues on this principle. A radical change would have to take its way *via* the transfer of sovereign rights to organisations with the approval of parliament, expressing the democratic will of the people and bringing stability and clarity to a complex field of law — if the time should come justifying such a transfer. Until then, it would be unwise — today, beyond the horizon of international co-operation — to anticipate such a development by sophisticated legal techniques. The limited relevance of acts of international organisations to municipal law is a reflection of the overall stand of international co-operation and its contradictions. If political solutions to these contradictions will be found, the law — as always — will follow. The law of supra-national organisations will show the ways and techniques — and thereby a general perspective.[50]

Summary *

1. Only decisions which by their own content aim at municipal legal orders of member-states may be of relevance to these orders.
2. Such acts may try to decide a single problem or they may be framed generally. They may be incorporated or transformed individually or generally. Direct applicability by the executive or the judiciary presupposes a "self-executing" character.
3. The international binding force of a resolution is neither a necessary nor a sufficient precondition of its relevance to municipal law.
4. The approval of the entry into an international organisation generally does not anticipate the transformation or incorporation of secondary organisational law. Resolutions modifying a founding charter in accordance with the rules laid down in the respective charter are to be qualified materially as treaty law, even if they occur in the form of a unilateral decision.
5. The Basic Law of the Federal Republic of Germany does not deal explicitly with decisions of international organisations if they cannot be qualified as international agreements, as expression of international customary law, or

[50] The author is grateful to Mr. *Ulrich Dieckert*, University of the Federal Forces, Hamburg, for helpful discussions.

* Summary by the author.

as general principles of international law. The fact that the Constitution is silent so far does not prevent municipal legal relevance of acts of an international organisation. The same is true with regard to general principles of constitutional law, like the principle of stability of law or the principle of the rule of law. All these principles refer to requirements which may materialize in a single case as constitutional barriers to the relevance of an international organisation's decision.

6. Decisions of international organisations may inspire national legislation in the form of parallel acts, of acts referring to decisions of international organisations, or of acts indirectly reacting to international normative demands. Limitations to such legislation are set by requirements of constitutional law and individual basic rights especially. The international origin of a norm of municipal law may have effect upon the interpretation of this norm later on.

7. Decisions of international organisations do not justify an interference with basic rights laid down in the Basic Law; they may contribute, however, to the understanding of such norms of municipal law, which justify such interference.

8. Decisions of an international organisation may also contribute to administrative-decision making, resulting in a mere benefit for the individual, not a burden. Constitutional law requires, however, that "essential matters" are decided upon by Parliament.

9. The judiciary may use decisions of an international organisation as guidelines for the interpretation of vaguely-fomulated blanket norms. Judicial self-restraint and strict respect of the prerogatives of Parliament as to legislation, and of Government as to foreign policy decision-making are required by constitutional law. International participation of the Federal Republic in the creation of the decision in question is a criterion which may justify direct judicial application.

10. A strict limitation of the relevance of acts of an international organisation to municipal law is found in the axiomatic decision of the Basic Law to connect a transfer of sovereign rights to an international authority with the approval by the competent legislative bodies. An essential upgrading of the present role of decisions of an international organisation in municipal law is dependent on the further development of international cooperation, which may bring about conditions under which such a transfer of rights would be acceptable. Until then, decisions, resolutions, and declarations may play a role primarily as secondary instruments for the interpretation of existing municipal law and as an inspiration to the legislator.

UN General Assembly Resolutions and Municipal Law

By Igor I. Lukashuk*

One of the characteristic features of the contemporary system of international relations is that it includes, as an integral part, a substantial complex of international organizations.[1] Without this complex the contemporary system of international relations could hardly function successfully. Therefore the increase in number of international organizations and their growing significance are objective tendencies which are backed up by the growing need for regulating international relations on a permanent organizational basis. International life puts forward an increasing number of problems which can be settled only by broad co-operation of States on such stable basis.[2]

The United Nations (UN), being a universal organization with unique competence, hold the central position in the whole complex of international organizations. It is underlined by many States that, as our Minister of Foreign Affairs said without the UN "it is not possible at all to imagine contemporary international relations"[3]. There is every reason to believe that the significance of international organizations, and of the UN in particular, will continue to grow. This tendency is determined by the urgent needs of the world community and is actively supported by many States. In the Communique of the (1986) Political Consultative Committee meeting of the Warsaw Treaty countries it is stressed as follows:

> The States represented at the meeting support the growing contribution of the UN and other international organizations to the cause of securing peace, disarmament, and ending the arms race, to the cause of solving all global problems facing humanity.[4]

Back in 1960, among the principles approved by the Conference of Independent African States, the first place was occupied by the follow-

---

* Dr., Professor of Law, Leading Researcher at the Institute of State and Law of the Academy of Sciences of the USSR.

[1] Doctrine of international law asserted this fact as early as in the 1960s, *see* *M. Lachs*, Wspólczesne organizacje międzynarodowe i rozwój prawa międzynarodowego, Pánstwo i Prawo 1963, 827 note 12.

[2] *See V. Moravetsky*, The Functions of International Organization (in Russian), Moscow 1976, 20.

[3] *E. A. Shevardnadze*, Speech at the jubilee meeting of the 40th UN General Assembly Session, in: Pravda (in Russian), October 25th, 1985; *see* also the speech of the Foreign Minister of Czechoslovakia *B. Chnoupek* at the same session, in: Pravda (in Russian), October 3rd, 1985.

[4] Pravda (in Russian), June 12th, 1986.

ing: "Inviolable adherence to and support of the UN Charter and respect for the UN decisions".[5] Some African lawers go even further insisting on giving the UN General Assembly powers to adopt legally binding decisions by the majority of votes.[6] Even in the countries which treat the UN with restraint, there are many experts speaking in favour of recognition of the role of this organization and its decisions[7].

Working out and adopting resolutions hold a special place among various forms of activity of international organizations. With the help of resolutions international organizations define their tasks, formulate principles and rules which member States are to follow.[8] Rule-creating activity plays an important part in the functioning of international organizations. International organizations have become an indispensable element of the international normative system. Under such system we mean a system of political, legal, moral, and other international rules based on the common goals and principles and created by the agreement of States for the purpose of regulating their relations with each other.[9] The UN General Assembly resolutions are taking part in the formulation and implementation of the whole variety of international rules. Therefore, they can influence municipal law through international law, moral, and political rules. These resolutions have also a considerable ideological influence on municipal law.

In this particular case we are only interested in the direct impact of the UN General Assembly resolutions on municipal law. It is known, that in international law doctrine there exist different views as to the binding force of these resolutions. Some authors claim that certain General Assembly resolutions bear a binding legal force.[10] But most authors presume that these acts are recommendations bearing no such force.[11]

---

[5] Independent Africa in Documents (in Russian), Moscow 1965, 41.

[6] *See T. O. Elias*, Africa and the development of International Law, Leiden/Dobbs Ferry, New York 1972, 46—62.

[7] Assistant Secretary for International Organization Affairs *Ch. Maynes*' statement: "Too often we have paid lipservice to the UN system, but not taken it seriously enough . . . President Carter is strongly committed to developing the full potential of multilateral institutions . . .", in: The Department of State Bulletin, no. 1986, July 18th, 1977, 100.

[8] *See Christoph Schreuer*, Recommendations and Traditional Sources of International Law, in: German Yearbook of International Law 20 (1977), 103—118 (103).

[9] *See I. I. Lukashuk, G. K. Dmitrieva*, Das Völkerrecht im internationalen Normensystem: Probleme des Völkerrechts, Berlin 1985.

[10] *See Jorge Castañeda*, Legal Effects of United Nations Resolutions, London 1969; *Louis B. Sohn*, The Development of the Charter of the United Nations: The Present State, in: *Maarten Bos* (ed.), The Present State of International Law and Other Essays, Deventer, The Netherlands 1973, 39—59 (55).

[11] *See G. I. Tunkin*, The Theory of International Law (in Russian), 2nd rev. ed. Moscow 1970, 184 *et seq.*; *Shinya Murase*, International Law Making for the New International Economic Order, in: Japanese Annual of International Law 25 (1982), 45—66 (51—53).

The UN Charter and the international practice prove the second point of view. That the Charter authorized the General Assembly to make recommendations and therefore to acknowledge its right to take legally binding decisions would mean to review the Charter. However, the fact that recommendations are devoid of the legal binding force does not mean that they lack any other binding force at all. A resolution having no binding force at all would be senseless, would contain *contradictio in adiecto*, and 160 States would hardly be making so much effort to elaborate the resolutions. The essence of a resolution is in reaching agreement between States, which takes the form of normative directions, aimed at putting them into practice. Among these resolutions, we should single out those which contain directions as to the settlement of a concrete problem. Such resolutions are capable of having direct legal consequences, both in international and municipal law.[12] Analysis of the practice shows that States consider the UN to be an important mechanism for "solving international problems"[13]. It is underlined that to fulfil the General Assembly recommendations is a duty of the member States.[14] The UN Secretariat holds the same position.[15]

Therefore, the General Assembly resolutions not being legally binding have nevertheless a binding force of some other kind. This binding force has a certain legal basis. Article 2 para. 2 of the Charter commits all Members to fulfil in good faith the obligations assumed in accordance with the Charter, in order to ensure to all of them the rights and benefits resulting from the membership in the Organization. Without respect for the resolutions of the General Assembly, this aim as well as other aims of the United Nations cannot be achieved. The UN would not be able to be a centre for harmonizing the actions of nations in the attainment of common ends. In other words: The very fact of States membership in the UN entails certain mutual obligations of co-operation and good faith pertaining to the fufilment of the resolutions adopted.[16] Respect for the General Assembly resolutions is therefore predetermined by the necessity of ensuring the functioning of these acts, the binding force of

---

[12] *See* Legal Consequences for States of the Continued Presence of South Africa in Namibia (South-West Africa), notwithstanding Security Council Resolution 276 (1970), (Advisory Opinion), I.C.J. Reports 1971, 50.

[13] *See* Soviet-Yugoslavian Communique, in: Pravda (in Russian), November 18th, 1976.

[14] *See A. A. Gromyko*'s declaration in New York, in: Pravda (in Russian), May 23rd, 1978; Memorandum of the US State Department Legal Adviser, in: American Journal of International Law 55 (1961), 701.

[15] *See* The UN General Secretary Report on the Work of the Organization, UN Doc. 1/A/37/1, 1982, 3.

[16] *See* Interpretation of the Agreement of March 25th, 1951, between the WHO and Egypt, (Advisory Opinion), I.C.J. Reports 1980, 93.

which are of moral and political character.[17] This force depends on how the recommendations accord with the UN Charter, its aims and principles, as well as on the extent to which it is supported by the Member States.[18]

Each member of the UN has the right not to support any resolution and, therefore, not to be bound by it. But systematically voting against the General Assembly resolutions which are accepted by the majority of votes may be considered as the abuse of rights, as contradicting the aims, principles, and spirit of the UN Charter.

Reflecting the urgent needs of international life and being accepted by the authoritative Organization to which the majority of existing States are members, some General Assembly resolutions may be more important and effective than certain treaties.[19] General Assembly resolutions now have greater impact on the policy, economics, *etc.* of the States. This is true even for those States which treat these resolutions without much respect.[20] Municipal law cannot remain outside the scope of this growing influence.[21]

*

Let us concentrate now on the problem of direct impact of the UN General Assembly resolutions on municipal law of States. There are facts proving that these resolutions had a considerable impact on the national

---

[17] *See G. K. Dimitrieva,* The Role of the UN General Assembly Resolutions in the Mechanism of Legal Regulation of International Relations (in Russian), (Kiev University Vestnik), International Relations and International Law 1985, note 20; *M. G. E. do Nascimento e Silva,* Observations, (Rapport provisoire, Les techniques d'élaboration des grandes conventions multilatérales et des normes quasi-législatives internationales), in: Annuaire de l'Institute de Droit International 57/II (1977), 71—74 (73); in his letter to Parliament of December 20th, 1984, the State Secretary for Justice of the Netherlands stated that "recommendations do not entail any binding legal obligation to observe them and that they have only moral force, i. e., that they command a particular course or courses of action to States which the latter are urged to take into account when preparing or pursuing their policy", *R. C. R. Siekmann,* Netherlands' State Practice for the Parliamentary Year 1984—1985, in: Netherlands Yearbook of International Law (NYIL) 17 (1986), 127—214 (131).

[18] *Jochen Abr. Frowein,* Der Beitrag der internationalen Organisationen zur Entwicklung des Völkerrechts, in: Zeitschrift für ausländisches öffentliches Recht und Völkerrecht 36 (1976), 147—167 (167).

[19] *See Schreuer* (note 8), 105; *Simone Dreyfus,* Droit des relations internationales, Paris 1978, 113.

[20] The above-mentioned US State Secretary Adviser *Ch. Maynes* writes: "The power center of American foreign policy has seldom taken the United Nations very seriously." That attitude is now changing, according to *Ch. Maynes,* because "UN decisions are suddenly having a much greater impact on the United States in the political as well as the economic field . . .", *Charles William Maynes,* A UN Policy for the Next Administration, in: Foreign Affairs 54 (1976), 804—819 (804, 805).

[21] *Petko Radoynov* writes about the growing impact of the international organizations on the national law of States, *Petkov Radoynov,* Law-Making Functions of the International Organizations (in Bulgarien), Sofia 1975, 22.

law including constitutional law. They have promoted the acceptance of certain principles of international law by the constitutional law of a number of States. This has been also done to the greatest extent by the Constitution of the USSR, which embraces all the main principles of international law. Major provisions of the Universal Declaration of Human Rights have been included into constitutions of very many newly formed independent States.

The resolutions which are aimed at setting certain rules of behaviour for the subjects of municipal law, physical and legal persons, first of all, have a direct impact on the national law. This is true for constitutional law as well. Thus, on the basis of the General Assembly Resolution of November 3rd, 1947, banning propaganda of war, the Statute on the Protection of Peace was passed in the Soviet Union in 1951[22].

There are resolutions calling upon the States to adopt certain laws. The General Assembly by Resolution 2465, adopted during its XXIII Session in 1968, thus proclaimed a criminal action the use of mercenaries against national liberation-movements and outlawed mercenaries as such. The Assembly called on the governments of all countries to issue laws which proclaim recruiting, financing, and training mercenaries to be criminal actions.[23] Special interest for the problems discussed present the Code of Conduct of Law-Enforcement Officers.[24] Having adopted this document, the General Assembly recommended to the governments to discuss the problem of its application as a code of principles within the framework of municipal law.[25]

Therefore, among the General Assembly resolutions there are such resolutions which cannot be put into effect without the help of municipal law. Some of them recommend to the States to include certain rules into their national law. In all these cases, provisions of the resolutions assume national legal force only after they have been implemented into the national law of the State and sometimes into the practice of this law.[26]

---

[22] *See Y. M. Rybakov*, Armed Agression — the Grave International Crime (in Russian), Moscow 1980, 86.

[23] Resolutions adopted by the General Assembly during its XXIII. Session, UN Doc./A/7218 (GAOR, 23rd sess., suppl. no. 18), 5.

[24] Code of Conduct of Law-Enforcement Officers (in Russian), New York 1979.

[25] In the Commentary to the Code it is mentioned: "The present Code is observed in all cases when it is included into the national law or practice", *loc. cit.*, 7.

[26] X v. *Inspector of Direct Taxes*, Supreme Court of the Netherlands of November 7th, 1984. The Universal Declaration of Human Rights is based on the power to make recommendations. "The Court may not therefore review the law by reference to the Declaration", *L.A.N.M. Barnhoorn*, Netherlands Judicial Decisions Involving Questions of Public International Law, 1984—1985, in: NYIL 17 (1986), 247—310 (253).

Resolutions concerning the settlement of a concrete problem, dealing with the legal status of a certain country or territory, may have great direct impact on municipal law. Numerous General Assembly resolutions on the *apartheid* regime in South Africa and on Namibia are a unique such example. In these resolutions, laws dealing with the *apartheid* regime have been more than once defined as tyranny.[27] The General Assembly in the Resolution of October 22nd, 1966, (2145/XXI) asserted that the South African Republic had failed to fulfil its obligations under the Mandate for South-West Africa and had "in fact, disavowed the Mandate". The Assembly decided that the Mandate "is therefore terminated, that South Africa has no other right to administer the Territory and that henceforth South-West Africa comes under the direct responsibility of the United Nations". By the Resolution of May 19th, 1967, (2248) the General Assembly established a United Nations Council for South-West Africa in order to administer South-West Africa until independence, to promulgate such laws, decrees, and administrative regulations as are necessary for the administration of the Territory. On December 22nd, 1978, the General Assembly accused the South African regime for conducting unilaterally elections contrary to the UN decisions and proclaimed the results of the elections having no legal force. The UN Resolution called upon the Member States "not to recognize in any way the representatives or organs created as a result of these elections"[28].

The implementation of these resolutions required to introduce changes to the functioning of the national legal, administrative, and judicial systems of the Member States with regard to the cases which concerned South-West Africa. From the juridical point of view, these changes were to be generated not by the Resolutions themselves but by the acts of municipal law. The facts mentioned above show diverse ways in which the General Assembly resolutions may influence municipal law. It is true, however, that the case with South-West Africa is a unique one and cannot be treated as typical. Nevertheless, somewhat similar cases may happen in the future. The General Assembly Resolutions on Cyprus prove this assumption.[29]

The growing influence of the General Assembly resolutions on municipal law necessitates theoretical investigation of the problem as well as its settlement in the international and national law.

[27] Note 23, 20.

[28] Pravda (in Russian), December 23rd, 1978.

[29] The Foreign Minister of Cyprus, *N. Rolandis*, speaking at the General Assembly XXXV. Session, said that the principles of the agreements of 1977 and 1979 "on the summit level and UN resolutions on Cyprus should be treated as basic, organizing elements of the federal republic", (in Russian), in: Cyprus Bulletin 1980, 7 note 20.

Analysis of doctrine shows that this problem has not yet attracted much attention.[30] Different points of view exist here. Some authors consider General Assembly resolutions of being capable of creating international law rules directly and primarily comparable with the rules of municipal law.[31] But most authors writing on this problem deny to the resolutions the direct operability within municipal law.[32]

International law does not contain special norms regulating the impact of General Assembly resolutions on municipal law. At the same time, this process must take place within the framework of international law and it is, therefore, regulated by this law to a certain extent. There exist principles and rules of international law essential for the process under consideration. First of all, according to the UN Charter, the General Assembly resolutions regulate relations between States exclusively, even if economic, social, cultural, and humanitarian problems are touched upon. According to Article 1 para. 3, the purpose of the United Nations is "to achieve international co-operation in solving international problems of an economic, social, cultural, or humanitarian character".

The above-mentioned is proved by the principle of non-intervention into domestic matters. According to Article 2 para. 7, "nothing contained in the present Charter shall authorize the United Nations to intervene in matters which are essentially within the domestic jurisdiction of any State".

A rule has been established in international law long since, according to which the choice of ways in which the rules of international law are realized, lies within the competence of a State. It is of primary importance to achieve the results presupposed by the rules.[33] Rules of international law should be employed at home within the framework of municipal law. These provisions are applicable to the implementation of General Assembly resolutions as well.

---

[30] Thus, provisional conclusions of the International Law Institute on the status of the General Assembly resolutions treat them as being of great importance for the international law-making process. Nevertheless, the problem of their implementation into the national law had not even been touched upon. *M. Krzysztof Skubiszewski*, Rapporteur, Resolutions of the General Assembly of the United Nations, Quatrième question: The elaboration of general multilateral conventions and of non-contractual instruments having a normative function or objective, in: Annuaire de l'Institute de Droit International 61/II (1986), 257—267 (260—265).

[31] *See Charles Cadoux*, La supériorité du droit des Nations Unies sur le droit des Etats-membres, in: Revue générale de droit international public 63 (1959), 649—680.

[32] *See G. I. Tunkin* (ed.), International Law (in Russian), Moscow 1982, 79; *P. Radoynov*, International Legal Problems of the Socialist Economic Integration (in Bulgarien), Sofia 1984, 35; *Christoph C. Schreuer*, Decisions of International Institutions Before Domestic Courts, London/Rome/New York 1981, 14.

[33] *See Roberto Ago*, Sixth Report on State Responsibility, in: Yearbook of the International Law Commission 1977, UN Doc. A/CN. 4/302 and ADD. 1—3, 4.

If we consider now municipal law, we shall see that it does not contain, so far, more or less clearly defined rules which regulate the impact of resolutions of international organizations on domestic law. It is nothing to be surprised about because legal regulation of domestic implementation of the rules of international law is still far from being perfect. The situation is worsened by the fact that those comparatively little positive results achieved in regulating the internaional law rules of implementation are applicable to General Assembly resolutions only to a slight extent. This is explained by the differences in the legal and non-legal acts which are especially tangible in the system of municipal law.

The national law makes only first steps on the way of domestic implementations of the organizations' resolutions. As an example, which may be followed by other countries, we may cite Article 93 of the Constitution of Spain (1978): "The General *Cortes* or the Government in accordance with their competence have the responsibility to ensure implementation of the treaties or resolutions issued by the international organizations"[34].

Legislative organs play the primary part in reflecting General Assembly resolutions in municipal law, while executive organs assume responsibility of their implementation. National courts hold specific positions with regard to the impact of the resolutions on the practice of the application of the municipal law. Analysis of the judicial practice shows that courts provide well-grounded reasons for differentiating between the impact of international legal acts and resolutions of international organizations on municipal law. It is stated in the decision of the High Court of Kenya in *Okunda and Another* v. *Republic* that principles regulating elimination of contradictions between international treaties and domestic law are not applied to elimination of contradictions between the domestic law and the law generated by the organ established on the basis of the treaty. To ground this thesis the Court has expressed the following opinions. The State signs the treaty being aware of its content and of its own law and juridical policy. This cannot refer to the rules adopted by the organ established on the basis of the treaty. The content of such rules which may be very broad, could not fall within the scope of vision of the parties at the moment of signing the treaty.[35]

The opinion mentioned above has the following sense: The content of the treaty is approved by the competent State organs, while the content of the resolutions is not. If it were otherwise the international organ would be able to carry out law-making functions in municipal law

[34] Spain, Constitution and Legislative Acts (in Russian), Moscow 1982, 62; similar norms are contained in the Constitutions of The Netherlands and Denmark.

[35] See International Law Reports 51 (1978), 414—423.

alongside with the corresponding State organs and would thus assume a supra-national character. This opinion is quite reasonable. The way out of this situation may be found in establishing the procedure of approving by the competent State organs those resolutions of the international organizations which are aimed at bringing changes into the municipal law.

Courts in some countries are governed by these opinions, not only when they consider General Assembly resolutions, but also when they deal with the legally binding decisions of the Security Council. The High Court of Australia in its decision of September 10th, 1973, decided that, as far as the Security Council resolutions were not introduced into practice in Australia by corresponding legislative acts, they cannot be taken as a ground for actions of the executive power which contradict the law.[36]

Therefore, the executive power has the right to take within its competence such measures which are necessary for the realization of the provisions of the resolutions of an international organ. But this provides no grounds to the executive for going beyond the limits of the existing laws. Only legislative organs may introduce into municipal law the changes requested by resolutions.

In most cases the courts, due to the unsettled impact of the international organs' resolutions on municipal law and its implementation, prefer not to consider problems which have to do with resolutions. In doing so they refer to the doctrine of political problems or give other reasons. Often courts justify their refusal to implement a resolution of the international organ by the fact that it is in contradiction of national law.

Having analysed the judicial practice in the USA, Professor *Christoph Schreuer* came to a conclusion that *Diggs* v. *Shults* (1972—1973) was the only one known case which contains a clear-cut conscious conflict between the decision of the international organ and domestic law. In this decision the court considered itself bound by the federal law which directly violated the UN Resolutions on sanctions against Rhodesia which the United States had to support in accordance with the UN charter.[37]

In the light of the above-mentioned, it is necessary to admit that the legal settlement of domestic implementation of resolutions of international organizations, including those of the General Assembly, is much

---

[36] *See Bradley* v. *Commonwealth of Australia and Another*, in: Australian Law Reports 1 (1973), 241.

[37] *See Schreuer* (note 8), 238.

desirable.[38] Thus, in spite of many obstacles, the General Assembly resolutions undoubtedly have an impact on municipal law and its implementation. This impact is factual and not juridical, formal. The resolutions of the General Assembly reflect the collective opinion of the UN Member States. They represent authoritative expression of political, legal, and moral conscience.[39] The impact by way of national juridical thinking is perhaps the main road of inducing the national law and the practice of its implementation. There is every reason to believe that this influence of General Assembly resolutions on municipal law will continue to increase, contributing to the process of internationalization, democratization, and humanization of the municipal law of many countries.

---

[38] *P. Radoynov*, Legal Nature and Significance of Legal Acts of the Council for Mutual Economic Aid (in Russian), in: *E. T. Usenko* (ed.), Legal Aspects of the Activities of the Council for Mutual Economic Aid, Moscow 1977, 89.

[39] *See Panoz Terz*, Die Normbildungstheorie, (Eine völkerrechtsphilosophische, völkerrechtssoziologische und völkerrechtstheoretische Studie), in: Acta Universitatis szegediensis, Acta juridica et politica 34 (1985), 48.

Discussion

Oppermann:

I want to express, Mr. *Chairman*, with your kind permission, my admiration for both speakers as I did already individually to them during the coffee break. Their subject was extremely difficult as regards the substance, because they had to treat the law character of non-law, so to speak. I followed with keen interest how Mr. *Kunig* demonstrated the indirect influence of these resolutions and other unilateral acts on the sphere of municipal law. You, Mr. *Lukashuk*, spoke in particular on the resolutions of the General Assembly. I am extremely interested in the international economic law side of these resolutions. I noted down all your clever formulas as to how to bridge that fundamental contradiction of transforming non-law into law: "These resolutions of the General Assembly have an ideological influence on national law. They have no legal force, but a certain obligatory force. They have some kind of force, a binding force of some other kind; they should be put into practice; they have an impact on national law; they have a factual, but not a juridical influence". I am not being ironic, but you can certainly see the problem. I want to put up one point in order to see if I have understood you correctly. One has to make a difference as far as the resolutions of the General Assembly are concerned. Namely, if they are taken by consensus (unanimity) or only by majority. The legal and moral value of majority resolutions seems to be rather shaky. Take, for instance, the situation of the vote on the Charter of Economic Rights of States in 1974. Here you had about 119 votes for the resolution and about 16, I think, abstaining or against it. But among these 16 dissenters were, economically speaking, very important States. Such a situation considerably weakens the importance of the resolution. One can speak of a "moral character" of resolutions of the General Assembly. In German we sometimes say that they constitute a sort of *Argumentationsrahmen* for the scope of a certain problem. But even this is only true if there has been real world-wide consensus on the resolution. The moral character of the resolution presupposes a sort of "moral use of the majority" inside the United Nations. There is sometimes the use of the so-called "automatic majority" of the Third World in the General Assembly. This automatic majority is very dangerous for the real value of the resolutions. If you just want to put through a sort of resolution with a big majority, without really bothering what the legal and political convictions in the different parts of the world are really like, you may get a very "impressive" resolution. But you will never get true acceptance of such a kind of resolution on the side of the dissenters. They regard the resolution from the perspective of Article 10 UN Charter as mere recommendations. This is a very important problem for the dignity of the UN system. The implementation of important resolutions of the General Assembly presupposes a generally convincing character of its contents. Only then can you expect that the resolution should be observed in good faith and put into practice. Thank you very much, Mr. *Chairman*.

Lukashuk:

It seems to me that Mr. *Oppermann* pointed just to the main problem. I believe that there is an international normative system which consists not only of international law, but international morality, international political rules, rules of international organizations, and so on. But principles of the system are, generally speaking, common aims and principles of the Charter. States often get to an agreement and often this agreement is not legal, not illegal, but not legal. It is some kind of policy rule. The main thing is to elaborate a rule. It is quite understandable because, as you know, international law does not have a special mechanism for implementation, or, there is one but which is far from perfect. That is why it is the most important thing to get to an agreement and then to implement this agreement into life. Of course, there are different ways of implementation, for legal agreements in one way, and non-legal agreements the other way. Still, take for example the Treaty of Alliance. It is an international legal treaty but to try to implement this treaty by legal means would be very difficult, because it is a highly political treaty. So very often States use another non-legal form. The resolutions of the United Nations General Assembly are a kind of agreement, not legal agreements of course, but still, at their basis lies agreement. You, (Mr. *Oppermann*), stressed properly that whenever you deal with legal acts then it is no question, for example, in parliament: What majority? If you have majority, then it is enough. Such resolutions as the General Assembly resolutions are of a moral, political nature. It is very important: how many States vote for the resolution, because the moral or political force depends on this majority. That is, why I was speaking of their having a special force. They are obligatory but not legally obligatory, they are of moral or political force, but I believe that in future the obligatory force of such a resolution of the General Assembly will get legal character. States will go on in this respect. Of course, it will not be tomorrow, but the day after tomorrow.

Then another thing: You, (Mr. *Oppermann*), stressed this point. Of course, no, we cannot adopt resolutions without participation of the main systems. We must co-operate, we must co-ordinate our wills, our interests, only then these resolutions will work. As you call it a "mechanical majority", it would develop nothing. Well, in some special cases it may have an ideological or propagandistic effect, and that is all. In order to regulate relations between States, somehow the resolutions must take into consideration lawful interests of all participants.

Simma:

First, I would like to make a compliment both to Mr. *Lukashuk* and to Mr. *Kunig* for their presentations, because they managed to keep me awake after an unusually lavish lunch, which is quite something to accomplish. I was struck by the very modern and pragmatic way in which both lectures dealt with the problem. I see here a certain parallel with the treatment of the question we discussed in the morning, namely the question of the relationship between municipal law and international law. I think that also there we had a certain period in the 1920s and the 1930s, when a lot of beautiful theories were developed and the main proponents of these theories did not particularly care about the facts, about State practice "behind" these theories. After World War II, certain authors have taken the view that most of these theories, like the debate between monists and dualists, are entirely besides the point. I think that overstates it, but it is certainly a good development that we are getting down to business and starting to dicuss the details, the technical questions of incorporation of various rules of international law. I think that the same is taking place here and this is a rather positive sign. There has been the question of the legal significance of General Assembly resolutions — the playground *par excellence* of legal theories for several decades. I think that now we are moving away from the theories and getting down to the basics, that we are observing what actually happens, and I would like to congratulate you for doing exactly that.

Mr. *Lukashuk* has said something which I think is of really basic importance for our question. He has said, if I understood him correctly, that only those General Assembly resolutions have a moral force or significance which are supported by all the main powers in the United Nations. This means that, for example, the Friendly Relations Declaration of 1970 has a much greater persuasive force than, for example, a resolution like the Charter of Economic Rights and Duties of 1974. This is something we have to keep in mind in the further discussion on this topic. I have a question to Mr. *Lukashuk*. I think it is probably going to be dealt with by my neighbour on Thursday, (Mrs. *Shinkaretskaya*), but I would still like to pose it to her: What would be the effect of General Assembly resolutions repeated many times, *i. e.* of whole series of resolutions on the *domaine réservé*, on domestic jurisdiction? Let us think of the impressive number of resolutions dealing with questions of human rights. Could we say that such General Assembly resolutions are a vehicle or an instrument by which domestic jurisdiction of UN member States is carved out, diminished, melted down? What is your view on that?

I have one last question to Mr. *Kunig*. In fact, it is more of the nature of an observation. In Germany there is the saying: *Wo ein Wille ist, da ist auch ein Weg* — where there is a strong interest, it will find it's way. As we all know, this is especially true for lawyers. So let me just mention two cases in which the *Bundesverfassungsgericht* has not had great problems in upgrading the legal status of international organizations or of decisions of such organizations, for obvious reasons. The first case was the *Eurocontrol* decision in which, I think, the *Bundesverfassungsgericht* had to make good what it did (or what it overdid) in the *Solange* Case, concerning the hierarchy between German Law and European Community Law. In *Eurocontrol* it paid tribute to European Community Law by having recourse to the law of a very modest and not at all supra-national organization which deals with flight control in, I think, heights of over 7000 metres. So *Eurocontrol* is supra-national only in the geographical sense, but certainly not in the legal sense. But as I said, you find there some kind of compensation — reparation for injuries, so to speak directed towards the European Communities. The second case, of course, is the case of the *Twin-Track* decision concerning NATO. As you remember, the *Bundesverfassungsgericht* took the view that NATO was an organization based on Article 24 of the German *Grundgesetz*, which means an organization to which the Federal Republic has transferred sovereign rights. This was a view which was neither taken by the fraction of the Greens in Parliament, nor by the distinguished professors representing the Federal Government before the Court. Thank you.

Mosler:

What I was going to say has already been said by my predecessor. First of all, I would like to congratulate the two speakers of this afternoon for their excellent presentation of a very difficult subject.

Now I want to ask a question to Mr. *Lukashuk*. There is a distinction between resolutions and resolutions. I share the view of Mr. *Simma* that one can explain the legal value of resolutions of the General Assembly as having persuasive authority. The question is whether all of the resolutions have equal persuasive authority. I will try to give examples: The Declaration on Decolonization — and the following resolutions in this field — has a wide effect and is widely accepted. The Declaration on Sovereignty on National Resources has also in principle a wide effect, although there are differences in detail. Then there is the famous Resolution on Friendly Relations. I think the main principles, the headlines of the various sections are generally accepted; their authority is really persuasive. As regards the detailed explanations printed under the headlines, there some difficulties arise. I think one can find a kind of scheme to differentiate between the various degrees of authority. This morning the *North Sea Continental Shelf* Cases have not been mentioned. In this judgment, which had to do with customary law of the sea, there the Court makes a distinction between countries which are particularly concerned by a rule and others which are not particularly concerned. It is obvious for example, that a law of the sea agreed upon only by landlocked States could not be effective. Can any similar distinction be made — and this is my question — with regard to the greater or lesser authority of General Assembly resolutions? Reference has already been made to the Charter on Economic Rights and Duties. Here is the problem that some States are asked to do something, while others want their wishes to be complied with.

Bernhardt:

Mr. Chairman, I share the admiration of the former speakers for the excellent reports, and I also admire the rapporteurs for having avoided the notion "soft law". Now, I would like to draw your attention to a decision of the Federal Constitutional Court which might be of certain interest in the present context. It is a decision of the Court of March 26th, 1987. The German Federal Constitutional Court declared that, in interpreting the basic rights provisions in the German Basic Law, account should be taken of the decisions of the European Court of Human Rights.

But now I turn to the more general question whether decisions of international organs are immediately binding in the internal legal order. This can only be accepted if two conditions are met. The first is that the international organ concerned has the power to accept binding decisions, and the second condition is that the national legal system provides for the internal validity. But there are even some problems in the case of decisions or resolutions which are not formally binding, and here, I agree that no clear answer can be given. The question of how far such resolutions can be taken into account in the internal order depends upon many different factors. It depends upon the substance of the resolution, the majority, or the adoption by consensus, *etc.* Even though the resolutions are not binding in certain cases, it can and should not be excluded that they may have some relevance to the internal legal order. They can be one element in the legal reasoning. Thank you.

Starushenko:

I would like to support this soft interpretation of the resolutions of the General Assembly given by Mr. *Lukashuk*. I think, that in our age of nuclear weapons and terrorism, and even of nuclear terrorism, it is very important to prevent the violation of the resolutions containing the norms of international law. And for this, it seems to me, that all kinds of methods taken are good. My question is: What do you think is the difference between the resolutions adopted by voting or those accepted by consensus? Do you think that the Definition of Aggression accepted by consensus in 1974, for example, has also a soft character, or do you think that all States must respect this definition?

Bothe:

I think we have become aware, on the basis of the two excellent reports, that we are dealing with a complex question. To reduce that complexity, I suggest four differentiations.

First of all, there are different kinds of obligations involved. There are cases where a resolution is really legally binding, such as a resolution of the Security Council adopted on the basis of Article 25 of the Charter. Outside the sphere of supra-national organizations, this power to adopt binding decisions is rather exceptional. Then we have cases where the basis of an obligation, if any, is consensus. But that may mean different things. Consensus may create a legal obligation. There are organizations where a unanimous decision is binding and, thus, a legal obligation results from this kind of consensus. It is questionable whether this amounts to a treaty obligation, but it is not doubtful that the basis for the obligation is consensus as recognized by law. On the other hand, we have the more vague field of political consensus where the obligation ensuing from consensus is merely political or moral, not legal. Finally, there are majority decisions where the basis of an "obligation" is only the political pressure exercised by the majority.

This leads me to my second differentiation. We are dealing with different kinds of subject matters. We are not only dealing, and this is quite clear from Mr. *Kunig*'s report, with the United Nations and obligations belonging to the field of international power politics. We are dealing with such matters as the protection of the environment, human health, social and working conditions, weather modification techniques, weather observation systems, and many other very technical matters. Those are sometimes dealt with by majority decisions. In this connection, we frequently encounter the rule that those who are against the majority or at least those who have no strong feelings about it, abide by the practical pressure exercised by the majority opinion.

This leads me to my third differentiation. We are dealing with different kinds of organizations having different procedures. We have the United Nations and the UN family, we have such organ as the Economic Commission for Europe, one of the most beneficial organizations created after the War. It made it possible for European States, at times when the relations between East and West were worse than they are today, to sit together and deal with practical problems. We have many smaller regional organizations. Eurocontrol has already been mentioned. We may go down to such institutions like the Trilateral Commission dealing with the pollution of Lake Constance, where we encounter exactly the same problems: Decisions are being taken, but there is no basis for a legal obligation. But the resolutions are nevertheless respected on the basis of national law, or the national law is modified accordingly. It is a pressure exercised by the reasonable character of a technical decision. Sometimes, common sense makes good law.

On the basis of these three differentiations, and that is my fourth differentiation, different kinds of national implementation are needed. In this connection, I would like to point out another kind of constitutional dimension of the problem. Mr. *Kunig* mentioned the question of individual rights. Where a decision affects individual rights, it must have a basis in law, in an act of legislature. This is one of the justifications for the rule we find in many constitutions, that treaties, before they are ratified by the State, have to be approved by the legislature. This is clearly the role of Article 59 para. 2 of the Basic Law of the Federal Republic. But this provision, and the same is true for similar provisions in other constitutions, only applies where the international norm to be created is a treaty, not in the case of other kinds of international obligations. The creation of such other obligations is really the hour of the executive branch of government. This should also be illustrated by an example, this time an American one. The Generalized System of Preferences was adopted by consensus in the framework of UNCTAD. But this was only a political consensus, the obligation stemming from it is not a legal, only a political one. One of the main reasons why that consensus was not put into the form of a legal agreement was the fact that it would have been impossible for the President of the United States to get this agreement through the Senate. The Senate would probably never have given, as required by the Constitution, its advice and consent, for reasons which we quite clearly see these days, namely the protectionist attitude of the American Congress. In view of this attitude, the solution consisted in the creation, by the executive branch alone, of an obligation which is not a legal one. Similar considerations apply to the extra-legal, or non-legal binding force of the SALT II agreement which also was never ratified by the United States' Senate, but was observed by both countries on a political basis. This is a development of obligations outside the traditional notion of legal obligations in international relations. This practice has become so frequent that, over the years, it has lead, in my view, to a remarkable modification of the international system of rule-making which has, this must be acknowledged, also left some traces on the constitutional division of powers within States. Thank you, Mr. *Chairman*.

Tunkin, Chairman:

We all agree, I believe, that resolutions of international organizations and specifically resolutions of the United Nations' General Assembly influence the behaviour of States. They function within the international system and the problem is to what extent they influence the internal legislation, the internal legal systems of States. But it is closely connected with a more general question. First, whether there is any legal element, element of legal force in the resolutions of the United Nations General Assembly. Our view, Mr. *Lukashuk*, is, that there is some element of legal force. First, this idea was advanced by *Malintoppi* in his excellent book "Le Raccommandazioni Internazionali" (1958), then it was supported by Mr. *Virally* in his book "L'organisation mondiale" (1972), and I also joined them in supporting this idea. Their argument is as follows: Resolutions of international organizations are the means of fulfilling their functions under the UN Charter, if we take this organization. All member States are bound to assist the United Nations in exercising its functions. Therefore, if a State has no regard at all to the resolutions adopted by the United Nations' General Assembly, it does contravene its Charter obligations. Of course, this is a very delicate problem, but still it seems that there is some legal obligation in the resolutions of the United Nations' General Assembly. That is one point. If there is such an element then it may influence in certain cases the internal law of States, the internal legal system in some cases, where applicable. Both rapporteurs have rightly pointed out that the influence exercised by the resolutions of international organizations is manyfold, not only through legal means, but by moral influence, and political influence. So there are in fact all other factual influences that a State considers it advisable to implement, to adopt, and to consider, and to follow to some extent even the rules contained in the resolutions of international organizations. If we take the International Labour Organization, it usually adopts, first of all, recommendations, and it has more than 150 recommendations adopted. Why? Because States are, in specific cases, not yet ready to accept legal obligations; so they adopt recommendations and many recommendations, with certain amendments, have become later on, conventions. And what that means is that they adopt recommendations, expecting that States will follow the recommendations to some extent. Mr. *Lukashuk* correctly pointed out that even the existence of a proclamation of a certain rule may influence the internal legislation of States.

Now the word is to the rapporteurs. Mr. *Kunig*, would you like to speak?

Kunig:

Thank you, Mr. *Chairman*. First of all, I would like to thank all speakers for their interesting comments, particularly for the further examples you provided in order to show how decisions taken by international organizations may gain whatever relevance on the level of municipal legal orders. Generally, I agree with what has been remarked in the discussion, and I see no reason for reply. Therefore I restrict myself to a few further remarks only.

To my mind, it is important that we did not only find a consensus as to the description of the current legal situation, but also in so far as where the difficulties and hindrances are to be found, which render further upgrading of the relevance of decisions of international organizations to municipal law a complex problem. I am convinced that one important aspect, in this context, is the question how we can isolate such resolutions and decisions which by their structure and by the conditions of their origin are appropriate for functioning on the municipal level. In my report, I tried to offer some potential criteria — others have been mentioned here during the discussion. Definitely, the degree of approval is a criterion of high relevance, but I would like to underline also that I consider the perspective of the national decision-maker as particularly important, I mean the decision-maker who asks himself whether he may make use of the decision. A national court, for instance, certainly has to take into consideration how the representatives of the respective State dealt with the resolution on the level of the international organization. Did these representatives vote in favour of the organization, did they just let it pass, without a positive reaction? What were the reasons for their behaviour? All the "loop-holes" we talked about whereby decisions of international organizations may reach the internal level, they are not constituted by norms directly referring to international decision-making — they are just norms which may be understood and interpreted in the light of such decision-making. It has to be avoided that national administrations or judges by reference to a resolution transform national foreign policy. It would certainly be of help if further criteria for qualifying decisions of organizations as appropriate reference norms for national decision-making could be elaborated. I do not yet have them at hand, however.

One aspect was, when listening to the discussion — I felt that most probably not all of us share identical views — the point Mr. *Tunkin* commented on at the end. You concentrated on the question, Mr. *Tunkin*, what really is the international validity of resolutions of the General Assembly of the United Nations. I more or less left this fascinating topic aside in my presentation, and I now take the liberty just to give some questions back to you. Do we have enough examples where a breach of a General Assembly resolution by the international community, or even by a majority of States, was held to be a breach of an international legal obligation? You underlined that paying no regard at all to a General Assembly resolution is not sufficent under legal terms. But this raises further questions: no regard at all to a certain individual resolution, no regard to a bundle of resolutions during a longer period of time, no regard to UN decisions generally? What we need here is the elaboration again of further criteria, which would enable us to handle individual cases. The question remains with me how we can differentiate between the general obligation to co-operate with other States and with the UN — an obligation laid down already in the Charter — from the obligations originating by secondary rules which — as we all would agree, I suppose — are not obligating in principle.

I tried to show in my report, however, that — notwithstanding international legal status — at any rate, there are roles to play in the municipal context also for non-binding norms, set by an international organization. Thank you.

Lukashuk:

First of all, I am to thank you for all your kind words and I believe, and I hope, that Mr. *Kunig* will agree with me that your remarks were at least not less precious than our reports. Of course, it would be very difficult to answer the whole problems and all your questions, so, if I am unable to answer some of them, please forgive me. Many speakers asked about consensus. You know it is a good invention, in a way. But you know in life everything has its setbacks — that is what concerns us; take for example the *Bundesrepublik Deutschland*. I do not compare of course two countries, you see, but maybe you would not agree and would not sign a treaty in the same context. But still, because all countries vote for this resolution, you need this vote for the resolution. So a consensus is good, of course, but it has some setbacks and we must notice this.

Starushenko:

Consensus is good — but the way to consensus?

Lukashuk:

I should propose that, first on an international level a committee of lawyers would be established, maybe independent lawyers — experts. They will look for implementation of General Assembly resolutions and every year they will prepare reports for the General Assembly.

Starushenko:

Would it implement General Assembly resolutions?

Lukashuk:

No, nothing happens at all. This is the first step. The second step is on the national level. Due to the law, some executive power must report to the parliament, or maybe to the government, about adopted resolutions of the General Assembly and make some recommendations. It may be very primitive first, but still it is some kind of mechanism to implement the resolutions.

You have noticed that two professors from two countries, which are not quite the same, they have got most of the same results. I hope that this is not the only example of how far we can co-operate and produce proper results by consensus or otherwise. Still we can produce proper results of such closer scientific research work or co-operation. Thank you.

Incorporation of International Treaties into Municipal Law*

By Albrecht Randelzhofer**

This report concerns itself with an important aspect in the area of the *auswärtige Gewalt* (foreign powers) of the Federal Republic of Germany. In spite of the positive law provisions in the *Grundgesetz* (German Basic Law), *i. e.* Articles 24, 25, 32, 59 of the Basic Law, there does not seem to be any uniform concept. The reason lies not only in the contradicting scholarly views on the particular questions at issue, but also in a certain lack of concurrence between the rules of law and practice. Supervening this are the principal difficulties which follow for the Federal state, Federal Republic of Germany, out of (1) the limited capacity of its member states in international law, the *Länder*, as well as out of (2) the undetermined extent of participation of the *Bundesrat* (upper chamber) as an organ of the *Länder* in the foreign powers.

I. The different international agreements according to the Basic Law

1. *The agreements of the Federation*

Article (Art.) 59 of the Basic Law deals with agreements which concern the foreign relations of the Federation. It binds the Federal President, who represents the Federation as a whole in international affairs, to an act of approval or co-operation of other leading state organs. According to the different procedures provided for in this Article, one can distinguish the following international agreements of the Federation:[1]

* The report given is an only slightly amended version of my publication "Domestic Law Procedures for Conclusion of International Agreements Transacted by the Executive in the Federal Republic of Germany", in: *Michael Bothe / Raul E. Vinuesa* (eds.), International Law and Municipal Law, Berlin 1982, 145—149. Notwithstanding, the *Editors* of the present volume wished its renewed publication in order to thereby prove the sequence of the Colloquy and because otherwise parts of the discussion would not have been intelligible.

** Dr. iur., Professor of Law, Director of the Institute of International and Foreign Law and Comparative Law, Free University of Berlin (West).

[1] There is no unity of opinion as to the types of international agreements in the Basic Law. *Cf. Albrecht Randelzhofer*, Innerstaatlich erforderliche Verfahren für das Wirksamwerden der von der Exekutive abgeschlossenen völkerrechtlichen Vereinbarungen, Archiv des öffentlichen Rechts 99 (1974) Supplement 1, 18—42 (19 *et seq.* with further references).

a) International agreements regulating the political relations of the Federation

In a broader sense every international agreement is concerned with the political relations of a state. But Art. 59 para. 2 has a narrower understanding. This provision is aimed at limiting the necessity of affirmative consent to international agreements. Out of that aim follows, according to the *Bundesverfassungsgericht* (German Federal Constitutional Court), that not all agreements which deal with public affairs, the public welfare, or state business are political, but only those which concern the existence of the state, its territorial integrity, independence, position, or its appropriate status in the community of states.[2] Moreover the content and purpose of such an agreement must be directed toward a "regulation" of the political relations of the Federation to other states, thus effecting a political arrangement. In this sense political agreements are, above all, those which affirm, consolidate, or extend the position of authority of the Federal Republic of Germany *vis-à-vis* other states. For example, the following belong to this category: treaties of alliance, mutual assistance, and deeds of accession to the most important international organizations.

b) International treaties affecting the Federal legislation; Art. 59 para. 2 sentence (sent.) 2, alternative (alt.) 2

The question whether such an agreement is at hand depends upon whether "in the particular case an act for giving effect with participation of the legislature is necessary"[3]. The content of an agreement is thus only then part of the Federal legislation if the fulfilment of the contractual obligations is solely possible through the enactment of a Federal statute.

c) Administrative agreements; Art. 59 para. 2 sent. 2

The term administrative agreement is controversial.[4] On the one hand one can consider the form, and on the other hand the content of the agreement. The prevailing opinion holds that all executive or depart-

---

[2] *Entscheidungen des Bundesverfassungsgerichts* (Federal Constitutional Court Reports — BVerfGE) vol. 1, 372—396 (380 *et seq.*) [hereinafter cited as: BVerfGE 1, 372—396 (380 *et seq.*)]; BVerfGE 36, 1—36 (13 *et seq.*); BVerfGE 40, 141—179 (164 *et seq.*); *Ondolf Rojahn*, in: *Ingo von Münch* (ed.), Grundgesetzkommentar, vol. 2, 2nd ed., München 1983, Art. 59, § 23.

[3] BVerfG 1, 372—396 (388); *Rojahn* (note 2), § 26; *Theodor Maunz*, in: *Theodor Maunz / Günter Dürig / Roman Herzog / Rupert Scholz*, Grundgesetz, Kommentar, München 1987, Art. 59, § 17.

[4] Above all *cf. Elfried Härle*, Die völkerrechtlichen Verwaltungsabkommen der Bundesrepublik, in: Jahrbuch für Internationales Recht 12 (1965), 93—139 (113 and n. 27).

mental agreements as well as all international agreements, which are not included in Art. 59 para. 2 sent. 1 of the Basic Law, come under this law.[5] The administrative agreements distinguish themselves from the agreements which affect the Federal legislation in that the fulfilment is affected in the form of administrative law (*i. e.* administrative regulations, administrative acts). Political administrative agreements differ from the political agreements which deal with public affairs, the public welfare in accordance with Art. 59 para. 2 sent. 1 alt. 1, in that they touch upon, but do not regulate, the political relations to foreign countries. In practice the differentiation is, however, often very difficult.[6] Agreements of such type have been concluded in some cases as treaties regulating political relations (the treaties of accession to the World Bank, to the IMF, and to the ITU), in other cases as administrative agreements (the treaties of accession to the UNESCO, the FAO, and the ILO).

d) Other types of agreements mentioned in the Basic Law

According to Art. 24 para. 1 the Federation can transfer sovereign powers to international institutions. This can only take place in concurrence with other states, that is by the signing of a corresponding agreement, as took place, for example, at the founding of the European Communities. For such agreements, however, there are constitutional particularities only in respect to the constitutional changes connected with them.[7] Moreover, they are treaties in the meaning of Art. 59, as they regulate the political relations of the Federation as well as they affect the legislation of the Federation because, according to Art. 24, a statute is necessary. To become effective in the domestic legal order, the same rules apply as for the agreements according to Art. 59 para. 2 of the Basic Law.

Also political treaties according to Art. 59 para. 2 are the agreements concerning peace treaties, the preparation of a peace treaty, or the abolition of an occupation regime for which Art. 79 para. 1 sent. 2 allows a modification of the requirement of an amendment to the text of the Constitution.

---

[5] *Rojahn* (note 2), § 55; *Härle* (note 4), 95; *Manfred Beer*, Staatsverträge und Verwaltungsabkommen im heutigen deutschen Staatsrecht, Diss. München 1960, 34 *et seq.*; *Rudolf Bernhardt*, Der Abschluß völkerrechtlicher Verträge im Bundesstaat, Köln/Berlin 1957, 133.

[6] *See Klaus Stern*, Das Staatsrecht der Bundesrepublik Deutschland, vol. 1, 2nd ed., München 1984, 502 with further references; *Rojahn* (note 2), § 59; *Härle* (note 4), 116 *et seq.*; *Fritjof Regehr*, Die völkerrechtliche Vertragspraxis in der Bundesrepublik Deutschland, Diss. München 1974, 217, concerning the *Transitabkommen* (access agreement) between the Government of the Federal Republic of Germany and the German Democratic Republic of December 17th, 1977 — concluded as an administrative agreement — which presents a borderline case.

[7] *Rojahn* (note 2), Art. 24, § 20; *Maunz* (note 3), Art. 24, § 14.

2. *The treaties of the states* (Länder)

The Federal Republic of Germany is a federal state for which the Basic Law provides, along with the power of the Federation, to conclude treaties, and also limited treaty-making powers for the *Länder*. However, the *Länder* rarely act as subjects of international law alongside the Federation so that the corresponding regulations have only little meaning in practice. According to Art. 32 para. 3, the *Länder* may conclude treaties as far as they are responsible for legislation, and have the consent of the Federal Government. It has been a matter of controversy, however, as to whether the *Länder* power is exclusive[8] within their respective spheres or whether the Federation has a concurring treaty-making power in the same fields[9] and, if one accepts the latter, whether the Federation has the power to apply such treaties domestically[10] or whether these powers remain with the *Länder*[11]. In practice the controversy has not been resolved by the so-called *Lindauer* Agreement of November 14th, 1957, but it has been considerably blunted by a *modus vivendi*.[12] In the *Lindauer* Agreement the Federation and the *Länder* concurred, without prejudice to their conflicting legal positions, that the Federation should be competent to conclude consular, commercial shipping, establishment, and trade and payment treaties, as well as treaties for the establishment of international organizations, even if such treaties contained typical provisions that would fall within exclusive legislative jurisdiction of the *Länder*, if the provisions are typical and normally included in such treaties and only constitute a subordinate component of the treaty. Moreover, the Federation would be competent to conclude cultural agreements, but only upon prior consent of the *Länder*.[13] In those instances where consent of the *Länder* is necessary

[8] Prevailing opinion; *cf.* the information in *Walter Rudolf*, Völkerrecht und deutsches Recht, Tübingen 1967, 186, n. 27.

[9] Information in *Rudolf id.* at 184.

[10] Thus *Wilhelm-Georg Grewe*, Die auswärtige Gewalt der Bundesrepublik, in: Veröffentlichungen der Vereinigung der Deutschen Staatsrechtslehrer 12 (1954), 129—266 (173); *Eberhard Menzel*, in: *loc. cit.*, 206.

[11] *Hermann von Mangoldt / Friedrich Klein*, Das Bonner Grundgesetz, vol. 2 (reprint), Berlin/Frankfurt 1966, Art. 32, § V 1.

[12] *Cf.* the text of the agreement in: *Maunz* (note 3), Art. 32, § 45. The *Enquête*-Commission for the reform of the Constitution suggested, in its summary report, that the fundaments of the agreement may be written into the Basic Law. As to the practice *see Bernhard Hartung*, Die Praxis des Lindauer Abkommens, Köln 1984.

[13] Accordingly the German-Polish Cultural Agreement makes the effectiveness of the agreement dependent on the necessary domestic provisions (approval by the *Länder*). The Minister Presidents of the *Länder* consented to Art. 4 under the condition that the Federal government explains that by the terms *hinwirken* (to influence) and *berücksichtigen* (to take into consideration) no obligation to accept the suggestions of the combined School Book Commission may be construed. *Cf. Ulf Dieter Klemm*, Völkerrechtliche Praxis der Bundesrepublik Deutschland im Jahre 1976, Zeitschrift für ausländisches öffentliches Recht und Völkerrecht 38 (1978), 286—337 (291).

it is given within the framework of the treaty-making procedure. The requirements depend on the constitutional provisions of the respective *Länder* which vary from *Land* to *Land*.[14] Most of the constitutions of the *Länder* speak only of *Staatsverträge* (state treaties); other constitutions[15] expressly lift the group of international treaties from those which affect the (state) legislation. If one takes a closer look one sees that the constitutions that speak only of state treaties — with one exception[16] — also make the distinction between treaties which affect legislation and such treaties which do not. Moreover, it is apparent that the *Länder* constitutions differentiate between treaties and administrative agreements without mentioning the term in every case (administrative agreement).[17] The label administrative agreement, however, has not been defined. There is something to be said for a material-content definition of administrative agreements in the area of the *Länder* and only those agreements affecting the area of the administration as opposed to legislation and government falling among it.[18]

In the area of treaty-making powers of the *Länder* one can distinguish the following types of international agreements:

a) international treaties affecting the *Länder* legislation;
b) other international treaties;
c) administrative agreements.

II. Domestic law procedures for giving international agreements effect in international law

1. Agreements of the Federation

a) International agreements regulating the political relations of the Federation and those affecting Federal legislation; Art. 59 para. 2, sent. 1 alt. 1, 2

Both types of treaties[19] must be ratified by the Federal President according to Art. 59 para. 1 sent. 2, regardless of whether the agreement

[14] Art. 50 of the Constitution of Baden-Württemberg from 1953; Art. 72 para. 2 of the Bavarian Constitution from 1946; Art. 43 of the Constitution of the Free Hanseatic City of Hamburg from 1952; Art. 103 of the Constitution of the State of Hesse from 1946; Art. 26 of the Provisional Constitution of Lower Saxony from 1951; Arts. 57, 66 para. 2 of the Constitution of North-Rhine-Westphalia from 1950; Art. 101 of the Constitution of Rhineland-Palatinate from 1947; Art. 25 of the Charter of the State Schleswig-Holstein from 1949; in the Constitution of the City-State of Bremen there are no express provisions, unwritten constitutional law has effect here.

[15] Hamburg, Lower Saxony, Schleswig-Holstein.

[16] Rhineland-Palatinate.

[17] Again with exception of the Constitution of Rhineland-Palatinate.

[18] On the other hand it can not be overlooked that, also in the practice of the *Länder* administrative agreements can be concluded which are in no way limited to the area of the administration, just the opposite, they contain, however, regulations which are political in their nature.

[19] *Cf.* section I. 1. a) and I. 1. b).

itself demands the requirement of ratification or not. He may not ratify before he has approval in the form of a *Bundesgesetz* (federal act) passed by the body specifically responsible for the agreement. Thus, this "treaty statute" empowers him, but does not obligate him, to ratify.

In this context it is controversial as regards the type and extent of participation of the *Bundesrat* (upper chamber) and *Bundestag* (lower chamber), the bodies responsible for Federal legislation. The question at hand is whether the law authorizing the ratification is an *Einspruchsgesetz* (act of objection) or a *Zustimmungsgesetz* (act of consent). The answer is simple for those agreements which affect the Federal legislation (Art. 59 para. 2, sent. 1 alt. 2). It is to be answered fully according to the part the *Bundesrat* plays in the normal domestic legislative procedure. If such a treaty contains a clause which, if it were enacted as a domestic law, could only be enacted by a *Zustimmungsgesetz*, then the law authorizing the treaty must have the consent of the *Bundesrat*. In all other cases a simple *Einspruchsgesetz* is sufficient and, in the event that the *Bundesrat* objects, such refusal is overridden by a second affirmative vote in the *Bundestag* (Art. 77).

The controversy bears its primary consequence in the area of the political treaties. Despite the basic importance of this question it played no part for a long time: in 1969 — particularly in connection with the so-called *Ostverträge*, treaties with the USSR, Poland, and the CSSR — when the majorities in the *Bundestag* and the *Bundesrat* became composed of different political parties, the dispute gained actuality.[20]

According to one view,[21] the *Einspruchsgesetz* only is necessary because the *Zustimmungsgesetz*, which requires consent by the *Bundesrat*, is always explicitly mentioned. In support of this view it can be referred to the treaty-making practice of the Federal Republic of Germany as well as to Art. 115 para. 3 which provides that a certain type of treaty, the peace treaty, does not need the approval of the *Bundesrat*. On the other hand, another view reaches the conclusion that political treaties as a rule do need the consent of the *Bundesrat* primarily because of the federalistic aspects of the foreign relations powers.[22]

---

[20] Regarding the participation of the *Bundesrat* for political treaties, the *Bundesverfassungsgericht* has not been called upon to make a decision.

[21] *Eberhard Menzel*, Bedürfen ‚politische Verträge' der Zustimmung des Bundesrates?, in: Juristenzeitung 23/24 (1971), 745—759; *Wilhelm Alexander Kewenig*, Bundesrat und auswärtige Gewalt, in: Zeitschrift für Rechtspolitik (ZRP) 4 (1971), 238—243; *Siegfried Weiss*, Auswärtige Gewalt und Gewaltenteilung, Berlin 1971, 146 *et seq.* with further references.

[22] *Dieter Blumenwitz*, Die Beteiligung des Bundesrates beim Abschluß politischer Verträge, in: Bayerische Verwaltungsblätter (1972), 29—36; *Michael Cieslar*, Bedürfen ‚politische Verträge' der Zustimmung des Bundesrates?, Diss. München

b) Administrative agreements

In order to give an administrative agreement international effect it must be ratified by the Federal President. This follows out of the absolute power of the Federal President to conclude treaties as expressed in Art. 59 para 1 sent. 2. According to the custom which has developed in constitutional practice, the Federal executive (for executive agreements) and the individual department minister (for departmental agreements) are implicitly empowered by tacit delegation to conclude administrative agreements where the Federal President would otherwise have this power.[23] As a rule, administrative agreements are internationally effective as soon as they have been signed. The ratification by the Federal President is only necessary when an administrative agreement explicitly calls for it, or the Federal President himself claims a title to ratification. A consent of the *Bundestag* is never imperative for giving effect to administrative agreements. But it is possible that the Government brings the administrative agreement before Parliament to receive its consent. This raised a controversy between the Federal Government and the opposition in connection with the Agreement on the Development of long term Collaboration between the Federal Republic of Germany and the USSR in the fields of Economy and Industry, signed on January 8th, 1978. This agreement was concluded as an administrative agreement. But then the Federal Government attributed to the agreement a high political value and intended to pass it through Parliament for consent. The opposition brought objections saying that such a procedure is not possible for constitutional reasons. The Government rejected this opinion but in fact resigned to pass the agreement through Parliament for consent. Economic agreements generally are treated as administrative agreements and therefore are not subject to the consent of Parliament in the practice of the Federal Republic of Germany. But to stress this once more, Constitution stands not against such a possibility.[24]

But the consent of the *Bundesrat* is essential in certain cases. Among those cases are those in which — according to Art. 59 para. 2 sent. 2 which in turn refers to Art. 83 *et seq.* — the administrative agreement contains measures or obligations which, according to Art. 83 *et seq.*, require the consent of the *Bundesrat*. This is especially the case when an administrative agreement contains general administrative regula-

---

1972, 15 *et seq.*; *Menzel* (note 21), 752 *et seq.* and *id.*, Die Ostverträge von 1970 und das Selbstbestimmungsrecht der Völker, in: ZRP 5 (1972), 35—41; *Maunz* (note 3), § 20.

[23] *Franz Josef Jasper*, Die Behandlung von Verwaltungsabkommen im innerstaatlichen Recht, Düsseldorf 1980, 162 *et seq.*, is of the opinion, that this is not a delegated power of the Government but a genuine one.

[24] *See id.*, 81 *et seq.*

tions, or when the agreement requires the enactment of general regulations and does not deal with a matter inherent to the Federal administration.[25]

c) Other expressly mentioned international treaties

We have already seen (*supra* I. 1. d)) that agreements which transfer sovereign powers to international institutions (Art. 24) and agreements concerning the preparation of a peace treaty (Art. 79 para. 2 sent. 2) are both international agreements in terms of Art. 59 para. 2 sent. 1. Consequently, they require ratification by the Federal President who in turn must receive the consent of the *Bundestag* before ratification. Furthermore, the *Bundestag* itself must receive the consent of the *Bundesrat* when the agreement contains provisions which can only be enacted domestically by a *Zustimmungsgesetz*.

In addition, the peace treaties,[26] expressly mentioned as political agreements in Art. 115 *lit.* 1 para. 3, require ratification by the Federal President. In contrast to the agreements, where in terms of Art. 59 para. 2 sent. 1 the Federal President is empowered to ratify by a formal act of the Legislature, the Federal President is, according to Art. 115 *lit.* 1 para. 3, obliged to ratify by the formal act of the *Bundestag*. This procedure is likewise essential in order for the peace treaty to have effect in international law. Hence, where peace treaties are involved, the Legislature holds not only a control function, but the inherent political decision.

2. *Agreements of the states* (Länder)

International agreements of the *Länder* require ratifications in order to become internationally binding: in most instances by the Prime Minister of the *Land*, in some instances by the *Land* Government as a whole[27].

a) Agreements affecting the legislation

In this instance the ratification may only ensue when the *Land* Parliament has given its consent. The approval by the Parliament generally results through a formal act, in some *Länder* by decree[28].

---

[25] *Cf.* Arts. 84 para. 2, 85 para. 2 of the Basic Law.

[26] On this point *Gerald Griessel*, Der Friedensschluß im Deutschen Verfassungsrecht, Diss. München 1973.

[27] In Hamburg, Bremen, and North-Rhine-Westphalia; in the latter two states the power can be delegated to the chief executive.

[28] In Hamburg, Bavaria, and North-Rhine-Westphalia.

b) Other international agreements

These agreements do not need the approval of the *Land* Parliament for ratification in those *Länder* whose express constitutional provisions foresee an approval only when legislation is to be affected.[29] However, in a number of *Länder* whose constitutional provisions make international agreements dependent on the approval of the *Land* Parliament, the provisions must be so interpreted as to mean only agreements affecting legislation.[30] In some *Länder* the constitutional situation is controversial and unclear on this point.[31] In one *Land* all international agreements must doubtlessly be approved by the *Land* Parliament.[32]

c) Administrative agreements

The administrative agreements of a *Land* do not need the approval of the *Land* Parliament.[33] As a rule, they may become binding in international law with the conclusion by the *Land*'s Prime Minister and the *Land* Government as a whole respectively, or, when a particular minister is empowered, by the minister.

III. Domestic law procedures for giving effect to international agreements in domestic law

1. Agreements of the Federation

International agreements of the Federation always need a special, but in detail different, act in order to become domestically binding. Without this act they cannot be recognized by any organ called upon to apply the law. This means that they are in that sense not self-executing and do not become domestically binding along with their international effectiveness. A domestic law effect also does not result from Art. 25. According to this Article the general principles of international law are an element of the Federal law and directly create rights and duties for the inhabitants of the Federation. It is, however, generally recognized that by Art. 25 in connection with the principle *pacta sunt servanda* the contents of international agreements under no circumstances automati-

[29] In Hamburg, Lower Saxony, and Schleswig-Holstein.

[30] As in Bremen, Hesse, North-Rhine-Westphalia; also in Saarland, however, the treaties affecting the political relations need the approval of the Parliament.

[31] As in Baden-Württemberg; also in Bavaria where one must accept the view that, except for the administrative agreements, all treaties need the approval of the *Landtag*.

[32] Rhineland-Palatinate.

[33] With one exception: Rhineland-Palatinate, where the administrative agreements also need the approval of the *Landtag*. *See Adolf Süsterhenn / Hans Schäfer*, Kommentar der Verfassung für Rheinland-Pfalz, Koblenz 1950, Art. 101, § 5.

cally become applicable domestic law. Art. 25 refers solely to customary international law and not to international treaty law.

a) International treaties according to Art. 59 para. 2 sent. 1

The necessary treaty law giving effect to an international treaty is at the same time the act which enacts the provisions in domestic law and makes them applicable in the given situation. The treaty act has a double function:[34] it empowers the Federal President to ratify and gives the treaty the domestic legal force of a formal statute.

According to the prevailing opinion, the provisions of international treaties are transformed into domestic law by the treaty act (*Transformationstheorie*).[35] Through this act they no longer have their legitimacy in international law but in the domestic law decree. Even without a corresponding reservation (*Vorbehalt*) the transformed domestic law is only then considered in force if the international treaty is also effective.

The *Vollzugstheorie*[36] accordingly, the treaty act is the sole requirement to give domestic effect to the provisions of the treaty. Pursuant to this view the international treaty has effect as such in the domestic legal order, however, only by reason of the legislation. The treaty is of course only then internally binding when the treaty is effective in international law. Due to both theories international treaties do not become binding domestically until they are effected by an act of state. The Basic Law, in particular Art. 59 para. 2 sent. 1, does not give an answer as to which theory is correct. The treaty law giving effect can be considered a "transformer" as well as an "order" to give effect. The *Transformationstheorie* has been adopted by the courts in the Federal Republic of Germany. The treaty provisions, thus incorporated into German municipal law, have the rank of a regular law enacted by the Parliament.

Along with the question of how the content of a treaty becomes transformed into domestic law, another question is to be presented: whether the contents of the treaty as a whole or only certain parts thereof are to be enacted. According to the prevailing opinion, such parts of the treaty are transformed or ordered into effect which are self-executing.[37] Only those treaty provisions are considered self-ex-

[34] BVerfGE 1, 396—415 (410); *Rojahn* (note 2), § 40; *Rudolf* (note 8), 200 *et seq.*

[35] BVerfGE 1, 372—396 (389); BVerfGE 1, 396—415 (411); BVerfGE 6, 290—300 (294 *et seq.*); BVerfGE 29, 348—401 (360); *Rudolf* (note 8), 150 *et seq.*

[36] *Karl Josef Partsch*, Die Anwendung des Völkerrechts im innerstaatlichen Recht, in: Berichte der Deutschen Gesellschaft für Völkerrecht 6 (1964), 19 *et seq.*; *Gerhard Boehmer*, Der völkerrechtliche Vertrag im deutschen Recht, Köln/Berlin 1965, *passim*.

[37] *Rudolf* (note 8), 173 *et seq.*, 207; *Partsch* (note 36), 106 *et seq.*; *Boehmer* (note 36), 77; *Bernhardt* (note 5), 25 *et seq.*, 135 *et seq.* The German Constitutional Court applied the *Transformationstheorie* for its decision in BVerfGE 29, 348—376 (360).

ecuting which can create domestic legal effects in an unchanged wording and without regress to further sovereign acts. The prevailing opinion accordingly equates domestic effect with domestic applicability. On the other hand, a more recent view distinguishes between domestic effect, which refers to the whole treaty, and domestic applicability which is limited to the self-executing parts of the treaty.[38] In my opinion, this view speaks of domestic effect where the problem to be dealt with is that of the international obligation of national bodies to create domestic law which is in conformity with international law.[39]

b) Administrative agreements

The legal status of administrative agreements is not clear. One has to accept the view that they, too, do not gain domestic effect along with their international effect. A special act of a domestic organ is required in order to give them domestic effect. This act is not, however, a formal law. It differs from instance to instance and depends on the contents of the specific administrative agreement at issue.

If, for example, the provisions of an administrative agreement require a statutory order, the conversion into domestic law is carried out by the empowered administrative official[40] (usually the Federal Government or a Federal Minister) in the form of a statutory order. Recently the domestic effect has been expressly — previously implicitly — made dependent on the international effect of the administrative agreement. In instances according to Art. 80 para. 2, and those are most of the cases, the *Bundesrat* must approve such statutory orders. Administrative agreements containing provisions which are to be enacted in the form of administrative regulations obtain domestic effect by the application order of the authority responsible for the enactment of the administrative regulations. These also require the approval of the *Bundesrat* in the instances according to Arts. 84 para. 2, 85 para. 2.

The parts of the agreement which become domestically applicable have the rank of the acts creating their effect; in the aforementioned instances they have the rank of a statutory order or an administrative regulation.

c) Other specifically mentioned treaties

The treaties enumerated in Arts. 24, 79 para. 1 sent. 2, 115 *lit.* 1 para. 3 display no particularities concerning the procedure for bringing them

---

[38] *Albert Bleckmann*, Begriff und Kriterien der innerstaatlichen Anwendbarkeit völkerrechtlicher Verträge, Berlin 1970, 59 *et seq.*, 65 with further references; *Rojahn* (note 2), § 41.

[39] The difference is apparent in BVerfGE 29 (note 37).

[40] For further details concerning this complex *cf. Randelzhofer* (note 1), 33 *et seq.* in n. 48.

into effect in domestic law. I can refer to my statements made *supra* (section III. 1. a)) since the above mentioned treaties are treaties in the meaning of Art. 59 para. 2 sent. 1. Concerning the treaties according to Art. 24, let me note that regulations, decisions, and under certain circumstances also directives of the European Communities, do not need a domestic application order or transformation for domestic effect (*see* Art. 189 of the EEC-Treaty and Art. 161 of the Euratom-Treaty). These acts have direct effect in the Federal Republic of Germany. Their rank is controversial but the view which sees a higher rank of application of the European rules of law is almost generally accepted today.[41]

As to resolutions of the Security Council of the United Nations (UN), imposing sanctions under Chapter VII of the Charter and binding for the Federal Republic as a member of the UN (*see* Art. 25 of the Charter), a legal act of a domestic organ is necessary to give effect to UN-resolutions in domestic law. In the case of economic sanctions, this legal act would be a regulation based on the *Außenwirtschaftsgesetz* (Foreign Trade Act), as for instance in the case of economic sanctions against Rhodesia in 1966.

2. *Agreements of the states* (Länder)

The problem of the domestic effect of international agreements concluded by the *Länder* has not been thoroughly researched and out of the very sparse practice one cannot draw reliable conclusions. It is fair to say, however, that except for administrative agreements, the legal situation is here much the same as in the Federation.

a) Treaties affecting the legislation

Concerning the domestic effect and applicability of these treaties, the statute or decree of the *Länder* Parliaments authorizing ratification, at the same time, effects the domestic force of the treaty at the rank of *Länder* law. Only those provisions needing no implementation by additional legislative acts are applicable.

b) Other political treaties

The question concerning the domestic effect of political treaties in the *Länder* does not pose itself here — save for the exceptions already named — as there is no domestic act to empower for ratification.

c) Administrative agreements

Concerning the domestic law procedure for giving administrative agreements effect, the legal situation is difficult to survey. It is, however,

---

[41] *Rojahn* (note 2), Art. 24, § 43 *et seq.* with further references.

possible to discern some differences in contrast to the Federation. In Rhineland-Palatinate, the transformation and the order of domestic application, respectively, and also for administrative agreements, is effected by a formal act of Parliament. In Bavaria, the administrative agreement is given domestic effect by the decree of the *Land* Government. In other *Länder*, the view is apparently that administrative agreements come simultaneously into force in domestic and international law.[42] In the other *Länder*, as in the Federation, the administrative agreements come into force by a special act whose content is determined by the treaty. Administrative agreements which come from an area where the executive can regulate by means of a statutory order and which contain corresponding regulations (*i. e.* regulations domestically possible by statutory order), one can be sure that the domestic force is to be effected by a statutory order.

Concerning the applicability of the administrative agreements of the *Länder* the principles remain the same as for the administrative agreements of the Federation.

IV. Remarks to some remaining problems

A special problem, which plays a role concerning the international as well as the domestic effectiveness of treaties and therefore should be treated separately, is the question of whether the so-called parallel treaties need approval by law according to Art. 59 para. 2 sent. 1, concerning both the international and the domestic effectiveness. Parallel treaties are the treaties whose contents correspond to already existing domestic law. Those treaties can be applied domestically without such a law as there is already Federal law addressing the same subject matter.

The perhaps still prevailing view[43] denies the posed question by referring to the intention of the treaty act as a guarantee of the domestic execution, not needing to be fulfilled due to the already existing parallel provisions. The other opinion stresses, that the intention of the treaty act is the control by the legislative body of all government measures, which could irrevocably shape foreign relations.[44] The practice extensively confirms the latter view, though not without exception.[45]

[42] *Cf. Rudolf* (note 8), 232 *et seq.* and 236 concerning Baden-Württemberg and Lower Saxony.

[43] *Maunz* (note 3), § 44; *Boehmer* (note 36), 6 *et seq.*; *Herrmann Meyer-Lindenberg*, Zum Begriff der Verträge, die sich auf Gegenstände der Bundesgesetzgebung beziehen (Art. 59 Abs. 2 Satz 1 GG), in: *Karl Carstens / Hans Peters* (eds.), Festschrift für *Herrmann Jahrreis* zu seinem 70. Geburtstag, Köln 1964, 269—288 (277 *et seq.*).

[44] *Rudolf* (note 8), 218; *Herrmann-Wilfried Bayer*, Die Aufhebung völkerrechtlicher Verträge im deutschen parlamentarischen Regierungssystem, Köln 1969, 177 *et seq.*

[45] *Regehr* (note 6), 64 *et seq.*

As to the amendments of treaties, they need the approval of Parliament under the same conditions and to the same extent as the conclusion of a treaty, whereas the denunciation of, and reservations to, a treaty require no such approval and can be expressed by Government alone.[46]

V. Conclusion

The foregoing statements have led to the conclusion that, in spite of guidelines recognized in the meantime in the area of the *auswärtige Gewalt* (foreign powers) in the Federal Republic of Germany, and in particular in the specifically treated sector of the domestic law procedure for giving effect to international treaties, there are still many ambiguities and controversies. Lastly, these are founded on the fact that the pertinent provisions of the Basic Law must be considered as unsuccessful, both in their wording and in their systematic combination. A uniform clear practice, that could have done away with these deficiencies, has not crystallized in all problem areas.

The *Enquête*-Commission set up by the German *Bundestag* in order to reform the Basic Law had concerned itself with Arts. 24, 25, 32, and 59 of the Basic Law. It reached the conclusion that the wording of these provisions did not always correspond to the actual practice and the usual international practice. However, the Commission did not hold a change as being necessary as insurmountable difficulties or intolerable inadequacies have not arisen. It held that, before an amendment is enacted, one should await the further developments.

---

[46] *See Johannes Höppner*, Die verfassungsrechtliche Zulässigkeit der Durchführung von völkerrechtlichen Verträgen mittels Verordnungsermächtigungen, Diss. Göttingen 1979, 141 *et seq.*

Discussion

Bernhardt, Chairman:

I would like to make two introductory remarks. First, Mr. *Starushenko* has asked for the floor in order to make a statement which is not directly connected with our subject, but he should be given the opportunity to speak now. Secondly, I would like to ask my German colleagues not to have a long discussion on the German Constitution, instead, our Soviet colleagues should have the possibility to put questions and ask for further clarification. So, at first please, Mr. *Starushenko* would you take the floor?

Starushenko:

Dear colleagues: The relationship between international law and municipal law is not only of academic, but also of practical interest. To illustrate this, I shall refer to the question that arises in the process of bringing national legislation in conformity with the obligations of States, undertaken on acceding to the International Convention on the Elimination of all Forms of Racial Discrimination. I am a member of the Committee on Elimination of Racial Discrimination and I work in collaboration with Mr. *Partsch*, he represents your State in our Committee.

My communication may give some illustration to the ideas expressed by Mr. *Kunig* and Mr. *Lukashuk* yesterday, I hope.

The above-mentioned Convention is one of the oldest and the most effective instruments for the protection of human rights in the system of international co-operation. It is a treaty open for the accession of State members of the United Nations and non-member States alike.

First of all, I should underline the importance of conventions as a form of implementation of norms of international law. The existence of an international norm *per se* is not regarded by some States as sufficient cause for its strict observance. Unwillingness to do so is not the only reason. Every State may have serious difficulties of a political, economic, ideological, and other nature. While favouring the adoption of international agreements, such as the Universal Declaration of Human Rights or the Declaration on the Elimination of all Forms of Racial Discrimination (1963), some States, nevertheless, did not work systematically against racial discrimination or especially for its prevention in future.

The situation has changed after the Convention, not after the *Declaration*, but after the *Convention* was drafted and signed. The adoption of the Convention is one of the most effective ways of carrying into effect all the rules and norms of international law and international obligations. It makes it possible, first, to formulate them accurately; second, to make reservations in respect of certain articles, unacceptable to some of the States; third, to check on the compliance with the assumed obligations by the setting up of a control mechanism and bringing the matter to the attention of the public. Now 124 States have acceded to this Convention, more than to any other similar international agreement in the field under consideration. However, 46 States made a reservation. From the above follows the first conclusion: At this time, the drafting and conclusion of treaties — additional to the operating instruments of international law — is both permissible and desirable. The reconstruction of international relations on the basis of the law is a slow and difficult process, which constantly calls for additional efforts.

Implementation of the Convention presupposes the fulfilment by States of their obligation to suppelment and improve the national legislation. The Convention has not been acceded to by some States in which racial discrimination has apparently been in practice. For example, speaking at the 64th Annual Assembly of the American Association of International Law, *Rita Hauser*, a former United States' representative in the United Nations' Commission on Human Rights, said that her country was not going to become a party to the Convention because her country found unacceptable Article 4, banning the propaganda of racism, as well as Article 5, making it binding on the States to guarantee the right of citizens to equality in social and economic fields, including the right to work, protection against unemployment, and equal pay for equal work. Apart from the United States, some other States, such as the Republic of South Africa and Turkey, have not acceded to the Convention. Other States believed they did not have any serious problem of racial discrimination today, and that their municipal law was mainly in accordance with the Articles of the Convention. But they failed to give attention to measures for preventing racial discrimination and ethnic tensions in the future. Naturally, this impaired the effectiveness of the Convention.

Publicity is a factor urging the States to adopt legislative and other acts contributing to the fulfilment of their obligations assumed under the Convention. In accordance with the Convention, the Special Committee has been established to check on compliance with the provisions by the State Parties. The Committee holds all its sessions in public. Its annual reports to the General Assembly of the United Nations and its work is covered by the press releases and the mass media. The countries where racial or ethnic tensions are growing are also interested in giving wider publicity to measures they have taken and to their participation in the Convention.

Various methods are being employed to promote legislation against racial discrimination by the State Parties to the Convention. This includes above all considerations by the Committee of the reports presented by the State Parties, discussion of the Committee's report to the session of the General Assembly, and others. The State Parties submit a report every two years (Article 9 of the Convention). But the Committee may request further information if it is necessary. I want to underline that our Committee is not empowered to use in its discussions any material not presented by a government, adopt decisions condemning a government, organize international anti-government campaigns, or to take similar actions. An exception is made with regard to the actually outlawed *apartheid* regime, which the Committee resolutely condemned in its special decision. The Committee calls the State Parties to the Convention resolutely to take a number of measures against the Republic of South Africa designed to abolish the *apartheid* system and to implement radical changes in South Africa.

The Committee may also influence the implementation processes in the States by making suggestions and general recommendations, but this only on the basis of the report and information received from the State Parties. For example: Considering the fact that many States have not adopted the laws to ensure the implementation of Article 4 of the Convention (the Article speaks about the necessity of forbidding any activity of racial organizations). The Committee recommends that the State Parties do so, and reports how, and to what extent they have done it. An indirect method of pressure on a State, to make it comply with its obligations under the Convention, is the right of other State Parties to report its non-compliance to the Committee.

It is seen from the above that the actions provided for by the Convention, and practised by the Committee, and which are conducive to the implementation of international agreements, are in the nature of international co-operation. Continuing this tendency, the Committee seeks to adopt all decisions on important matters by consensus.

Allow me the right to draw the second and last conclusion. The Convention and the Committee's experience show that international co-operation in the field of human rights can develop successfully without any intervention into a State's internal affairs. This kind of co-operation helps to strengthen the international legal order and to improve international security and stability.

Bernhardt, Chairman:

Thank you, Mr. *Starushenko*. Please, Mr. *Lukashuk*.

Lukashuk:

Now we understand the reason why we have waited so eagerly for Mr. *Randelzhofer*; I think, that your State system for ratification is not complicated but very simple. What I do not understand is that I always thought that ratification means an act of the highest authority only, and you were talking about ratification by ministers, by government, and so on, and so on. Maybe I misunderstood this point.

Randelzhofer:

Only as far as treaties of the *Länder* are concerned.

Lukashuk:

So ministers are empowered to ratify administrative agreements?

Randelzhofer:

That is true in so far as so-called "administrative agreements" are concerned. The correct view, in my opinion, is that the ratification power still is with the Federal President, without having formally transferred this power by delegation to the ministers. In reality it is not that in substance the power to ratify has been transferred from the President to the prime minister, or to the Federal Government, or to a government minister. It is a form of delegation, but not in substance, only in exercise.

Lukashuk:

But still you call it ratification?

Randelzhofer:

Yes.

Lukashuk:

Thank you.

Bernhardt, Chairman:

I would like to add that the notion "ratification" is used with two different meanings. The word is sometimes used only for the confirmation of most important treaties by the head of State. But the notion is also used in a broader and more unclear sense, and then it means confirmation of a signed treaty whenever such an additional confirmation is necessary.

Lukashuk:

In both cases.

Randelzhofer:

But that is not a peculiarity of mine. That is a common view among German scholars.

The last question of Mr. *Lukashuk*, I think, is a very important one. I think it is really necessary to stress that the correct view, even in the case of administrative agreements, is that ratification are done by the President. But there exists the other view that in substance the ratification power is passed to the Chancellor, or to the Government as a whole, and in this connection we can speak — as Mr. *Bernhardt* pointed out — of ratification in the broader sense. In my view of the problem, ratification is still restricted to the act of the Federal President. In the case of the two former categories he does it personally, in the case of administrative agreements it is done by the Government *on his behalf*.

Bernhardt, Chairman:

One more point, we all know that there are a great number of agreements of minor importance which do not need any confirmation. Immediately upon signature they become binding conventions.

Klein:

Perhaps I may add another clarification. Nothing depends on the pure denomination. Mr. *Randelzhofer* has distinguished three types of agreement within Article 59 para. 2 of the Basic Law: treaties regulating political relations of the Federation, treaties relating to matters of Federal legislation, and administrative agreements. Now, take the case that the Government treats an agreement as administrative agreement, but its content is such that it regulates the political relations or relates to matters of the Federal legislation — in this case, of course, the special prerequisites of the Article come into force.

Randelzhofer:

I perfectly agree with Mr. *Klein* that the denomination in itself is not decisive. The substance of the agreement is crucial, about which prerequisites of Article 59 are really to be fulfilled.

Oppermann:

Mr. *Chairman*, may I presume to offer a few words after several German colleagues have done so, although this time had obviously been reserved to the Soviet guests. It is just a question addressed to our Soviet guests. Mr. *Randelzhofer* said a lot about the foreign power of our German *Länder*. I would be interested to hear something from the Soviet side about the external relations of your Republics in the Soviet Union. How far, for instance, does the treaty-making power of the Republics go? We know that the Ukraine and Byelorussia have a seat in the UN General Assembly, and this had certain political reasons, very understandable reasons, in 1945. Are there other comparable foreign powers of the Republics in the Soviet Union?

Tunkin:

I would like to put a question to Mr. *Randelzhofer*: Would you tell us what agreements and how many of those have been concluded by the *Länder*?

Randelzhofer:

Without your question, I was about to add to the question of Mr. *Oppermann* that it would be necessary to give a picture of the practical relevance of the regulation of Article 32 para. 3, that, in practice, this Article is not of primary importance. I am not able, although they are rather few, to tell you the number of treaties concluded by our *Länder* with foreign States. In general we have to admit that this is a more, but not only, theoretical regulation in our Constitution, and that in practice, the consent of the Federal Government necessary for the conclusion of such a treaty is not very often granted.

Bernhardt, Chairman:

The number of such agreements is small, but it is difficult to know the exact number, some agreements are never published.

Oppermann:

In cultural affairs, for instance, we have a treaty between the Government of the Saar and the French Republic on the establishment of a Franco-German secondary school (*Gymnasium*) in Saarbrücken.

Randelzhofer:

We have a treaty of Bavaria and the Holy See as to the embassy of Bavaria there.

Bernhardt, Chairman:

There are even agreements concerning the hunting of certain birds on the Lake of Constance.

Randelzhofer:

I think one can fairly sum up that it is not of great practical importance, but to resolve smaller problems concerning borders, such as review of boundary delimitations and so on — these treaties exist, but they are not published.

Hilf:

I want to add a question which concerns the denouncement of treaties. Under German constitutional law it is a disputed subject whether Parliament has any influence on a decision of the Government which denounces a treaty under public international law. The prevailing opinion is, that the denouncement of treaties is a prerogative of the Government. The Constitution does not require any participation of the Parliament. Are there any similar controversies in the constitutional law of the USSR? What is the internal procedure for denouncing a treaty?

Lukashuk:

There are two aspects of the problem. The first aspect is juridical. As for this juridical point of view, everything is perfect. We have our Federal Constitution which recognizes the rights of the Republics to conclude any treaty. We have Constitutions of the Republics where there are articles which recognize the same right. If we take international law, the only rule was prepared by the International Law Commission in the Draft on the Law of Treaties. The wording was that the problem of federal organs participating in treaties is to be decided by a federal constitution. From the point of view of international law or a national constitution it is allright, but the Ukraine is a better example. The Ukraine is a party to more than 100 treaties. Almost all of them are UN treaties, and the Ukraine participates along with the Soviet Union and the Byelorussian Soviet Republic. As for bilateral treaties, there are not many. For example, there was a treaty between the Ukraine and Poland over the exchange of citizens. There is an agreement about supporting the mutual borderline. But there are not many such agreements, and it is not a real wish of the Soviet Union. Because our partners say, why should we conclude an agreement with the Ukraine or Byelorussia; it is much more convenient for us to conclude an agreement with the Soviet Union without any juridical interpretation and so on. Maybe in some years it will be changed. But I do not think it will happen soon.

As for denunciation of treaties: We have a nine year old law on international treaties. Treaties are to be ratified — they are ratified by the Presidium after conclusions made by parliamentary commissions.

Tunkin:

Not always!

Lukashuk:

I know; but for major treaties — just like in your country — there are administrative treaties concluded by ministers and so on, here we are speaking about main treaties. But to renounce a treaty we need the consent of Parliament. The Government may ask a commission of Parliament about it, but it is not obligatory.

Schweisfurth:

I have a question for Mr. *Lukashuk*. Will there be in the realm of the Soviet Union pursuant to the now undergoing *perestroika* also a *perestroika* in the Federal system of the Soviet Union? I ask you because, as you know, there has been introduced already a certain decentralization of the external economic powers of the Soviet Union. Until now it was possible only for the Soviet Union itself to set up organizations for foreign trade. Now the Union Republics have received the right to establish foreign trade organizations. This is a quite new development. My question is, whether this development may be pointing into the direction where the foreign relation powers of the Union Republics may gain. You mentioned that the law regulating the treaty-making powers of the Soviet Union is nearly ten years old. Looking at Article 80 of the Soviet Constitution of 1977 where the external powers of the Union Republics, and amongst them the treaty-making power, are formulated, I am awaiting for almost a decade now laws of the Republics concerning their treaty-making powers. Will there be such laws issued in the near future?

Lukashuk:

I do not think that we will reconstruct our Federal system at once. There is so much to do with this *perestroika*, and, first of all, our economic enterprises may go abroad with permission of the Republics only — if there would be any need for Republics to enter public treaties and agreements; I do not see it yet.

Bernhardt, Chairman:

Thank you.

Content and Limits of 'Domaine Réservé'

By Galina G. Shinkaretskaya*

The problem of the limits of domestic jurisdiction of the State has long been posed in the science and practice of international law — ever since international law took shape and need appeared for differentiating the spheres of the operation of international and municipal law. There was a time when much was written on the subject, but finally the jurists seem to have lost interest in it, qualifying it as not offering anything substantial for general conclusions. However, in our time it is worthwhile to return to this problem for the following reasons.

The spread of international law regulation to the fields, which in the past were not even called in question, is due to the growing interdependence of the peoples and the realization that there are a number of universal human values, the primary of which is life itself threatened by an incredible stockpile of armaments. There are also a number of global tasks (economic, energy, food, and others) on the solution of which the destiny of the human civilisation depends in the long run. More and more urgently needed is the co-ordination of actions of States and their mutual control in such "sacred" spheres as the level and quality of armaments, disposal of such natural resources as water and the air, etc. A controversial but interdependent, and in many ways integral world is taking shape through the struggle of opposites.[1]

*

The category *domaine réservé*, or "domestic jurisdiction", appeared as a means of restricting the right of international organizations or individual States to interfere in the decisions, or the consequences of decisions, taken by a State. It was fixed in Article (Art.) 15 para. 8 of the League of Nations Covenant, and was included into Art. 2 para. 7 of the United Nations (UN) Charter and into regional agreements of a general character. A survey of bilateral agreements of a general and political character likewise reveals a rather frequent recurrence of decisions obliging States to refrain from interference. The provision

* Senior Researcher at the Institute of State and Law of the Academy of Sciences of the USSR.

[1] *See* Resolution of the XXVII Congress of the CPSU on the Political Report of the CPSU Central Committee; *Mikhail Gorbachev*, Political Report of the CPSU Central Committee to the XXVII Party Congress, Moscow 1986, 136.

concerning domestic jurisdiction is firmly established also in customary international law as proved by the decision of the International Court of Justice in the *Military and Paramilitary Activities in and Against Nicaragua.*

Thus, international law records mutual recognition by the States of fields of jurisdiction which are closed to interference by other States and also other subjects. Clearly, domestic jurisdiction refers to the right of each State to freely — independently of other States and international organizations — exercise its legislative, executive, and judicial jurisdiction. Its existence is the consequence of State sovereignty and the right of nations to self-determination. The principle of State sovereignty as the starting point of international law inevitably requires recognition of a field in which the State retains exclusive domestic jurisdiction. Being a consequence of State sovereignty, domestic jurisdiction is in the *domaine* of the State and is inherent in it alone. However, neither the documents nor doctrine of international law contain a uniform definition of the concepts "domestic jurisdiction" or "matters that lie essentially within domestic jurisdiction", or give a clear answer to the question as to the limits of domestic jurisdiction; nor is the term itself quite correct. In the English "domestic jurisdiction" the combination of the words "domestic" and "jurisdiction" gives ground to speak of its tautology,[2] though it appears logical in the English system of law. However, when the term is taken over by other legal systems and is incorporated into the vocabulary of general international law, the use of the word "jurisdiction" adds to the ambiguity of the term as a whole, due to the growing diversification of the concept "jurisdiction" itself. From this point of view, the Russian term including the word "competence" is more precise. However, taken as a whole, the Russian term is not quite precise either, (literally: "powers within a state"), and this lack of precision seems to have played its role in confusing the concepts "matters that lie essentially within domestic jurisdiction" and "domestic matters".

And so, what is domestic jurisdiction? The easiest way of answering the question, it would seem, is to enumerate matters belonging to domestic jurisdiction. However, the inevitable failure of this attempt was recognized back in 1954,[3] and the view was established among jurists that the field of domestic jurisdiction is juridically indeterminate and indeterminable. Nonetheless, from a number of documents it is possible to deduce an approximate range of matters in relation to which States assume the pledge to refrain from interference. The richest material can be gathered from the 1970 Declaration on Principles. It recognizes as

[2] *See Ian Brownlie,* Principles of Public International Law, Oxford 1973, 417.
[3] *Cf.* Annuaire de l'Institut de droit international 43 (1950), 21.

unlawful actions as follows: (a) violating the sovereignty of a State and its political, economic, and cultural foundations; (b) limiting sovereign rights; (c) aimed at changing the system, or (d) depriving the people of the form of its national existence; (e) having the aim of depriving the State of its inalienable right to choose its political, economic, and cultural systems. Though the resolutions and declarations of the UN General Assembly, strictly speaking, are no treaties, the provisions of the Declaration on Principles have special juridical force as repeatedly pointed out in Soviet and Western literature. These provisions of the Declaration, however, are usually reproduced in other international documents dealing with the question of non-interference in domestic jurisdiction.

It is not difficult to see that matters interference into which is declared unlawful in the Declaration concern questions bearing on the independence of States and their very existence. New elements of the problem appeared in the last decades, when States gaining political independence realized the special importance of upholding their economic independence. Art. 1 para. 1 of the Charter of Economic Rights and Duties of States specifies:

> Each State has the sovereign and inalienable right to choose its economic system as well as its political, social and cultural systems in accordance with the will of its people, without outside interference, coercion, or threat in any form whatsoever.

Further on, the Charter says directly that each State has authority over foreign investment and the operation of foreign companies within its national jurisdiction, each State has the right to nationalize foreign property, and that itself regulates its external economic activity.

In our time the struggle for natural resources has branched out from the general problem of the struggle for economic independence, though the importance of natural resources was felt long time ago.[4] The importance of protecting natural resources from plunder by foreign companies was reflected in the UN General Assembly Declaration on Permanent Sovereignty over Natural Resources, adopted in 1962. Jurists of developing countries stress that the 1962 Declaration gives grounds for regarding questions connected with the exploitation of natural resources as belonging to the domestic jurisdiction of the State, the sovereign, and in support they invoke Art. 2 of the Charter of Economic Rights and Duties of States.[5]

---

[4] 250 years ago, *M. V. Lomonosov* wrote that "Russia's wealth would multiply owing to Siberia", having in mind Siberia's natural resources, and in 1835, *de Tocqueville* prophesied that the USA and Russia would become the mightiest powers of the world owing to their natural treasures.

[5] *See*, for instance, *S. Azadon Tiewul*, The Evolution of the Doctrine of Permanent Sovereignty, in: University of Ghana Law Journal 15 (1978—81), 55—84.

The preoccupation with the problem of authority over natural resources was clearly seen in the course of the UN Third Conference on the Law of the Sea and is evident in the major legal instrument of our time — the UN Convention on the Law of the Sea of 1982. The Convention contains carefully formulated provisions determining the rights and prerogatives of States in relation to natural resources. This is clearly seen in the Articles referring to the continental shelf and the exclusive economic zone. The rights to explore for and exploit living and mineral resources in these areas of the World Ocean are exclusive and have a two-fold nature: On the one hand, they are a consequence of sovereignty (since they belong *ipso facto* to States and only to States)[6] and, on the other hand, they originate in international law (being the product of a treaty). The Convention contains one more provision which confirms the exclusive character of the sovereign rights of a coastal State, and actually leaves it for this State to decide whether it regards these rights as lying within domestic jurisdiction. As laid down in Art. 297, in the event of a dispute, with regard to a coastal State's exercise of its sovereign rights or jurisdiction over natural resources of the continental shelf and exclusive economic zone, it may refuse to submit it for judicial consideration or arbitration. No other act, apart from the Convention on the Law of the Sea, seems to contain such a clear regulation concerning both the distribution of the rights of States, and the appropriate definition of the subject of jurisdiction of international court organs.

The view of States on the volume of domestic jurisdiction is clearly expressed in cases where it is a question of the right of international courts to deal with a specific case. The Permanent Court of International Justice and the International Court of Justice of the United Nations' Organization have built up an imposing record in this respect. It has been analysed in detail in literature, so that I can confine myself to a few remarks.

The first case in which the question of domestic jurisdiction arose dates back to the early 1920s, immediately after the formation of the Permanent Court of International Justice, when it was to give its advisory opinion on the Anglo-French dispute in connection with the nationality decrees in Tunisia and Morocco.[7] The Court's argumentation and position became characteristic of the activity of the Court itself and, later, the International Court of Justice. In Western literature this Case and the Advisory Opinion are qualified as classical instances and are frequently quoted. Indeed, it was the first inquiry into the relationship

[6] According to the Convention, these rights may belong also to nations that have not yet gained statehood.

[7] *Nationality Decrees issued in Tunis and Morocco* (Advisory Opinion of February 7th, 1923), P.C.I.J. 1923, Series B, no. 4, 7 *et seq.*

of the prerogatives of an international organization, international court, and a State in setting the limits of domestic jurisdiction. In the course of this investigation the theory of "provisional approach" to domestic jurisdiction took shape, considerably influencing the procedural aspects of the activity of the Permanent Court of International Justice and the International Court of Justice. The quoted opinion also formulated the conception of the primacy of international law in determining domestic jurisdiction.

The cases that followed: *Treatment of Polish Nationals in Danzig*,[8] *Losinger and Co.*,[9] *Electricity Company in Sofia and Bulgaria*[10] — all concerned questions as matters belonging to domestic jurisdiction, which had to do with relations between the State, on the one hand, and physical and juridical persons, on the other. The view became established in literature that relations between the State and the population constitute an indisputable field of domestic jurisdiction.[11] After World War II the picture became more variegated. Questions concerning physical and juridical persons continued to remain among cases referred to domestic jurisdiction. Such was the argumentation of the USA in the *Interhandel* Case.[12] We should not, of course, overlook the fact that in another case the position of the USA was quite different. I mean the US' initiative with the inquiry of the UN General Assembly on fulfilment of the peace treaties with Bulgaria, Hungary, and Rumania in 1947.[13] Although a purely procedural question seemed to be raised before the International Court of Justice, its political load was quite visible. But, the important thing for us now is, that the USA indicated the following position: Relations of the State, not only with foreigners, but also with its own citizens, cannot be exclusively a matter of domestic jurisdiction.

In the post-war period a series of new phenomena on the question of domestic jurisdiction appeared in international law. Thus, in the *Certain Norwegian Loans* Case[14] Norway insisted on its right to determine the forms of loan repayment. A completely new category of cases belonging to domestic jurisdiction was made up of cases connected with the

---

[8] *Treatment of Polish Nationals in Danzig* (Opinion of 4 February 1932), P.C.I.J. 1932, Series A/B, no. 44, 4.

[9] *Losinger and Co.* Case, P.C.I.J. 1936, Series C, no. 78.

[10] *Electricity Company of Sofia and Bulgaria* Case, P.C.I.J. 1939, Series A/B, no. 77, 64 (Judgment — Preliminary Objection — of April 4th, 1939).

[11] *See Charles Rousseau*, L'independence de l'état dans l'ordre international, in: Recueil des Cours 73 (1948/II), 167—253 (239—246).

[12] *Interhandel* Case, I.C.J. Reports 1957, 15.

[13] *Interpretation of Peace Treaties with Bulgaria, Hungary and Romania* (Advisory Opinion of March 30th, 1950), I.C.J. Reports 1950, 65.

[14] *Certain Norwegian Loans* Case (Fra. v. Nor.), (Judgment of July 6th, 1957), I.C.J. Reports 1957, 9.

struggle of the young States against the colonial legacy. In the *Anglo-Iranian Oil Company* Case,[15] Iran, applying *Albéric Rolin*'s conception of "three zones", declared, that the nationalization of a foreign private company is a matter of its domestic jurisdiction and stems from the exercise of its sovereignty. In this instance, though in form it was a question of Iran's relations with a foreign private company, Iran in fact asserted its right to self-determination and economic independence.[16] There was one more dispute that was a by-product of colonialism — the dispute about the right of passage over Indian territory.[17] In this instance India upheld its sovereignty and territorial integrity and, basing itself on international law, sought to liquidate the consequences of British colonial domination.

Of interest to our investigation is also the recent Case *Concerning Military Activities in and Against Nicaragua*,[18] in which the International Court of Justice devoted much attention to non-intervention,[19] and declared that the interference of the USA in Nicaragua's affairs on the pretext of preventing the establishment of a "communist dictatorship" was contrary to international law. In its decision the Court stated that the attachment of a State to any specific doctrine is not a breach of international law. A different approach, it said, would make nonsense of the fundamental principle of State sovereignty on which international law rests as a whole.

*

The question of the limits of domestic jurisdiction of the State is traditionally posed as the alternative: international law *versus* national law. But who defines this boundary?

In Western literature, to this day most popular, it seems, is the reply which originated in English law and was formulated by *C. H. M. Waldock* back in the early 1950s: The domain of domestic jurisdiction begins where international law ends[20], and it is international law that

---

[15] *Anglo-Iranian Oil Company* Case (Judgment — Preliminary Objection — of July 22th, 1952), I.C.J. Reports 1952.

[16] *See Eduardo Jiménez de Aréchaga*, International Law in the Past Third of a Century, in: Recueil des Cours (RdC) 159 (1978/I), 1—344 (297).

[17] *Right of Passage over Indian Territory* (Por. v. In.), (Judgment — Preliminary Objection — of November 26th, 1957), I.C.J. Reports 1957, 125.

[18] Case *Concerning Military and Paramilitary Activities in and Against Nicaragua* (Nic. v. US), (Judgment of June 27th, 1986).

[19] *Stuby* sees the analysis of this question as a part of the Court's general contribution to the development of international law; *see Gerhard Stuby*, Staatliche Souveränität und internationale Gerichtsbarkeit: Zum Urteil des Internationalen Gerichtshofes in Haag vom 27. Juni 1986 in der Sache Nicaragua / USA, in: Demokratie und Recht 14 (1986), 401—408 (407).

[20] *C. H. M. Waldock*, The Plea of Domestic Jurisdiction before International Tribunals, in: British Yearbook of International Law 31 (1954), 96—142 (142).

decides where it should come to an end and give way to domestic jurisdiction. *Ian Brownlie* writes: "The limits of this domain depend on international law and change with its development."[21] Such approach leads the limits of domestic jurisdiction into diffusion, and it seems that such is based on the notion of absolute power of international law in the process of advancement towards a world law. But this is merely so at first glance. In reality, this approach perceives both international law and domestic jurisdiction as being absolute.[22] Perhaps, this was justified when one system of law was in domination. Besides, before World War II, and even after it, the balance between international law and national legislation reflected the opposition of the interests of one State to the interests of another State, or even all other States.

International life of the 1980s poses many problems in a new way. The situation in the world is such that we should not speak of the opposition of interests, but their merging. Theorists of science say that the time of change in the scientific paradigm, replacement of the earlier established system of axioms, has come, and that one universal human value must lie at the basis of the whole of international law and law in general for that matter. As is known, the Soviet Union advanced the idea of a non-violent, nuclear-free world, the basis of which can be only the merging of the common interests of all nations. Disarmament specialists say, that the paradigm of international law must be the right to freedom from mass destruction weapons. Environmentalists say, that at the basis of everything must be the concern for the preservation of such conditions on our planet which would ensure the existence of humanity. There is the idea that human life is of universal value. Be it as it may, the time has come for solving all international problems from the viewpoint of all interests of mankind as a whole. This means, that many questions on which international law was indifferent in the past are becoming meaningful for it. A vivid example is the problem of the level of armaments. Though the level of armaments is traditionally referred to the internal matter of State, we see how many types of weapons are becoming subject to international law regulation, namely, all types of mass destruction weapons.

All this leads to the necessary expansion of the sphere of operation of international law and to the inevitability of also establishing the limits of domestic jurisdiction. As it is, there can be no exceptional and unilateral determination of domestic jurisdiction. There is the well-known *Connally* reservation to the US' declaration of acceptance of the

---

[21] *Brownlie* (note 2).

[22] *Waldock* wrote for one that domestic jurisdiction is "one of the last refuges of the dogma of absolute sovereignty"; *Humphrey Waldock*, General Course on Public International Law, in: RdC 106 (1962/II), 1—251 (173).

International Court of Justice's compulsory jurisdiction. Accordingly, the jurisdiction of the International Court of Justice does not extend to disputes connected with matters that belong to the domestic jurisdiction of the United States "as determined by the United States". It is known that this reservation was actively criticized by American officials, members of the International Court of Justice, and authors. The main point of criticism is, that the reservation actually means the usurpation by the US of the right to interpret whether particular cases are within the jurisdiction of the International Court of Justice, already after they had been submitted to it, which means the replacement of the Court's jurisdiction by the jurisdiction of the USA.[23] In the Encyclopedia of Public International Law it is guardedly stated that a number of ambiguities appear in connection with this reservation.[24]

On the other hand, a thereto directly opposite tendency operates in international relations. The principle of State sovereignty is increasingly realized as a condition essential for the establishment of effective law and order in the world: More and more often the norms of international law are realized at the national level. One of the examples of this is the sphere of economic interests of States. In connection with the problems of the new international economic order, one author writes the following:

> Developing countries are in a position to enact legislation containing norms specifically tailored to fit their own specific conditions and levels of development. This is within the domain of the sovereign rights of developing countries, for which they do not need the consent of developed countries nor a negotiated consensus of other developing countries.[25]

A long-lasting and interesting discussion is under way on the question of the relationship between international law and municipal law in the field of protection of human rights. Although we may regard as firmly established the recognition of relations between a State and citizens as a matter belonging to the domestic jurisdiction of a State, on record are attempts to apply the question of human rights to aims that are not quite plausible. *Anthony D'Amato*, reflecting on the possible ways of justifying the US aggression against Nicaragua, frankly admits that grounds for this activity cannot be found in public international law and if it is possible to find support for the US position, it can only be found in the sphere of international law dealing with human rights.[26] Rather

---

[23] *See Herbert W. Briggs*, Reservations to the Acceptance of Compulsory Jurisdiction of the International Court of Justice, in: RdC 93 (1958/I), 223—366 (328—363).

[24] *Rudolf Dolzer*, Connally Reservation, in: *Rudolf Bernhardt* (ed.), Encyclopedia of Public International Law, instalment 1, Amsterdam *et al.* 1981, 55, 56 (55).

[25] *M. Bulajić*, Principles of International Development Law, Dordrecht 1986, 57.

[26] *Anthony D' Amato*, Nicaragua and International Law: The "Academic" and the "Real", in: American Journal of International Law 79 (1985), 657—664 (659).

popular now is the idea of "transnational protection" of human rights.[27] However, it is perfectly clear that:

> human rights are unthinkable and do not exist beyond a State. Each person enjoys only those rights and freedoms — social, economic, political, civil, and cultural — which are envisaged by the constitution and laws of the country where he lives.[28]

When an international tribunal decides the question of whether a particular matter should be referred to domestic jurisdiction, the point at issue is not the availability or absence of a respective international norm, but the existence of an international obligation of a State, *i. e.*, the obligation towards other members of the international community voluntarily assumed by this State (otherwise this obligation is insignificant). Of course, a State may subject any of its matters to international law regulation. Rather popular among Western jurists is the judgment of the Permanent Court of International Justice in the Case of nationality acts of Tunisia and Morocco[29], to the effect that there is no question that could not be regulated by international law. This idea has long been purely theoretical, and for its refutation we would have to seek in international documents not what is said in them, but what is left unsaid. Now, definitely we can say that the States a number of problems either do not subject to international law regulation, or agree not to do so.

The connection between municipal and international law regulation is the same as between State sovereignty and international law. Through its sovereignty, a State demands from international law independence in deciding a variety of questions, while the international law principle of State sovereignty assures the protection of international law for the field of law regulation where the will of the State itself prevails unchallenged. This field lies beyond the limits of international law, though the State may voluntarily subject some of its matters in this field to regulation by international law.

A State takes a decision and international law fixes this fact, or the decision is taken at an international level and then the State fulfills the norm of international law in its internal system in accordance with its own obligations.

---

[27] Arguments in support of this idea were clearly set out in the paper presented by Professor *Shimon Shetreet* from the University of Jerusalem. *Shetreet*, Transnational Protection of Human Rights (Report for the XII Congress of the Academy of Comparative Law), Australia, August 1986.

[28] *A. P. Movchan*, Human Rights and International Relations (in Russian), Moscow 1982, 20.

[29] *See* note 7.

Discussion

Bernhardt, Chairman:

Thank you for your most interesting speech. I would like to abuse my position as chairman for a moment to make some provocative remarks. I think the notion of "domestic jurisdiction" is to date more misused than correctly used; the notion has two aspects. The first concerns the subject matters which belong to domestic jurisdiction, the second question is, what means can be employed to try to influence situations in another State. In accordance with the Advisory Opinion of the Permanent Court of International Justice of 1923, I think that the notion of domestic jurisdiction can only be a relative one, and it can only be used where there are no obligations under international law. There are no subject matters which are totally excluded from international concern by their nature. Even in fields where in former times there was no international law rule whatsoever, new international law can impose limits on State sovereignty. Take the activities of the International Labour Organisation concerning the freedom of association of State officials. In former times, this was quite obviously a question of domestic jurisdiction. Take another example: The system of elections in a State has been considered to be a matter of domestic jurisdiction. Now, in an additional protocol to the European Convention on Human Rights, we have a special provision concerning free elections. We also all know that *apartheid* is now a matter of international concern. In our times international law can and often does regulate matters which have been left to domestic jurisdiction before. This is the one aspect, the subject matter aspect. I think we should also take into account the word "intervene" in Article 2 para. 7 of the Charter of the United Nations. This is very important insofar as even where a subject matter belongs to the domestic jurisdiction, I have doubts whether this excludes international discussions, protests, *etc.*, either by international organizations or by other States.

Please, Mr. *Tunkin*.

Tunkin:

First referring to the rapporteur: It seems to me that in the report there are some notes of juxtaposition of international law and State sovereignty on the one hand, and international law and domestic jurisdiction on the other. Such juxtaposition is very frequent, but in my view it is absolutely unjustified. Really, the norms of international law are created by sovereign States and it is up to them to choose what they will submit to international regulation. Therefore, it is quite right, but I do not agree with your critical remarks with regard to *Waldock* and *Brownlie*, because — I myself wrote a little report, some thirty years ago in this sense — the notion or the extent of domestic jurisdiction changes with the development of international law. There is no doubt about that, and Mr. *Bernhardt* gave just one of the examples to that effect.

One remark with regard to your thesis, Mr. *Bernhardt*, that there are no matters excluded from international regulation by their nature: It is *Kelsen*'s idea, but in my view it is not completely correct. It is correct to a certain extent only, because there are in my view matters which are, by their nature, taking into consideration all the circumstances of the present day situation, excluded from international regulations. These are matters of social systems. You cannot imagine that there may be norms say, prohibiting socialists or capitalists systems. So, to a certain extent, there are in my view, matters which are by their nature excluded from international regulation.

Wolfrum:

I would like to congratulate our rapporteur for her most challenging presentation, although I do not agree with her in all respects. I very much appreciate that Mr. *Tunkin* has clarified the starting point, in so far we are on common ground. The content of the *domaine réservé* is specified by international law. According to this concept, States may submit every aspect of their national legal system to international regulation. International law does not foreclose them in accepting the respective obligations as long as the submission to the international instrument in question has been taken place voluntarily. If, however, States have accepted an international agreement on human rights, for example, which provides that the citizens may invoke that treaty directly in national courts or *vis-à-vis* the national administration, then a reference to *domaine réservé*, with the view to mitigate or abandon the obligations entered into, is clearly excluded. Let me now proceed to another aspect.

Yesterday morning Mr. *Tunkin* spoke of general international law and that it even may develop without all States participating in its development, although it may become binding upon all. Given this concept of general international law, how can it be harmonized with the concept of *domaine réservé*? If I understood correctly what you said yesterday, then we have a growing tendency to establish these general international rules. They will limit the sovereignty of States and accordingly will narrow the scope of the *domaine réservé*. Let me come to my last more minor point.

Mrs. *Shinkaretskaya* mentioned the *Connally* amendment, really criticizing it. To a certain extent I agree with you. However, for me Article 297 of the Law of the Sea Convention is nothing else but a *Cornally* amendment, though limited to the law of the sea. It does make no sense, especially not with respect to the outer limits of the continental shelf. The more you extend them, the more you restrict what is meant to be kept for the international community. Hence, I believe that this exemption of the jurisdiction is not logical, taking into account the basic principles of Part XI of the Law of the Sea Convention. Thank you, Mr. *Chairman*.

Simma:

My charming colleague has concluded her report by pointing out that the methods of dialectics have been born in Germany. So let me try to get behind the miracles of the dialectics which you use. In my view, the third step of that dialectic is still missing in our discussion. We have had a strong thesis and we have heard some very strong antitheses being developed, but I still cannot see a synthesis on the horizon. I think, in essence, you have enumerated an impressive list of subject matters which could be labelled by the words "leave me alone". I think, what you have done is more an empirical study in the course of which you have assembled a list of questions in which States either have told, or are still telling, other States to leave them alone. For example, natural resources, continental shelf exploitation, treatment of nationals, even treatment of aliens as far as property is concerned, and so on. But at the end you have stated more than once that, of course, if States by their free will determine to subject an issue to international regulation they can do so. To use an example you dealt with, the problem of limitation of armament: The United States after having concluded a treaty with the Soviet Union on the elimination of, let us say, some type of missiles, you would certainly object very much to the United States arguing that — since this armament is vital to the life of the nation — objections on the part of the Soviet Union on how the United States goes about performing its treaty obligations would be *ultra vires* because they would interfere with the domestic jurisdiction of the United States. What you have presented in effect is a list of subjects in which, empirically, States have had problems with international regulations. But I think in all these subject matters — and this is a repetition of what Mr. *Bernhardt* has said — there remains the possibility, and in some instances the reality, of international law on the matter being created and giving all the contracting parties of a treaty, or certain other States, or all other States, in case of customary obligations, a *ius standi* — namely the right to ask the State concerned on how it goes about fulfilling its obligations. This, of course, is of particular importance with regard to human rights. Such a view has nothing at all to do with absolutism. It has nothing at all to do with a world State rising at the horizon, as long as we stick to the view that international law is created by — if I may use Mr. *Tunkin*'s words, a free co-ordination of the wills of States. If we have a free co-ordination of the wills of States to the effect that they have to live up to human rights and not to torture *etc.*, the question whether we have torture in these States, or the killing of political opponents, is out of the *domaine réservé* for good. I would go as far as including even Mr. *Tunkin*'s, let us say, *ultima ratio*, into the list of matters which, of course, empirically speaking, will not easily come under international regulation, but which, theoretically, could also become a matter of international concern. I would like to transform this into a question to Mr. *Tunkin*, admittedly a very academic question: Assume a treaty is concluded by the Soviet Union and by the United States in which those two States agree to adopt, for instance, some kind of middle ground between their social systems — let us assume some type of social democracy —, would you consider that such a treaty — concluded freely and in accordance with constitutional requirements, *etc.* — would be invalid, legally speaking? I agree with you that it will be very improbable, but I think that it would be entirely valid. In my view, human rights treaties are nothing but treaties for the purpose of outlawing the cases of excess of social systems. Thus, I agree that the International Covenant on Economic, Social and Cultural Rights is a treaty which serves a good purpose in limiting the excesses of the capitalist system. *Vice versa*, you could consider the Covenant on Civil and Political Rights as a treaty which has a very important role to play in fettering certain excesses of the socialist system. Thank you.

Tunkin:

I would very briefly like to answer the questions put to me. The last question by Mr. *Simma:* You know, I said, that I had in mind certain circumstances because everything changes, and in certain circumstances there are certain things which by their very nature cannot be subject to general international law regulation. This, I believe, is correct and your example, for instance, theoretically is possible, but we know as well that the wills of States are conditioned by the circumstances. To say "everything is possible" means nothing. But of course, one may say that nobody can prove the contrary. Still it is an empty phrase. So,

I said, that in the present day circumstances, there are certain things and namely socio-economic systems which cannot be internationally regulated by general international law. We do not know what will happen in 300 years.

Then Mr. *Wolfrum* put a very difficult question. I stated yesterday that general international law develops not only through custom but also through international treaties. And there are norms of general international law which are for some States treaty norms, for other States customary norms. Some States are parties to the treaty. Other States accept this treaty and show by their practical steps that they are applying this treaty, and therefore they do recognize norms of this treaty, maybe not all, but some of them. This creates norms which for some State parties to the treaty are treaty norms, for those who accepted them by customary way they are customary norms, but they are the same norms. You ask how this may be viewed in the light of domestic jurisdiction or *domaine réservé*. Well, there is no contradiction whatsoever, because any norm of international law is created by the co-ordination of the wills of States. I believe, you mean that when the majority of States have accepted the norm and some States still hesitate, or at least it is not proved that they accept this norm — what will be the problem of *domaine réservé* in regard to this State? Now, I may say that once I visited Professor *Charles de Visscher* at his home and he read my book, when I came in, "Droit international public: Problèmes théoriques" (1965), the French edition of my book. He said: "How do you, in this case, if you consider that general international law norms require the consent of all States, prove that all the States accepted this norm?". Well, I showed him a passage where I say — referring to *Strupp*, who said, I believe in 1932 — that when the majority of States accept a certain norm of international law there is presumption that all other States do accept this norm and it is binding on them. But of course the contrary may be proved.

Lukashuk:

It seems to me that almost all of us agree that there is such a reserved zone or domain, an exclusive zone of internal affairs. This zone where you cannot enter without knocking. But international regulation is getting deeper and deeper in internal life, just like Mr. *Simma* said. But still I wonder if there are some affairs which could not be regulated by international law. I want to say that I should not be happy if some day my family-life were to be regulated by international law. So, maybe, we have such a *domaine réservé* where international law cannot enter at all. But it seems to me that this notion of reserved domain is not an absolute notion. We must choose a more correct, a more exact notion. And there is such a notion. Would this mean subject matter of international regulation? You say, human rights, and so on, and so on. No — the subject matter of international legal regulation is relationships, international, inter-governmental, inter-state relationship; internal relations between physical and juridical persons are the subject matter of municipal regulation. Then everything will be just at its place, because interrelations between physical and juridical persons could never be regulated by international law. For example, the Soviet Union decided to build a plant. It is an internal matter. The Soviets and Africans settled this problem. Afterwards they concluded an agreement with West Germany about some support in this field. Thus, not the plant will be the subject matter of this agreement. But international co-operation, international relations between our States will be the subject matter of this agreement. It becomes quite clear, just the same as with human rights. Whenever we enter into an agreement on human rights, it is an agreement on inter-state co-operation. Every State will be obliged to support some human rights, but the subject matter there will be inter-state relation. If we take this concept, it will be much easier to settle and then internal relations will never get the subject matter of international law.

Bernhardt, Chairman:

I must say one sentence: At the end of this month, the European Court of Human Rights will decide three British cases. The question is whether the State has unduly interfered with family life.

Randelzhofer:

It is a challenge.

Lukashuk:

. . . it is a special event in the European Community.

Randelzhofer:

May I just add one second sentence. The Soviet Union not being bound by the European Convention is bound by the UN Convention on Human Rights and Political Rights. I draw your attention to Article 3 of the German Basic Law where, too, we have regulations concerning family-life — not direct regulations. For example, not that you are obliged to bring your wife breakfast to bed, but for example, that men and women are free and have to be free in the decision to enter into marital relationship. So that you cannot say that family-life is a *domaine réservé*, which is unable to be regulated by public international law.

Lukashuk:

But it is not my obligation — it is the obligation of the Soviet Union to ensure . . .

Randelzhofer

No, those things are shaped as personal rights of the individual. The individual has a right to oppose to the State . . .

Lukashuk:

Well, would you bring your State before the court?

Oppermann:

Excuse me, I did not want to interrupt! Only two short remarks: the first one — I wish to help Mr. *Tunkin* against Mr. *Simma*, although Mr. *Tunkin* knows to defend himself. I think there was deep wisdom in your remark, Mr. *Tunkin*, that the free choice of the social system is really at the very core of State sovereignty. The choice of the social system is the one thing which cannot be internationalized. In other words, this fundamental decision is quite near to a right highly cherished by all of us, and included at the beginning of the two UN Covenants on human rights of 1966. I speak of the right to self-determination of nations.

Tunkin:

. . . not the specific system, it means anything.

Oppermann:

Yes, but it belongs to the very heart of the decision on the choice of the social system. There is no dispute on the abstract principle. The big question we cannot treat here is, who is really the holder of this right. Is it the State, the nation, the people, and so on? As we all know, the real difficulties start at this point.

Now I want to turn to Mrs. *Shinkaretskaya:* You started with international economic law and you cited Professor *Brownlie* in this context, namely that, generally speaking, international law limits the scope of *domaine réservé*. There is much truth in that. The problem is that international law is not static. You gave a very interesting example for this when you chose "permanent sovereignty over natural resources and economic wealth", a principle very dear especially to many developing countries. But, on the other hand, you have another very important economic principle which runs contrary to the first, namely the "common heritage of mankind". Who decides which part of natural wealth falls under the regime of permanent sovereignty — coal, oil? Which natural wealth, on the other hand, is regulated by the principle of common heritage — the deep sea minerals? I just want to pose this fundamental question: Who decides this? Of course, international law does, but this is a very complex process. Not all of the 160 States are always of the same opinion whether the one principle applies, or the other. You cited the famous Article 2 of the Charter of Economic Rights and Duties of States. This is a very shaky norm, because it is exactly due to this article that the Charter did not find a convincing majority. Mr. *Tunkin* and myself were present in Seoul at the ILA-Conference discussing the problem of that Article within the Committee on a New International Economic Order. It was very interesting that even lawyers from the developing countries are slowly moving back from their views of the 1970s to former classical opinions, as far as the scope and importance of international law in the field of foreign investment, nationalization, and compensation is concerned. I just cite this here as an example of the steadily changing borderline between national and international law. Necessarily this is also true for the framework of internal affairs of a State. Thank you very much.

Bothe:

There seems to be an agreement around the table on what constitutes the *domaine réservé*. Mr. *Simma* defined it very aptly saying it means "a right of the State to be left alone".

To be left alone by whom? That is the first question where we have to differentiate. It makes a great difference whether nasty things about a foreign State or a foreign State official are said by an official of another State, or in a newspaper or television comment. In one case, you have a State actor, in the other a private actor. Coming to the question whether international organizations may debate certain events taking place in a State, this is probably more the question of the organizations' legal powers then that of *domaine réservé*. An international organization has no other powers than those conferred on it by its constitution and the law developed under its auspices. This also applies to the power of debate. This is my first differentiation, concerning the actors in question.

The second differentiation was rightly pointed out by Mr. *Bernhardt:* "What are the subject matters in relation to which a State has to be left alone?" One criterion defining these matters has not been mentioned, but it should be made clear. This is the effect of certain State actions. the question whether a certain behaviour of States produces an effect outside their national boundaries. Mr. *Lukashuk* just mentioned the case of building a plant. This is in principle a matter belonging to the internal sphere. But when we find out that the operation of a plant has some outside effect, it can no longer be considered as a matter of the *domaine réservé*. The dispute will often be a factual one — whether there is indeed any significant outside effect. But once there is such outside effect, the subject matter concerns also other States, namely those affected. This question of outside effects is one of the main themes of international environmental law. The development of international environmental law, prompted by the development of our knowledge about transboundary effects of certain human activities, has greatly contributed to a drastic change in the concept of *domaine réservé*. It has indeed considerably reduced this notion.

The second criterion is the existence of international legal norms. Everybody around this table will agree that nothing which is subject to a valid international legal norm could belong to the *domaine réservé* of a State. We have, however, quite often difficulties in agreeing on what the norms are. Let us take permanent sovereignty over natural resources as an example. The real controversy here is whether there are any international norms concerning the nationalization of foreign property, and what they are. If there are such norms, these questions do not belong to the *domaine réservé*. The sovereignty is a sovereignty bound by legal norms.

The same hold true, in my view, for human rights. The special and new difficulty with human rights in international law is that they belong to a new dimension. Traditional international law was concerned with practical matters of State intercourse. Human rights protect some fundamental values. Many practical matters of State intercourse, traditional objects of international regulation, are to a great extent value neutral. But in some traditional subject matters dealt with by international law, we are already close to the question of human rights, for example the treatment of prisoners of war. In the field of the protection of human rights, the law having the function of protecting fundamental values, we are very close to the question of social systems. Here again our major difficulty consists in the controversy about the exact meaning of the law. The question is not so much whether any subject matter is *in abstracto* or *a priori* excluded from international regulation.

This brings me to the fundamental dispute we had around this table about rules concerning social systems. I would like to try a synthesis between the dialectic thesis and antithesis. I think, Mr. *Bernhardt* is right in legal terms and Mr. *Tunkin* in sociological terms. Legally, rules concerning social systems are possible, sociologically they are not, the international community being what it is.

I now come to a third criterion for defining the sphere of subject matters where a State has the right "to be left alone". There are cases where the State behaviour in question is not regulated by an international legal norm, but there is international political concern. As our system of international relations has developed, certain phenomena have become a question of international concern. Non-legal approaches are adopted concerning such matters, non-legal, moral, political obligations are created with respect to such phenomena. Thus, there are areas where even without the existence of international legal norms, an international concern exists which makes it impossible to characterize this area as *domaine réservé.*

Finally, I come to a third and important point also mentioned by Mr. *Bernhardt*. This is the question of methods. The fact that there is a valid international concern because a State behaviour produces outside effects, because it is regulated by international norms, does not mean that the reaction or action by other States is completely free. There are also procedural rules about how it is possible to invoke this concern. We cannot discuss the whole problem this evening, but I think it is one of the most difficult and most fundamental themes in international law. What is legitimate political influence or a legitimate attempt to modify a stance taken by another State and what is undue pressure which we may call intervention? It is a question which has been discussed in the United Nations probably from its beginning. It was discussed in connection with the Friendly Relations Declaration, but not solved by this resolution. What that Declaration has to say about the question really does not mean very much. Thank you, Mr. *Chairman*.

Klein:

I would like to approach the core of our discussion in another way than it has been done up to now. I was much impressed by the presentation by Mrs. *Shinkaretskaya*, how she described the process of the emergence of global concerns, of objective values in international law. But what are such values, what do they mean? We have, for example, the prohibition of force, it is valid, of course, not only in Central America; the elimination of racial discrimination and *apartheid*; the maintenance of an ecological balance; the limitation of the arms race, or even arms reduction; and so on. But what is common to all these values? I think we may discover it in the perspective of the well-being of mankind, the well-being of the single person, of the individual. But if the well-being of mankind is in the heart of international law — like it is in the heart of all law — then, in my view, it is cogent that international law may not be excluded, in principle, from the protection of human beings — be it foreigners, or stateless persons, or even citizens of the own State. I think, to say it again, from this deliberation the conclusion is to be drawn that it is at least not logical to exclude international law from the relation between the State and its own population. Of course, legal norms may not exist in concrete circumstances and for concrete cases, but in my view, it is not at all convincing to say that they cannot or must not exist. Thank you.

Bernhardt, Chairman:

Thank you. And now you have the floor, Mrs. *Shinkaretskaya*.

Shinkaretskaya:

Now, I think, I have to thank not only Mr. *Chairman* but all the audience. At the very beginning of my presentation, I said, that I will maybe put more questions than I will try to give answers. I gained great success, because it appears that here we have almost as many opinions as in the United Nations' General Assembly. Every participant seems to have his own opinion on the question, and I dare not hope for another symposium on this, but at least, I hope, to have the opportunity to read something of it in any language. And what is quite valuable to me is, that my German colleagues possess, I would say, a very clear and legalistic way of thinking. This pure legal mind gives me great profit, because it somehow differs from my way of thinking and in combining this, I think, I myself will produce something valuable, too. I do not think that what was said here were questions put to me. Most of them were just reflections and I would like to make several remarks by beginning at the very end. I very much thank Mr. *Klein* because he saw the "heart of the matter". This is the contradiction between the urgent values common to all mankind and the sacred principle of State sovereignty, which we cannot somehow abolish, and still we cannot but base the whole of international law on the principle of State sovereignty. I see that my position was illogical, and maybe that an illogical way could lead to a success if I say, let us all the nations allow to solve all problems together. But is it real; I doubt it. I would just like to say some words on the dilemma pointed out by Mr. *Oppermann* concerning the "principle of permanent sovereignty" and the "common heritage of mankind". I do not see any contradiction here, because common heritage is the principle which I think flows directly from the principle of permanent sovereignty over natural resources. The developing nations just want to get profit from both, and the principle of the common heritage of mankind embraces only those things which are not covered by sovereignty. In legal terms it is, in my opinion, expressed only concerning the deep sea values. When we speak here of the balance between a common relation, between international law and national legislation, I am not sure that it is proper to take examples from the European Community, because I would say it is a quite special legal system.

The Law-Creating Activity of the CMEA and Soviet Law*

By Eugeny T. Usenko**

A clear conception of the differences between the principles and methods of integration in a socialist or a capitalist way is necessary in order to explain the special features of the law-creating activity of the Council of Mutual Economic Assistance (CMEA).[1] The capitalist way of integration on the model of the European Economic Community (EEC) presupposes a certain limitation of sovereignty of the Member States with respect to the formation of a supra-national organ. The socialist integration, on the other hand, is based on the respect for the sovereignty of the States participating in the international organization and does not lead to a supra-national organ.

The particularities of the two types of integration mentioned have provoked different definitions of integration. In western literature an idea of integration is often propagated, which has been linked to the structures developed in the EEC, but which is not proven right. The CMEA is also an organization, within and through which an integration of the socialist Member States is put into practice. But still, the Council is no supra-national organization and its organs do not dispose of a supra-national power.

The juridical acts created by the CMEA bear the character of international law. Therefore, one cannot speak of a "Law of the CMEA" in the same way as one does about the law of the EEC, which is actually created by a supra-national power. However, the juridical acts of the CMEA are in no way inferior to those of the EEC, as far as efficiency is concerned. In this context let us briefly look at the law-creating mechanism of the Council.

The CMEA is entitled to adopt two types of acts according to its Charter: decisions and recommendations.[2] Decisions are made regarding

---

* *Editors'* note: The paper was presented in German and has been translated subsequently.

** Dr., Professor of Law, Scientist of Merit, Chief of Division at the Institute of State and Law of the Academy of Sciences of the USSR.

[1] Basic materials on the CMEA in English are provided by: *William E. Butler*, ed., transl., A Source Book on Socialist International Organizations, Alphen aan den Rijn, The Netherlands 1978.

[2] Article (Art.) IV, Charter of the Council of Mutual Economic Assistance, in: *Butler* (note 1), 124—135 (126, 127), (*see* Documentation, 197).

matters of organization and procedure. Recommendations concern matters of the economic and scientific-technical co-operation of the Member States. They may only be adopted by the central organs of the CMEA. All recommendations in the Council are only adopted with the approval of all the States interested in the matter. If a State declares that it has no interest in the matter or does not want to participate in the recommendation on this matter, the recommendation can be adopted without this State (or States). If a Member State declares itself interested in the subject and votes against the recommendation, the recommendation will not be adopted by the Council.[3] Thus the principle of qualified unanimity is valid for the Council. The Member States are informed for consideration of the recommendation taken by the Council. Upon submittance of the recommendation the State may reject it, irrespective of the fact that its representative voted in the Council for the adaptation. This is, because the State through its representative partakes in the Council only in the sense of forming the intention of the Council, and this intention is expressed in the recommendation itself. At this point the recommendation is a unilateral act of the CMEA.

But the Charter does not only grant to the Council the right of making recommendations to the Member States. It links legal consequences to the acceptance of a recommendation in the Council, which are of a kind not to be found in other international organizations. The act of acceptance of a recommendation in the Council has the meaning of a juridical fact, which — in accordance with the Charter and the rules of procedure — brings about certain formal legal relations. One of the most important ones of these legal relations is the obligation of the State addressed to consider the recommendation and to inform the Secretariat of the CMEA within 60 days about the results of the considerations. The Secretariat will then notify the other States on these communications.[4] This obligation of the State addressed to consider and inform the Secretariat, whether it wants to accept the obligations resulting from the recommendations, is an important particularity of the recommendations of the CMEA in comparison with resolutions of the United Nations and resolutions of many other international organizations. This special feature goes to prove the qualified character of the CMEA recommendations and their potential to generate legal relations between the Member States.

The law of the USSR stipulates that the decision of acceptance of the recommendations of the CMEA rank among the competences of the

[3] *Loc. cit.*, para. 3.

[4] *E. g.* Rule 25, Rules of Procedure for the Session of the Council of Mutual Economic Assistance, in: *Butler* (note 1), 149—157 (155).

Government.[5] Of course, this is true for matters concerning the powers of the Government only. If the object of the recommendation forms part of the competence of the ministries, it is the ministries which decide.

If the States addressed by a recommendation accept it — which is normally the case — a new legal fact is created: the accepted recommendation. Thereto the Charter links the formation of a new legal relation: Every State which accepted the recommendation is obliged to comply with it and keep the Council informed about the process of compliance.[6] Thereby the character of the recommendation of the Council reaches its highest point of legal status. On the basis of such qualified and particular character of the recommendations and the binding nature of the approval, the creation of international treaties *sui generis* is rendered possible. It is obvious that such a treaty is formed due to the relation resulting from Article 2 of the Charter between the unilateral acceptance of each State to fulfil the recommendations and alike manifestations of will of the other States. This Article requires the consent of each Member State.

The intention of Council organs to offer to the States the conclusion of an international treaty by accepting the recommendations of the Council, is generally expressed by presenting the substantive contents of the recommendation in a separate document, *e. g.* the General Conditions for Delivery (G.C.D.),[7] the Programme of Integration, the Programme on Scientific-Technical Progress of 1985, *etc.*

The concept of treaty obligations arising from the recommendations of the CMEA, which was developed as a doctrine of international law in the Socialist countries,[8] has been reaffirmed by State practice. Thus the USSR, Hungary, and Czechoslovakia have ratified as an international treaty the General Terms of Specialization and Co-operation upon recommendation of the Council.

International treaties resembling in form, origin, and other special features those recommendations of the CMEA, are not identical with common international treaties and are therefore classified as inter-

---

[5] Art. 15 paras. 2, 4, Law on the USSR Council of Ministers, Vedomosti SSSR (News Bulletin of the Supreme Soviet of the USSR) (1978), no. 28, item 436, as amended by Vedomosti SSSR (1981), no. 26, item 839, in: *William E. Butler*, comp., transl., Collected Legislation of the Union of Soviet Socialist Republics and the Constituant Union Republics, vol. 1, Dobbs Ferry, New York 1985, I—4, 3—26 (13).

[6] Art. 2 para. 4 lit. a, d, Charter of the CMEA, in: Butler (note 1), 124—135 (125); Art. 1 para. 1 lit. h, Statute on the Secretariat of the Council of Mutual Economic Assistance, in: *Butler* (note 1), 187—191 (188), (*see* Documentation, 198).

[7] General Conditions for the Deliveries of Goods between Organizations of COMECON Member Countries (1968), in: *Butler* (note 1), 925—968.

[8] *See* among others *E. T. Usenko*, On the CMEA Agreements' Competence (in Russian), in: Sowjetstaat und Recht 6 (1979), 98—106.

national treaties *sui generis*. But they belong to the group of international treaties by their nature, representing the consent of the States and the resulting legal force of State obligations. Consequently, these treaties are subject to the imperative provisions of the international treaty law, of which the *pacta sunt servanda*-principle forms a very important part of.

We also have to look at the fact that these treaties not only differ from common international treaties in form and origin, but also because they remain linked — besides by their origin — with the organization and with the initial act by which they are created. These essential particularities also presuppose an appropriate area of application. They are widely used in practice in the case of basic documents (*e. g.*: Programme of Integration, Programme of Scientific-Technical Progress, Programmes for the Purpose of Cooperation), for the realization of which several acts have to be adopted lateron. To this end the help of the CMEA will be necessary day in day out. They are also used as a simplified type of treaty, when periodical changes and supplements — achieved with the help of the CMEA — become necessary, as is the case with the G.C.D.

They are also used in analogy, in other cases. Often the treaties resulting from recommendations of the Council are combined with ordinary treaties, and the other way around. The fact that one may not speak of the "Law of the CMEA" in the same way as one speaks of the "Law of the EEC" was already mentioned. That is true, because the binding clauses of its recommendations do not attain their legal force — as we tried to show above — by virtue of an act of a supra-national organization, but because of the voluntary assent of its Member States. If we look at this matter not from the point of view of the validity of the sources of the clauses in question, but from that of the attachment to the CMEA, we witness the creation of the "Law of the Council". It is a compact bulk of binding clauses which is linked organically to the Council of Mutual Economic Assistance. This is especially true for acts which unify the general terms of the commercial, technical, and scientific relations between the Member States of CMEA, such as the G.C.D., the General Terms of Specialization and Co-operation, the General Terms on Construction Jobs, *etc.*

All these and similar acts form part of the "Law of the CMEA", a block of international treaties of the same kind. Therefore, opinions are voiced in doctrine on the efficiency of carrying out to systemize and to put down in a separate act all general clauses of civil law, which are binding in the same way for economical relations. The recommendations of the Council — as well as the therefrom resulting treaties of a special kind — do not have an "immediate effect", as do the acts of the EEC.

According to the Charter of the CMEA, they are decisions made by the governments for other competent organs of the Member States and put into practice pursuant to the legislation of these States (Art. 1 para. 4).

In the Soviet Union, the transformation of international acts of unification of this kind are made *en bloc*, that is, such an act takes effect as a whole without being changed in order to adapt it to municipal law. By means of the corresponding acts of transformation, the above-mentioned G.C.D. of the CMEA became obligatory for Soviet foreign trade organizations, and other economical organizations, if they conclude commercial contracts with organizations of other Member States. Insofar, the relation between the different terms of the G.C.D. and the contracts mentioned is put on an equal footing with the relation of a given foreign trade contract and Soviet law.

Because the above-mentioned international acts unify civil law norms, the matter of adequacy is decided in Soviet law according to Article 129 of the Fundamental Principles of Civil Legislation of the USSR and Union Republics.[9] The first paragraph of this Article reads:

> If other rules have been established by an international treaty of the USSR than those which are contained in Soviet civil legislation, the rules of the international treaty shall be applicable.[10]

By virtue of this clause, all matters which are laid down in general terms of delivery — especially matters of economic relations — are ruled by these very terms and not by Soviet civil law terms. According to section 110 para. 1 of the G.C.D.,[11] in matters which are not, or not completely, laid out by these terms, the law of the selling State is applicable.

One can deduct from the above-mentioned facts that the law of the CMEA entirely consists of acts of international legal nature. But, at the same time, it becomes the internal law of the Member States. One has to agree with Professor *L. A. Lunz*'s statement, insofar, that the fact that rules of the international acts attain the force of national law does not integrate them into the system of internal law, and thus not into the system of Soviet law. Therefore, the technical vocabulary of the G.C.D. is not to be interpreted according to the legal conception of the law of the individual Member State. Thus, *e. g.*, the G.C.D. may have a different meaning elsewhere than they do in Soviet civil law.

A still more important consequence of the divergence between the law of the CMEA and the laws of the member States is the fact that up

---

[9] Vedomosti SSSR (1961), no. 50, item 525, as amended by Vedomosti SSSR (1981), no. 44, item 1184, in: *Butler* (note 5), II—1 (61, 62) (*see* Documentation, 191).

[10] *Ibid.*

[11] *See supra* note 7, 968.

to today the G.C.D. have had no, or little, effect on the regulation of relations between organizations and other subjects of law within the States. For instance, the G.C.D. are not applicable to the relations between the Soviet foreign trade organizations and the Soviet organizations for import or export.

The separateness of the "Law of the CMEA" from the national laws of the Member States — and the legal lay-out as a whole (in the sense of inner unity) within the framework of the above-mentioned acts — creates a possibility of transformation *en bloc* into the laws of the Member States, without adaptation to the individual legal system of the States at all.

However, one has to clarify that the "Law of the CMEA" and the national normative systems are supplementary to one another. This is true not only in the sense of filling in the "gaps" in the G.C.D. by means of subsidiary application of national law, but also, mainly, because the international economic relations, which are regulated by the "Law of the CMEA" stem from and seek to refine the municipal laws.

One can assume that the realization of the task of the XXVII. Congress of the Communist Party of the Soviet Union to support the direct relations between organizations and undertakings of the Member States of the CMEA will lead to a still stronger union between the unified system of norms of the CMEA and the Soviet law.

The Relevance of Acts of International 'Supra-national' Organizations to Municipal Law: The European Community

By Meinhard Hilf*

Since the creation of the European Community (EC)[1] it has been a constant challenge to determine the relevance of acts of the EC for its Member States. Throughout the relatively short history of the EC the answers have been different, and will be different in the future. This is due to the particular and ever changing character of the EC. It is the so-called "supra-national" character which shall be clarified first. The second part of the paper will focus on the relevance of the various acts of the EC institutions in regard to their legal effects on the legal orders of the Member States. The concluding remarks then will deal with some questions relating to legal protection, and to effective and eventually forced execution of EC law within the Member States.

I. The supra-national character of the EC

1. The Founding Treaties of the EC

The Founding Treaties are silent as to the precise definition of the EC. In the original text of the Treaty, establishing the European Coal and Steel Community of 1951, one still could find an expressed reference to the notion of "supra-national" community. For whatever reasons, this formular was abandoned in 1965.[2] And now?

One may compare the EC with a rather large oceanliner which, after a celebrated launching, put to sea from its home port with six captains and is now sailing under the command of twelve different captains. Some of them dreamed of far horizons and of reaching one day the paradise of a genuine federal state of Europe. Others were more hesitant and, once on the open sea, began to feel rather seasick and — at the same

* Dr. iur., Professor of Law, Chair of Public, European, and Public International Law, University of Bielefeld.

[1] The designation EC will be used to simplify reference to the three European Communities: The European Coal and Steel Community (ECSC), the European Economic Community (EEC), and the European Atomic Energy Community (EURATOM).

[2] *See* Art. 9 al. 5 and 6 of the original text of the ECSC Treaty which has been altered in 1965.

time — homesick and hoped to stay as close as possible to their home countries. Unfortunately they had agreed to change the captain at the helm every six months and to decide all major questions by unanimity. It is certainly tempting to go more into detail and to try to determine the ship's precise position in 1987. We only know that they have not reached paradise. Yet, we also know that they are already too far from home so that any attempted escape by one of them could hardly be survived. However, they have succeeded in agreeing on various amendments to their original agreements. In July 1987 the Single European Act (SEA) entered into force, after the Irish population consented to its ratification. This Act, amending again the three Founding Treaties and integrating the loose European Political Co-operation (EPC) into the common institutional framework, is an important step forward. Certainly, the Act primarily is a consolidation of the present state of the Community, but it also expresses a renewed consensus to reach a common market by 1992, and, above all, the Act may develop its own dynamics.[3]

From the Preamble of the Founding Treaties of 1951 and 1957 two important elements may help answering parts of our question: In reading these texts it becomes evident that the basic aim of these Treaties is a political one.[4] After the end of World War II the agreed economic integration appeared to be only a tool — but certainly an important one — to contribute to an "organized and vital Europe", which was supposed to substitute the age old rivalries by merging their essential interests. Given this political aim the second element adds a dynamic approach. The Preamble of the EEC Treaty underlines the determination of the Founding States to lay the foundation for an "ever closer union" among the peoples of Europe. Of course, one could argue that an "ever closer union" at the same time means a never obtainable union.[5] I want to leave aside further possible reflections as to the content and legal character of these texts. I only want to underline that the Community is on its way. However, its final legal form is still undefined. The Community finds itself in a continuing process of integration, and already some authors are of the opinion that this process is irrevocable and

---

[3] For the text of the Act *see* Official Journal June 6th, 1987, no. L 169/1; for comments *cf. Pierre Pescatore*, Some Critical Remarks on the "Single European Act", in: Common Market Law Review (CML Rev.) 24 (1987), 9—18 (10 *et seq.*), and *Claus-Dieter Ehlermann*, The International Market Following the Single European Act, in: CML Rev. 24 (1987), 361—409. The Irish Supreme Court, *Crotly* v. *An Taoiseach et al.* April 9th, 1987 (forthcoming), held that prior to a ratification a referendum is required.

[4] *Cf. Ulrich Everling*, Das Europäische Gemeinschaftsrecht im Spannungsfeld von Politik und Wirtschaft, in: *id.*, Das Europäische Gemeinschaftsrecht im Spannungsfeld von Politik und Wirtschaft, Ausgewählte Aufsätze 1964—1984, Baden-Baden 1985, 53—85 (54 *et seq.*).

[5] *Roland Bieber et al., Introduction, in: Roland Bieber et al.* (eds.), L'Europe de demain, Brussels/Luxembourg 1985, 7—14 (8 *et seq.*).

one remote day it will necessarily end up in something like the United States of Europe.[6] The present situation is by far not that of a federal state. It is only recognized that its specific character distinguishes the EC from any other international organization in existence. Already in 1962, the Court of Justice of the European Communities (ECJ) highlighted the legal elements which determine the supra-national character of the EC. These elements are the following:

— the limitation of national sovereignty
— the direct applicability of Community law in regard to the Member States and to individuals and
— the supremacy of Community law over any national law, guaranteeing its uniform application throughout the Community.[7]

These elements have been, up to now, formulated most prominently by the ECJ in 1964:

> By creating a Community of unlimited duration, having its own institutions, its own personality, its own legal capacity of representation on the international plane and, more particularly, real powers stemming from limitation of sovereignty or a transfer of powers from the States to the Community, the Member States have limited their sovereign rights, albeit within limited fields, and have thus created a body of law which binds both their nationals and themselves.

And the Court went on:

> The integration into the laws of each Member State of provisions which derive from the Community, and more generally the terms and the spirit of Treaty, make it impossible for the State, as a corollary, to accord precedence to a unilateral and subsequent measure over a legal system accepted by them on a basis of reciprocity.[8]

This statement of the Court is recognized as being a precise description of the supra-national character of the EC.

In the case law of the ECJ, these elements have been defined yet in some 2000 decisions. In 1964 the ECJ still referred to the powers of the EC as being "within limited fields". From this statement, as well as from the wording of the Treaties, the underlying principle of limited

---

[6] For a discussion of this question *see Ulrich Everling*, Sind die Mitgliedstaaten der Europäischen Gemeinschaft noch Herren der Verträge?, in: *Rudolf Bernhardt / Wilhelm Karl Geck / Günther Jaenicke / Helmut Steinberger (*eds.), Völkerrecht als Rechtsordnung, Internationale Gerichtsbarkeit, Menschenrechte, Festschrift für *Hermann Mosler*, Berlin/Heidelberg/New York 1983, 173—191 (190).

[7] *Cf.* Case 26/62 *van Gend & Loos* (1963) ECR 3; *see* the comment by *Martine Schlüter-Lapierre, Van Gend en Loos Case*, in: *Rudolf Bernhardt* (ed.), Encyclopedia of Public International Law (Instalment 2), Amsterdam/New York/Oxford 1981, 287—290.

[8] Case 6/64 *Costa* v. *Enel* (1964), ECR 1251; *see* the comment of *Meinhard Hilf, Costa* v. *Enel*, in: *Bernhardt* (note 7), 67—69.

attribution of powers has been formulated.[9] Yet, it is difficult to indicate the limits of these powers, given the drastic expansion of the Community's activities and the frequent use of the more sweeping powers in Articles 100 and 235 of the EEC Treaty. In every case, in which acts were based on these provisions, the powers of the Community were expanded. The Member States may not further act in these fields and the given rules may only be abolished by a new and unanimous decision of the Council of the EC. Even fields which, for a long time, seemed to be within the exclusive powers of the Member States are now affected by Community law: Examples are the fields of education, culture, national administration, or even political relations, as in the case of economic sanctions against third States. The Council, in agreement with the ECJ, interprets, in rather broad terms, the given powers of the EEC in the light of the general aims of the Community as formulated in Article (Art.) 2 of the EEC Treaty. The general principle of subsidiarity, which is supposed to be able to restrict the exercise of the powers of the Community and which is now expressly referred to in the SEA[10], will have practically no effect, since one will hardly find the ECJ willing to annual an unanimous act of the Council on the ground of this principle.

2. *Co-operation and integration within a para-federal structure*

If it does not appear to be adequate to speak of clearly defined or limited powers of the EC, do we then already have the general power to distribute powers on the side of the Community? This is not the case. The Member States may still interfere within the Council, and try to amend the Treaties, and limit the expansion of the powers of the EC. But if there is no unanimity, then only the *status quo* may be upheld by vetoing any further progress. The ECJ does not seem to be willing to act as a stronghold of the powers of the Member States. In no case the Court, so far, ever has anulled an act of the Community on the grounds of excess to powers. To be exact, in only one case the Court has annulled an act of the European Parliament (EP) because there was no Community power to spend money in favour of political parties within the framework of elections of the EP.[11] In all other cases, the Court decided *in favorem integrationis*.[12]

---

[9] *See Bengt Beutler / Roland Bieber / Jörn Pipkorn / Jochen Streil*, Die Europäische Gemeinschaft — Rechtsordnung und Politik —, 3rd rev. ed., Baden-Baden 1987, 76 *et seq.*

[10] *Jean-Paul Jacqué*, Preamble, in: *Francesco Capotorti et al.*, The European Union Treaty, Oxford 1986, 25 *et seq.*

[11] Case 294/83 *Les Verts* v. *European Parliament* ECR April 23rd, 1986 (forthcoming).

[12] *Joseph H. H. Weiler*, Eurocracy and Distrust, in: Washington Law Review 55 (1987), 1103—1142 (1119).

What then distinguishes the supra-national Community from a federal State? In regard to powers, the Community may affect nearly all fields of activities of the Member States, but only in regard to, or in connection with, economic questions. Thus the large areas of education[13], culture, public order, defense, and foreign political relations, and, above all, of national administration are in their essence not affected by the Community. Member States still nearly have the monopoly of executive powers. No Community official has the right to exercise police powers within the Member States or any power within the forced execution of Community decisions. When, in January 1987, Community officials wanted to verify the books and files of a German chemical company (*Hoechst*), in view of a supposed offence against the EC rules on competition, they had to be accompanied by German officials with the exclusive right to break up doors and filing cabinets if the company refuses to give the relevant informations. And of course, this can happen only on the basis of prior authorization by a court.[14]

Apart from unlimited powers, the Community lacks its own territory. Thus Greenland, in 1984, could have become an autonomous territory only upon the decision of Denmark alone.[15] And the Community lacks its own nationality. A Community citizenship — as referred to in Art. 3 of the proposal of the EP of 1984 for the founding of a European Union — would refer only to the sum of rights and obligations of individuals under Community law.[16] Only the Member State is to decide which individual may become its national. And above all, only the institutions of the Member States are based on full democratic legitimation. Council and Commission are also based on this national democratic basis. And as mentioned before, Member States alone decide on the revision of the Treaties, though they are not entitled to denounce their membership in the Community.[17] The interrelationship between the Community and

---

[13] Thus the field of education has connections with economic formation; *see* Case 293/83 *Gravier* v. *City of Liège* (1985) ECR 606. This judgment, however, meets with opposition in some Member States, for example in the Federal Republic of Germany by the *Oberverwaltungsgericht* (Higher District Court on Administrative Matters) Berlin, July 15th, 1986 (forthcoming). A detailed analysis is given by *Thomas Oppermann*, Europäisches Gemeinschaftsrecht und deutsche Bildungsordnung, "Gravier" und die Folgen, Bonn 1987.

[14] This is to be considered a general principle of constitutional law, which finds its expression for example in Art. 13 of the German Constitution, in Art. 10 of the Belgian Constitution, in Art. 72 of the Danish Constitution, and in Art. 9 of the Greek Constitution. *See* also Art. 8 al. 1 of the European Convention on Human Rights.

[15] This decision has led to the Treaty of March 13th, 1984, amending the Community Treaties, *cf.* Official Journal February 1, 1985, no. L 29/1.

[16] *Cf. Francesco Capotorti*, in: *Capotorti* (note 10), Art. 3, 36—38.

[17] For extraordinary circumstances under which a denouncement of the Treaty may be considered *see Meinhard Hilf* in: *Hans von der Groeben et al.* (eds.), Kommentar zum EWG-Vertrag, vol. 2, 3rd ed., Baden-Baden 1983, Art. 240, (9 *et seq.*).

its Member States may be considered to have some para-federal elements. A European federal state, however, does not exist and will not arise from the existing Treaties.

Before discussing the relevant acts of the institutions of the EC, one has to distinguish two different categories of actions: the categories of co-operation and of integration.[18] Both have their particular relevance in regard to acts which may be taken by the Community. Whereas co-operation is the classical instrument in relation to international organizations and leads, in general, only to non-binding acts unless ratified and incorporated, integration refers to acts taken by the common institutions which may have a binding and direct effect on the Member States and their individuals.

Arts. 6 and 103 *et seq.* of the EEC Treaty limit the institutions of the Community to giving recommendations concerning the co-operation of the Member States in the field of their general economic and monetary policies. These in substance remain within the powers of the Member States. The EPC, now formally included in Art. 30 of the SEA, again leads only to non-binding consultations and engagements between the Member States. It is astonishing, if not a misinterpretation, that on April 9th, 1987, the Irish Supreme Court decided that this incorporation of the EPC constitutes a further limitation of sovereignty and an infringement on the policy of neutrality of the Republic of Ireland. Such a limitation could only be agreed upon by a referendum of the Irish people.[19]

Finally, co-operation is taking place "at the edge" of the Community, that is in fields where it is not clear whether the Community has exclusive powers. Especially Art. 220 of the EEC Treaty explicitly refers to the conclusion of international treaties between the Member States. The institutions of the Community are at times involved in these negotiations. Member States even have designated the ECJ to give preliminary rulings on some of these international instruments.[20] It is an open discussion whether these treaties again only reflect the technique of international co-operation or whether, due to their connection with the law of the Community, they have a more specific legal nature.

The specific supra-national character of the EC is attributable to the technique of integration. The limitation or transfer of sovereignty in

---

[18] For this *summa divisio cf. Léontin-Jean Constantinesco*, Das *Recht der* Europäischen Gemeinschaften, vol. 1: Das institutionale Recht, Baden-Baden 1977, 123—135.

[19] *See* note 3.

[20] *See* Protocol concerning the interpretation by the Court of Justice of the Convention of 27th September 1968 on jurisdiction and the enforcement of judgments in civil and commercial matters, Official Journal August 2nd, 1975, no. L 240/28, and Official Journal October 30th, 1978, no. L 304/10.

favour of the Community leads to an integrated decision-making process. It leads to legal acts which are to be distinguished from acts of co-operation by their uniform and direct applicability in all Member States.[21] The uniform application has two consequences: the first is, that the exclusion of one or more Member States from the application of any of the commonly decided policies is contrary to the very idea of Community law. The ECJ, in 1977, declared incompatible with Community law a proposed international agreement of the Community, in the execution of which only some of the Member States would have taken part in.[22] Opting out from common and, thus, uniform policies is only permitted if there is a general agreement and if it is a case of limited importance. The new Art. 8 *lit.* c of the EEC Treaty permits exceptions only within a limited period of time.[23]

The second consequence is that the law of integration is directly applicable and, thus, takes precedence over any legal rule of the Member States. Only the ECJ may interpret or annul legal acts of the Community. No national institution may interfere in this matter — even if it is the Supreme Court of a Member State. It is along this line that the *Bundesverfassungsgericht* (German Federal Constitutional Court) has refused, after an initial period of hesitation, to decide on the validity or at least on the applicability of acts of the Community within the Federal Republic of Germany, especially in regard to the protection of fundamental rights. The Court still maintained a reservation in the case that, in the future, the Community "runs wild" and disregards fundamental rights of the individuals which the Community is bound to protect.[24] This decision of the German Court has been welcomed, for it acknowledges the specific character of the law of the Community. One may have, however, some doubts as to the legality of the continuing reservation. Within the integrated system, no national institution shall have the power to interfere in the rule-making process of the Community. In extreme cases, such as viewed by the German Federal Constitutional Court, it will be the Member State as such which could, and — under the constraints of the national constitution — should, bring the con-

[21] At first underlined by the ECJ, *cf.* note 7.

[22] Opinion 1/76 Draft Agreement Establishing a European Laying-up Fund for Inland Waterway Vessels (1977) ECR 741.

[23] *Cf. Meinhard Hilf*, in: *Capotorti* (note 10), 142—144; methods of differentiated integration are discussed by *Claus-Dieter Ehlermann*, How Flexible is Community Law? An Unusual Approach to the Concept of "Two Speeds", in: Michigan Law Review 82 (1984), 1274—1293; and *Eberhard Grabitz* (ed.), Abgestufte Integration, eine Alternative zum herkömmlichen Integrationskonzept?, Kehl am Rhein/Straßburg 1984.

[24] Decision of October 22nd, 1986 in: *Entscheidungen des Bundesverfassungsgerichts* (Federal Constitutional Court Reports, - BVerfGE), vol. 73, 339 (hereinafter cited as: BVerfGE 73, 339); *cf. Christoph Vedder*, Ein neuer gesetzlicher Richter?, in: Neue Juristische Wochenschrift 40 (1987), 526—531.

tinuing membership gradually to an end. In this context, the constitutionality of the national act of approval, voted upon by the national parliament in agreeing to join the Community, can be, at any time, controlled by the national constitutional court — if there is one.[25]

If it is not clear whether an envisaged policy has to be transformed into legal acts by the technique of co-operation or integration, the Community may, together with the Member States, agree upon the conclusion of a mixed act, which leaves the qualification of this act unresolved. Eventually, the courts will have to decide on its precise legal nature.[26]

3. *Institutions and law-making procedures*

Prior to the qualification of the acts of the Community in their relevance for the Member States, one general observation has to be underlined. This refers to a particular quality of Community law which is essential for the functioning of the Community as a whole. Community law reflects the common values and traditions of all Member States. This is due to the particular composition of the institutions as well as to the specific decision-making process. In a permanent comparative atmosphere the legal values of all Member States are confronted with each other. The representatives of the governments of the Member States within the Council give their consent to any legal act of the Community only, if they are convinced that this act reflects and does not violate any of their fundamental legal traditions under national law. The EC Council, in search of consensus and compromise, is even legally obliged not to act in conflict with fundamental national legal or constitutional principles.[27] This is pertinent to the general principle of solidarity which underlies the Community as such and which finds its expression in Art. 5 EEC Treaty. It binds the Community in regard to the Member States and *vice versa*.[28]

This permanent comparison of legal principles of national law is important for the Commission when it elaborates its proposals. In the

---

[25] Discussed by *Meinhard Hilf, Solange II:* Wielange noch Solange? in: Europäische Grundrechtezeitschrift 14 (1987), 1—7 (6).

[26] In the case of *international* mixed agreements with third States the ECJ has decided in *Demirel* v. *Stadt Schwäbisch Gmünd* that the Court has power to interpret the entire agreement, and not only those parts which are based on the powers of the Community: *cf.* Case 12/86 *Demirel* ECR September 30th, 1987 (forthcoming).

[27] For the consideration of fundamental rights *see* Case 4/73 *Nold* v. *Commission* of the EC (1974) ECR 491.

[28] Case 192/84 *Commission* of the EC v. *Greece* ECR December 11th, 1985; Case 44/84 *Hurd* v. *Jones* ECR January 15th, 1986 (forthcoming); Case 52/84 *Commission* of the EC v. *Belgium* ECR January 15th, 1986; and Case 84/85 *Commission* of the EC v. *Belgium* ECR March 3rd, 1986 (all forthcoming); for a discussion of the principle of solidarity *cf. Albert Bleckmann*, Europarecht, 4th ed., Köln/Berlin/Bonn/München 1985, 135 *et seq.*, and *Beutler* (note 9), 81.

end, the ECJ, composed of judges from all Member States, will have to pronounce itself on the validity of these general principles of Community law. Thus, in essence, Community law is not autonomous, artificial, or a foreign law for the Member States. Member States do recognize their own values and traditions within the new legal order of the Community. They will accept it as a common law which is close to their own legal convictions. The specific character of Community law, which emerges from its multi-national institutions, is an essential condition for the following:

— the acceptance of EC law by and within the Member States
— the effective execution of EC law by the Member States and
— the continuing adherence and respect for the principle of priority of EC law over national law.

But, is this concept in accordance with the rule of majority-voting within the EC Council, which more and more is practised in the decision-making process of the Council? In 1986 the Council decided 92 cases by majority. This rather recent development is pursuant to the enlarged Community and to the renewed political will to establish a common market by the year 1992.[29] No Member State, however, would consent to such a vote by majority, if it did not have the assurance that its basic legal values and traditions would be taken into account and would be duely considered before a decision is taken within the Community framework.

With this more general observation in mind, we may turn to the various acts of Community law and determine their relevance for the law of the Member States. Leaving the Treaties aside, one has to refer to nine different categories.

II. The relevance of acts of EC law for municipal law

1. Regulations

The legal effects of regulations come close to the effect of the provisions of the Treaties. According to Art. 189 alternative (al.) 2 EEC Treaty "a regulation shall have general application". A regulation "shall be binding in its entirety" and "be directly applicable in all Member States". The same may be said, for example, in regard to Art. 30 EEC Treaty which prohibits quantitive restrictions on imports and all measures having equivalent effects within the common market.[30] A regulation, ranking below the Treaty, is, in its legal effects, similar to

[29] *See Claus-Dieter Ehlermann*, in: Bitburger Gespräche — Jahrbuch, München 1988.

[30] *Cf.* Case 178/84 *Commission* v. *Federal Republic of Germany* ("Purity of Beer") ECR March 12th, 1987 (forthcoming).

a national act of parliament. It is the primary instrument of achieving uniformity of rules throughout the Community. However, a regulation is not decided upon by a parliament, but by the executive institutions of the Community. Therefore, the Treaties have chosen the more modest designation of "regulation", instead of calling it a law or an act.

From the text of Art. 189 al. 2 EEC Treaty the ECJ has deduced the supremacy of regulations over any national law.[31] Of course, the ECJ may not decide a case of conflict. It is only called upon to decide measures concerning the interpretation or the validity of Community law. It is up to the national courts and administrative authorities to guarantee that regulations are of general and direct application. In a case of conflict they have to set aside any conflicting national rule. Art. 189 al. 2 EEC Treaty does not require the invalidity of any conflicting national rule.[32] In addition, Member States may not alter unilaterally, or even interpret a regulation, or transform it into national law. Transformation especially would lead to considerable confusion as to the legal nature of a regulation.

A particular problem arises from the differences between the rules of administrative law in the various Member States, which have to be applied in order to execute the regulations of the Community. For example, time limits for bringing an action against administrative decisions may vary from one month to thirty years. National rules on administrative discretion or on equity are different. How is it possible then to assure uniform and direct application? The Community has no power to harmonize the entirety of national administrative law. It certainly can try, and has already done so, to lay down uniform time limits for the application of specific regulations.[33] But in general one has to respect the sensitivity of the Member States in maintaining their own administrative rules. Thus, the ECJ had to acknowledge that the existing differences may not be overcome overnight. It only required that the Member States execute Community law on a non-discriminatory basis in regard to their respective national law, and that they do not hinder the general and uniform application of EC law by using their proper discretion or applying national rules of equity.[34]

---

[31] *Cf.* note 8; on the priority of Community law over national constitutional law *see* Case 1/70 *Internationale Handelsgesellschaft* (1970) ECR 1125; *Torsten Stein, Internationale Handelsgesellschaft Case*, in: *Bernhardt* (note 7), 140—142.

[32] This priority of application has been confirmed by the German Federal Constitutional Court in: BVerfGE 73, 339 (375).

[33] *Cf. Meinhard Hilf*, Möglichkeiten und Grenzen des Rückgriffs auf nationale verwaltungsrechtliche Regeln bei der Durchführung von Gemeinschaftsrecht, in: *Jürgen Schwarze* (ed.), Europäisches Verwaltungsrecht im Werden, Baden-Baden 1982, 67—92 (76, note 22).

[34] Case 66, 127 and 128/79 *Salumi* (1980) ECR 1237; Case 119 and 126/79 *Lippische Handelsgesellschaft* (1980) ECR 1863; Case 130/79 *Expressed Dairy Foods* (1980) ECR 1887.

2. *Decisions*

The element of general application is essential in order to distinguish the regulation from the decision. According to Art. 189 al. 4 EEC Treaty, a decision is only binding upon those to whom it is addressed. A typical example is an act by which the Commission imposes a fine on an individual company for having violated the rules on competition in accordance with Art. 85 *et seq.* EEC Treaty. Such a decision may be attacked directly before the ECJ as this act is of direct and individual concern to the complainant. This is the requirement to be fulfilled in view of the admissibility of such an action (Art. 173 al. 2 EEC Treaty). Even regulations may be of "direct and individual concern" if they affect only a defined group of individuals as it is quite often the case in the field of foreign trade law.

Though decisions have a binding effect, they may only be enforced by national authorities. Thus, Art. 192 al. 2 EEC Treaty provides that the enforcement of a decision shall be governed by the rules of civil procedure in force in the relevant Member State. Each national government has to designate the authority which has to append an order of enforcement to the decision. No other verification than in regard to the authenticity of the decision may take place. Whereas some national courts still verify whether a Community decision is in conformity with national constitutional law,[35] the German Federal Constitutional Court, by a decision of April 10th, 1987,[36] refused such an additional control. This judgment is the first which applies consequently the above-mentioned leading case *Solange II* of October 22nd, 1986.[37]

3. *Directives*

In theory the most interesting binding act under Community law is the directive. It is a typical act which is common to organizations composed of different entities on different levels. According to Art. 189 al. 3 EEC Treaty, a directive shall be binding, as to the result to be achieved, upon each Member State to which it is adressed. It shall leave to the national authorities the choice of form and methods. No other instrument has led to such controversies as have arisen between the ECJ and various national courts on the legal nature of directives.

Directives may be used primarily where uniformity is unnecessary, or where national interests prevent the adoption of a regulation. Thus, Art. 100 EEC Treaty authorizes the Council, acting unanimously, to issue

---

[35] *Landgericht* (District Court) Bonn, in: Neue Juristische Wochenschrift 39 (1986), 665—669.
[36] Not yet published.
[37] Note 24, BVerfGE 73, 339.

directives for the approximation of such national provisions which directly affect the establishment or functioning of the common market. Member States usually have two years to choose the form and methods to achieve the required result. Thus directives come rather close to international treaties which have to be transformed into national law.

What happens when a Member State does not react within the given time limit? In this case individuals may invoke the directive in their favour against their national authorities. The only condition is that the directive is clear, precise, and unconditional, for example, setting a precise technical standard for certain industrial products or for granting equal access for men and women to any profession.[38] In these cases, Member States may not invoke as a defence their own failure to implement the directive in time. This does not mean that the directive is of general and direct application, but that it may have a direct effect under certain circumstances.

This is the essence of the rather limited case law of the ECJ,[39] which, nevertheless, is not followed by a number of national courts[40]. However, the ECJ has good reasons for its case law. The ECJ itself has ruled, that this jurisprudence is not applicable to relations between private parties.[41] Thus, a private employer is not bound by a clear and unconditional directive if his State has failed to implement the directive within the given time limit. Only the Member States are notified of directives which are not pronounced in the section of the Official Journal, in which legally binding acts have to be published in accordance with Art. 191 al. 1 EEC Treaty. This, certainly, is a rather formalistic reason which limits the possible direct effects of directives only in relation to the public authorities. The ECJ thought that it should not push too far this case law, which is hardly covered by the wording of Art. 189 al. 3 EEC Treaty. Consequently, the Court ruled that directives which are not implemented in time may only create rights in favour of individuals, but not obligations for individuals.[42] The German Federal

---

[38] *See* for example directive 76/207, Official Journal February 14th, 1976, no. L 39/40; for a detailed discussion of this case law *cf. Ulrich Everling*, Zur direkten innerstaatlichen Wirkung der EG-Richtlinien: Ein Beispiel richterlicher Rechtsfortbildung auf der Basis gemeinsamer Rechtsgrundsätze, in: *Bodo Börner / Hermann Jahrreiß / Klaus Stern* (eds.), Einigkeit und Recht und Freiheit, Festschrift für *Karl Carstens* zum 70. Geburtstag, vol. 1, Köln/Berlin/Bonn/München 1984, 95—113 (98 *et seq*).

[39] *Cf.* Case 14/83 *von Colson* v. *Land Nordrhein-Westfalen* (1984) ECR 1891; Case 286/85 *McDermott* ECR March 24th, 1987 (forthcoming).

[40] *Cf.* Conseil d'État December 22nd 1978, in: Europarecht 14 (1979), 292—294; *Bundesfinanzhof* (German Supreme Court on Financial Matters) April 25th, 1985, in: Europarecht 20 (1985), 191—198.

[41] Case 152/84 *Marshall* ECR February 26th, 1986 (forthcoming).

[42] Case 291/84 *Commission* v. *Kingdom of the Netherlands* ECR September 17th, 1987 (forthcoming); Case 80/86 *Attorney General* v. *Kolpinghuis Nijmegen* ECR October 8th, 1987 (forthcoming).

Constitutional Court followed this jurisprudence and underlined that the case law of the ECJ has been developed within the generally accepted function of courts to interpret the law and to adapt it to changed circumstances.[43]

4. Recommendations and programmes

Art. 189 al. 5 EEC Treaty provides that recommendations and opinions have no binding force. This is true for programmes which concern the future activities of the law-making institutions of the Community. Recommendations may refer to the economic or financial policy of the Member States. With the exception of the steel sector, where programmes are laid down for the limitation of production by means of binding acts, Member States are not legally obliged to conform to such recommendations. They have, however, a general obligation under the guiding principle of solidarity (Art. 5 EEC Treaty) to facilitate the achievement of the Community's tasks. This general obligation does not transform recommendations into legally binding acts. Only the substance of the recommendation and the convincing arguments in its favour may induce the Member States to adapt their national policies. As the Community is no super-power, non-binding instruments do not have any particular effect which may come close to a binding force. The pure wish of the Commission is no command which will have to be followed by the Member States.

5. International agreements

The Community may, in the exercise of its powers, enter into binding agreements with third States or international organizations. Such instruments are transformed or executed within the Community by specific decisions of the Council, normally regulations. These agreements are binding for the institutions of the Community as well as for the Member States (Art. 228 al. 2 EEC Treaty). Individuals may invoke such agreements before the courts if the agreement in question is precise, clear, and unconditional and, thus, may be considered to be directly applicable. According to the ECJ, this is the case for a number of trade agreements especially with States to which closer ties exist as, for example, under free trade agreements or agreements of association. In regard to the world wide General Agreement on Tariffs and Trade (GATT) and to the relevant codes, the Court, however, has denied any direct applicability for a number of reasons which, in the first place, refer to the more diplomatic and thus apparently unpredictable system of GATT.[44] In

[43] *See* German Federal Constitutional Court of April 18th, 1987 (forthcoming).

[44] Cases 267—269/81 SPI and *Sami* (1983) ECR 801; Cases 266/81 *Siot* (1983) ECR 731, confirming Case 21—24/72 *International Fruit Company* (1972) ECR

GATT, negotiations, according to the Court's appreciation, are playing a more important role than the strict application and enforcement of legal rules.

International agreements are binding upon the institutions of the Community. The ECJ deduced from this rule that any norm of international law has priority over any act which is taken by the Community's institutions. This opinion is hardly convincing, as in a number of Member States no such rule of general priority exists. This opinion has, at the same time, the negative effect that the ECJ is rather reluctant, hesitant, and cautious to consider treaties as being directly applicable. This is a rather regrettable consequence, as the day to day application of treaties by national courts as well as by the ECJ is important for the "grassroot effect", for their effective realization. By its constant jurisprudence, the ECJ hindered the direct application of some general principles of GATT which, consequently, have only little importance for the individual operator. In regard to national law, however, the binding effect of this agreement follows from the fact that the agreement is incorporated into Community law by a specific act of the Council.

6. *General principles*

The Founding Treaties of the Community could, by their very nature, not establish a complete legal order. It was their main aim to lay down the guiding principles on the basis of which a common market would have to be achieved. It soon became the task of the ECJ to fill gaps and to pronounce itself on the existence of general principles of law. The Court, in accordance with Art. 164 EEC Treaty, has to ensure that in interpretation and application of this Treaty "the law" is observed. This law includes the legal traditions which are common to the Member States. The legal systems of the Member States are the roots of the Community. Certainly, the Community has its distinct existence, its own legal personality, and has to follow its aims which are not the same as those of each individual Member State. However, Community law, once formulated and set into force, is going to be executed within, and by the legal orders of, the various Member States. This close connection and interdependence of the two sides, the Community and the Member

---

1219; *cf. Claus-Dieter Ehlermann*, Application of GATT Rules in the European Community, in: *Meinhard Hilf, Ernst-Ulrich Petersmann* (eds.), The European Community and GATT, Deventer *et al.* 1986, 127—140 (135); *Meinhard Hilf*, The Application of GATT Within the Member States of the European Community, with Special Reference to the Federal Republic of Germany, in: *op. cit.*, 153—186 (173 *et seq.*); *Marc Maresceau*, The GATT in the Case-Law of the European Court of Justice, in: *op. cit.*, 107—126, and *Ernst-Ulrich Petersmann*, The EEC as a GATT Member — Legal Conflicts Between GATT Law and European Community Law, in: *op. cit.*, 23—71.

States, justifies and makes it even necessary that the same fundamental legal principles apply to each side. Examples are the general principles of administrative law (principles of proportionality, of due process of law, of fairness, *etc.*) and the fundamental rights of the individual in regard to which the ECJ has developed a rich jurisprudence. The ECJ has taken a dynamic approach and has even taken into account principles which emerged only after the conclusion of the Founding Treaties. It may be referred, for example, to the European Convention on Human Rights (ECHR), which became a common set of rules only after the accession of France in 1974, and especially after 1981, when France recognized the possibility for individuals to bring complaints before the European Commission on Human Rights. All Member States of the Community are now parties to the ECHR. In the text of the ECHR, the ECJ, in addition to the various texts of the national constitutions, will find enough common ground for the formulation of adequate standards for the protection of fundamental rights of the individual.[45]

If, as in the *Hoechst* Case[46], it would appear that the relevant texts either of the Community or of national law do not provide for any prior authorization by a judge for an enforced search for books and files, the ECJ would probably be prepared to refer itself to the relevant constitutional principles of the Member States and of the ECHR. The Court would either declare illegal any enforced action until the relevant texts of the Community are amended, or, more courageously, the ECJ would declare itself competent to issue the necessary authorization after having convinced itself that the Commission is on solid grounds for a suspicion in regard to a breach of rules on competition. Such decision would be by far not the most courageous one which the Court would have ever taken. Anyhow, it would not be appropriate to oblige the Commission to ask twelve different national judges for approval, prior to any energetic effort — seldomly enough made! — to discover a joint infringement on the rules on competition by companies of various Member States.

The general principles are part of Community law and therefore take part in the supremacy of Community law over national law. The Court, when ruling on the legality of trade obstacles of national origin, may well apply the standards of the ECHR. By this backdoor, the ECHR will have an indirect effect on municipal law which it does not have in some

[45] *Cf.* Case 4/73 *Nold* (1974) ECR 491; Case 155/79 *AM & S* (1974) ECR 1575; Case 222/84 *Johnston* ECR May 15th, 1986 (forthcoming).

[46] Case 46/87 *Hoechst* v. *Commission* (not yet decided), together with four parallel cases from the Netherlands and from Spain. *See*, however, the refusal of the ECJ to issue interim measures in favour of Hoechst, decree of the President of the Court, March 26th, 1987 (forthcoming).

Member States of the Community, like in the United Kingdom and the Republic of Ireland.[47]

Summing up, the general principles of law form part of Community law and thus have to be observed in the legal orders of all Member States. This comes close to an effect of incorporation of fundamental rights under Community law into the legal orders of the Member States. But any such effect would be limited to the field of competence over which the Community has jurisdiction.

7. *The judgments of the ECJ*

The relevance of the judgments of the ECJ for municipal law is not without complexity, due to the various procedures under which the ECJ has jurisdiction. Within the review of the legality of acts of the Community, judgments have an effect *erga omnes*. Preliminary rulings are binding only for the specific courts that have referred the relevant question. Certain effects, however, which come close to an effect *erga omnes* are discussed in this context.[48] For further detail it has to be referred to Arts. 171, 176, and 192 EEC Treaty.

8. *Inter-institutional acts*

The so-called inter-institutional acts have, by their very nature, no legal effects within municipal law. Therefore, the question will have to be set aside whether these acts may have any legal effect at all. It has become a rather frequent and fruitful practice of the Community's institutions to settle inter-institutional disputes by more or less formalized common declarations and agreements. It may be considered to be an unwritten principle of Community law that the institutions are bound in their reciprocal relationships to observe such inter-institutional arrangements.[49]

---

[47] *Cf.* Case 60/84 *Cinéthèque* (1985) ECR 2618; Case 222/84 *Johnston* ECR May 15th, 1986 (forthcoming).

[48] Case 66/80 *International Chemical Cooperation* (1981) ECR 1191 concerning preliminary rulings on the validity of acts of the Community's institutions; *see Jochen Streil*, in: *Beutler* (note 9), 244 *et seq.*

[49] *Cf.* Joint Declaration by the European Parliament, the Council and the Commission, Official Journal April 22nd, 1975, no. C 89/1; Official Journal October 8th, 1976, no. L 278/10; Joint Declaration by the European Parliament, the Council and the Commission on various measures to improve the budgetary procedure, Official Journal July 28th, 1982, no. C 194/1; for further references *see Roland Bieber*, in: *Beutler* (note 9), 171—212 (195 *et seq.*), and *Meinhard Hilf*, Die rechtliche Bedeutung des Verfassungsprinzips der parlamentarischen Demokratie für den europäischen Integrationsprozeß, in: Europarecht 19 (1984), 9—40.

9. *Acts 'at the edge' of the Community*

In the given context one has finally to refer to acts which do not orginate from the Community's institutions, but which have a close connection to the body of Community law. I refer to decisions of the representatives of the governments of Member States. Such decisions may, as to their substance, be interrelated with Community law. The forms of these acts vary from genuine agreements under public international law, which may even necessitate a proper ratification under national procedures, to common understandings, or simple declarations of intent. The representatives of the Member States may meet inside or outside the EC Council, they may decide with or without a proposal of the Commission, the text may be published in the Official Journal of the Community, or only in national gazettes, or not at all. It is thus entirely open for discussion whether, and within what limits, the ECJ would exercise its jurisdiction and make a pronouncement on the legal nature of these acts.

A particular category are the engagements within the European Political Co-operation. Though this field of activity has been formally integrated in the framework of the Community by Art. 30 of the SEA, it has, however, not acquired any legal status similar to Community law. Whereas the procedural committments may be considered as being binding, the political engagements are not qualified as legally binding acts.

Having thus exhausted the various categories of acts and their particular relevance for municipal law, some elements as to the legal protection, the execution, and the legal enforcement of acts of the Community have to be mentioned.

III. Legal protection, execution, and legal enforcement

The ECJ has to ensure that the law is observed. In its case law the ECJ has developed its proper procedural law as laid down in the Treaties and has tried to adapt it to the development of the constitutional law of the Community.[50]

The subject of legal protection, execution, and enforcement again is closely linked with the intense inter-relationship between Community law and the law of the Member States. It is not the exclusive task of the ECJ to provide for judicial protection. At the same time the courts of the Member States have to grant judicial protection for the individuals. These courts control the executing decisions of the national authorities.

[50] *Cf.* Case 294/83 *Les Verts* v. *European Parliament* ECR April 23rd, 1986 (forthcoming).

The link between the national legal orders and the legal order of the Community is assured by the preliminary procedure under Art. 177 EEC Treaty. This procedure can only function on the basis of an intense, reciprocal co-operation between the national courts and the ECJ. The latter is the judge of Community law; it has no jurisdiction to rule on the validity of national law. The responsibility as to the conformity of national law in regard to Community law lies in the hands of the national courts.

A similar connection exists in relation to the supervision of the fulfilment of the obligations of the Member States. Art. 169 EEC Treaty offers to the Commission the possibility — and some say: the obligation — to bring an action before the ECJ against any Member State which has failed to honour its obligations under the Treaties. This procedure is certainly important for the effective implementation and execution of Community law by the Member States. The Commission, in more recent years, has used this procedure more and more. Since 1980 there has been a considerable increase. In 1985, for example, the Commission submitted 503 (1980: 227) supposed failures to the attention of the national governments, it gave 233 (68) reasoned opinions, and finally brought 113 (28) cases before the ECJ.[51] This increase is due to numerous directives which have not been implemented in time by the Member States. Even individuals have discovered this procedure in order to seize the Commission with legal problems for the solution of which they have no direct access to the ECJ.

Als impressive these figures may be, the effective execution of Community law does not depend on this formalized and complicated procedure, but rather on the decentralized day to day application of Community law by the national courts and administrations.[52] It is up to the individuals to invoke their rights and to avail themselves of all the possible remedies which are at their disposal. Only when this happens, Community law will have the necessary relevance which has been discussed so far on a more abstract level.

IV. Summary

It has been tried to review the supra-national character of the Community and to highlight those elements which may distinguish the Community from any other international organization. We have looked at different categories of acts and their particular relevance for municipal law. We discovered the profound connection and increasing interrelationship between the legal order of the Community and the national

[51] *Cf.* Official Journal September 1st, 1986, no. C 220/14.

[52] *Cf. Ehlermann* (note 29).

legal orders of the Member States. It has become evident that this system can only function under the participation of States which have rather homogeneous legal traditions and economic systems. The legal equality of all Member States is one of the basic elements of the Community. The decisive question as to which legal order has priority can be answered in theory. In practice, however, Member States are not prepared to surrender unconditionally to the agreed rules of Community law. It does not harm the entire system if the dividing line in the field of sovereign powers remains obscure: This obscurity may cause the Community and its Member States to treat each other with the necessary degree of mutual consideration.

Discussion*

Randelzhofer, Chairman:

Now we may open the floor for discussion. Mr. *Oppermann* is pressed to leave us a little bit earlier, so he will have the floor now.

Oppermann:**

Thank you, Mr. *Chairman*. As I am — partly at least — addressing Mr. *Usenko*, and as Mr. *Hilf* knows the German language, I take the liberty of speaking in German.

Both papers were definitely enriching, and for us on the German side especially that by Mr. *Usenko*. This does not mean any criticism of yours, Mr. *Hilf*, but as all of us in Germany are more or less permanently engaged in European Law, you had to give us a lecture on basic structures of things we are familiar with. However, I found it very interesting to witness once more your special statement on European Law, which I fully sympathize with. We bear, of course, in mind that Mr. *Hilf* was working for some time in Brussels, the Capital of Europe. There he fully absorbed the spirit of Europe whereas the rest of us who stayed in the home countries, and sometimes we have trouble "living up to that spirit". On the whole, however, I fully agree with you.

I just want to work out one point of principle which illuminates the common and different character of both papers. Mr. *Usenko*, you correctly noted it at the very beginning, the same definitions were used here: "supra-national", or, in the Law of CMEA: "social economic integration"; "integration", "supra-national" — the same words, and yet, with very different backgrounds and contents. First of all, we should — just for the record — state that, for us, in the EEC this European Community Law, neither with regard to regulations, nor, partly, with regard to directives, no longer means international law in this direct transformation. Nor is it public law, constitutional law, intra-state law, municipal law; it is something "between" all that. The European

* *Editors'* note: The discussion has partly taken place in German and was translated subsequently, which is thus not a verbatim record. The relevant statements are indicated where appropriate.

** *Editors'* note: The contribution was made in German and translated subsequently by the participant.

Community Law has, of course, its aspects of international law. You have mentioned the commercial contracts by which the EEC makes agreements of international law with third countries. However, on the whole, in German and French universities we give lectures on "European Law", which is a different lecture to the one on international law. Neither does European Law belong to the lecture on international organizations. Here, too, the interrelated character becomes visible, which is especially reflected in the "supra-national" character of the Community Law. This supra-nationality is not a single factor, but a combination of different characteristic features, which constitute the special "mixture" of supra-national European Law. You mentioned the "transfer of power", and the direct applicability of the Community Law by the Member States. We could also add the special nature of Community financing, *i. e.* by its own income. For each of these elements we can always find an example which has its counterpart elsewhere — even the International Monetary Fund is self-financed; the Commission of Navigation on the Danube had already in former times international norms for direct application at hand, *etc.* However, the accumulation, the combination of different elements in one single organization forms the supra-national element. *Vice versa*, I had the impression — but I will give this back to you as a question, Mr. *Usenko* — that, after all, the Law of the CMEA is dealt with by the law of international organizations, if I now look at it scholarly — with a certain particularity of this compact mass of norms of the Council Law, as you have described it concerning the recommendations of the CMEA. Sometimes, I had the impression that a slight breeze of supra-nationality, in our sense, was already blowing through the CMEA. But it was no more than a very delicate spring breeze. If I am not mistaken, the law of the CMEA is in its core, after all, international law, although a specific part. Indeed, also from our perspective there is agreement that the EEC is no State, no federal State. The term "Community" has not become existent by chance, which obviously summarizes this stronger density of organization, this density of law. The European Community is situated somewhere between the State on the one hand, and the classical international organization on the other. We could recognize very easily from the two excellent papers that, on the contrary, the law of the CMEA has probably not yet been accepted as "emancipated" so far by its Member States: The same definitions, and yet, very different contents! Thank you very much.

Tunkin:

Either to Mr. *Hilf* or Mr. *Oppermann*: Is there a generally accepted opinion with regard to the European Community, that it is not an international organization? Is the so-called Law of the European Communities international law? Rather, I put it like this: The Law of the European Communities is not international law and it is not national law, of course, it is something in between, a new type of law. Is this the generally accepted opinion?

Randelzhofer, Chairman:

It is not the commonly shared view, it is the prevailing view, especially of the international legal scholars dedicated to European law. My very personal view is, it is still public international law, but public international law of a special type. It is possible, as the European Communities demonstrate, to develop public international law to a very high level and, in my opinion, the European Community law is such public international law on a very high level. But most of my colleagues specialized on European Community law concentrate on the idea that it is something in between. For example, the decision of the Federal Constitutional Court mentioned by Mr. *Hilf*, the so-called *Solange II*, is much in favour of the superiority. The immediate applicability of European Community law is reviewed basically in an affirmative way by our *grand seigneur* of European Community law, *Hans Peter Ipsen*. But he could not resist blaming the Court for — in a very gentle way, I must admit — that it had used in one term the phrase that in the way of incorporating European Community law you have to root too, not only, but too, on the interpretation of public international law. *Ipsen* says, that this is the one and single fault of the decision, because nothing of European Community law has anything to do with public international law. That is one position. It is not mine, and not everybody's.

Oppermann:

I should say it is a prevailing view that it is something else, but again you have to differentiate. Of course, it says the European Community is an international organization as well, as far as outside relations are concerned. I mean there is much of public international law, the treaty-making powers of the Community, and so on. But in internal affairs, the European Community is dealing with so many matters, and in a way which is no longer pure public international law; if you see the effect, for instance, of the EC Law for the immigration of workers from one community country to the other and so on. But Mr. *Hilf* is still a little bit more European than I, and therefore he may interpret this best.

Lukashuk:

First of all, I want to stress, it was a pleasure to listen to Mr. *Hilf*'s lecture. It was really highly talented, and a "European Symphony". The day for Mr. *Hilf*'s report should have been the 5th of May — the European-day.

I want to ask some questions first. One of the differences between federation and confederation is, that a federation has direct power over citizens. In this case it is not a federation, it is not a confederation, still it has direct power in some respect. We very often forget that the European Community is an economic community and the subject matter of co-operation is the economy, but not policy in general. This is the economy of some community. Further, you said that there is no need for transformation of many acts of the Community. Maybe there is some general municipal rule, written or unwritten, about general transformation that such and such acts of the Community must be observed by a municipal legal order. It is municipal custom. I would like if you could answer this question.

*Schweisfurth:**

You have dealt with the law-generating activities of the CMEA in such a comprehensive manner that I would neither like to add something nor criticize anything of your paper. I will only refer to your introductory remarks where you placed the capitalist integration to the socialist integration in a somehow antithetic manner, and where you pointed especially to the different mechanisms of law-making. I believe that such an antithetic conception of both integrations is not quite correct, if we look at the CMEA historically. Mr. *Oppermann* just said that we are used to look only at the European Communities and that we do not see what happens elsewhere. This is true also for the temporal dimension. Sometimes I have the impression that we look at international organizations as they exist in the moment, but not at how they came into being. You certainly know that in our press we often read that the CMEA is "the EC of the East". This is already historically not the case, because the CMEA's origin is as early as 1949, when it was founded as an organization being a counterpart to the OEEC, that is, as a counter-measure to the *Marshall* Plan. And the CMEA . . .

*Usenko:**

Well, I did not say that . . .

*Schweisfurth:**

Of course, you have not said so. I only want to recollect this. In essence the main principle of the CMEA, which you have mentioned,

* *Editors'* note: The contribution was made in German and translated subsequently by the participant.

namely the principle of being interested, has been taken from the mechanism of the OECD, from its regulations. If you look at the Statute of the OEEC of 1948 you will find there just this principle, and the OEEC was certainly a pure "capitalist" organization. I think therefore, looking at this origin, you can find the "principle of interested States" in international organizations of States with market economies, as well as in those the members of which are States with state-planned economies. And if we then proceed in the history of the CMEA we suddenly meet the notion "socialist integration". You know, that this notion was not used by the CMEA countries originally. It was not until 1971 that this notion appeared in an official document of the CMEA, namely in the Complex-Programme. Since that time the term "socialist economic integration" is officially used. Since then, we may ask ourselves what "integration" designates, in the Eastern and what in the Western part of Europe.

When the CMEA continues to cling to the principle of consent of all only "interested" States, indeed the reason may be pertaining to the nature of the States' systems. The reason is the state-planned economies, or — more precisely — the ranking of the national jurisdiction in matters of economic planning. The economic planning is regarded as one of the most important functions of the State and therefore as an indispensable attribute of State sovereignty. Questions of economic planning, therefore, shall not be excluded from domestic jurisdiction. The Complex-Programme knows only "common planning" of certain industrial branches by "interested" member States. But if the CMEA would gain supranational functions then it might become possible, in the course of further development of the CMEA, that matters of economic planning may leave the realm of domestic jurisdiction. In order to prevent this from the very beginnings, the member States of the CMEA, I believe, stick to this mechanism of the "principle of interested States" which, as I said, originates from the regulations of the OEEC.

*Danilenko:**

I have one question to Mr. *Usenko*. Recently, at the highest political level an understanding was reached that the socialist countries should promote closer co-operation, especially in the framework at the CMEA. Are there any plans to alter or to modify the existing process of decision-making? Could the Socialist countries achieve the proclaimed political goals without any change in this area?

---

* *Editors'* note: The contribution was made in German and translated subsequently by the participant.

Simma:

First, I want to make a remark relating to Mr. *Tunkin*'s question. I think that also with regard to the question which you put, namely the relationship between Community Law and international law, or the nature of Community Law as a particular system of international law, or rather a something "in-between", there has been a shifting of the attention away from very theoretical discussions. You know the old-fashioned internationalists trying to force Community Law into the *Procrustes*' bed of international law and, on the other side, authors like *Hans Peter Ipsen*, who did not want Community Law to have anything to do with the — according to their view — rather sick and slow-working system of international law. As I said, we are observing a shift away from that to more pertinent and more pragmatic questions, and I want to mention only one, namely the question: Under what circumstances, at which point, public international law principles and rules could come into play if certain community procedures are exhausted? For example, we have had cases in the European Community where two court actions, according to Articles 169 or 170 EEC Treaty, against Treaty breaches by Member States took place before the problem was solved. Here, of course, the question arises whether, after all Community procedures have been exhausted, rules of general international law would become applicable in the relations between Member States, for instance, rules on retortion or reprisal.

My second question* goes to Mr. *Usenko:* You have stated at the outset that, even though COMECON is working with much more modest juridical means compared to the EEC, the effectiveness of the law of COMECON comes close to that of European Community Law. The terminology which you have used sounded as if you wanted to equate the EEC with the "allopathic" method of integration, while COMECON follows a rather "homeopathic" course. Now my question: What are the factual, the sociological reasons for such high effectiveness of COMECON law, despite its "soft" legal methods?

*Klein:***

I also would like to put a question to Mr. *Usenko*. You have discussed the problem of those treaties *sui generis* which generate from a recommendation of the Council, after the governments of the member States have agreed. But what is about modification and termination of such treaties? Does this happen exclusively, at least in practice, by the

---

* *Editors'* note: This part of the contribution was made in German and translated by the participant subsequently.

** *Editors'* note: The contribution was made in German and translated subsequently by the participant.

repetition of the same procedure by which the treaties are made; what would mean that the Council has to recommend it and the member States have to consent to this resolution?

*Usenko:**

I would like to make some closing remarks. If I have some time left, then I would also like to comment on the legal nature of the EEC law. Yes, I stated that the effectiveness of the CMEA and EEC acts might be the same. I tried to substitute this proposition. Mr. *Hilf* asked how it is possible to achieve with less complicated methods the same results. I would not agree that the methods of the CMEA are less complicated. These methods may even be more complicated than the methods employed by the EEC. Because our integration is based on the "principle of sovereignty of States", we have to apply those complicated but successful methods.

Mr. *Schweisfurth*, I did not say that the CMEA was established as a counterbalance to the EEC. In reality, the CMEA was established as an economic security organization to counteract the discrimination on the part of some States back in 1949. That was the first goal of the organization. With the passage of time, however, this goal was losing in importance and the need to create an independent organization for the integration of the socialist countries was more urgently felt. Factual integration began even prior to 1970, when the special programme for the integration of the CMEA States was formally adopted. This process was adequately described in the socialist doctrine. To summerize, as a process, the socialist integration has started much earlier.

I would not agree that acts of the CMEA create only treaty relations that are governed by treaty law. The Vienna Convention on the Law of Treaties stipulates that its provisions do not apply to special rules created by international organizations. I have stressed this point in my presentation. The *sui generis* treaties established by the CMEA acts have strong ties with the CMEA organization. For instance, they cannot be modified by participating States. Such a modification should be accomplished through the CMEA machinery. The major point, however, is that CMEA acts are based on the consent of the interested States and that these acts have the same binding force as other international treaties. There are some CMEA instruments that stipulate directly that the adopted recommendations have the same force as international treaties.

As to the question of Mr. *Danilenko*, I would like to say that the promotion of the effectiveness of the CMEA is one of the main problems

* *Editors'* note: The contribution was made in German and translated subsequently by the participant.

discussed at this stage. All members of the organization are called upon to submit specific proposals that will be discussed, I think, during the Council's meeting in July of 1987. The Soviet Union also prepares some proposals. As far as I know, there are proposals to alter some CMEA structures. Whether the suggestions of this kind will be adopted is not clear yet. At least the aim was proclaimed to streamline the structure, so as to make it more effective. It is possible that to this end even some alterations in the Charter of the CMEA will have to be approved. I am, however, quite sure that the "principle of interested States" will remain.

As to the legal nature of the EEC acts, I agree with Mr. *Oppermann*. This is a complicated question, of course. A part of what is called EEC law is undoubtedly international law: the Treaty of Rome and some other treaties. It is difficult to define the nature of the internal EEC law that is created by the supra-national organs. I think that we have to see the difference between the principles of the EEC and the practice. According to the principles, the supra-national organs should, in the first place, take into account not the interest of the Member States, but that of the organization. However, in practice even acts that, from the legal point of view, are supra-national have to take into account the interest of the Member States. Because the interests of the Member States are taken into account, from the factual point of view, the EEC law can be defined as a special kind of international law. I agree with Mr. *Oppermann* that this law is not international law, nor is it municipal law. It lies between those two forms of law. Where would this special kind of law lead to? To the law of a federation, or to international law? As yet it is difficult to answer this question. Thank you.

Randelzhofer, Chairman:*

I thank you very much for this closing statement, Mr. *Usenko*, by which you were examining once again our issues in an extraordinarily well-balanced way. Now, prior to Mr. *Hilf*'s closing word, Mr. *Simma* wants to have the opportunity to add a short explaining remark to his question.

*Simma:**

Mr. *Usenko*, when I asked you why the law of COMECON, in spite of its "modesty", reached the same degree of effectiveness as EEC law, I intended to apply the word "modest" not in the sense of "primitive" or "unsophisticated", but in the sense of more indulgent to State sovereignty than EEC law.

* *Editors'* note: The contribution was made in German and translated subsequently by the participant.

*Usenko:**

Yes, that was also my understanding.

*Hilf:**

Thank you very much, Mr. *Lukashuk*, for your kind comments. You considered my contribution to be a "European Symphony". I do not know whether my contribution would have been welcomed in genuine European circles in Brussels. I think I have underlined that one hardly can speak of an autonomy of the law of the EC. The law of the EC still is linked to the legal orders of the Member States. There is a reciprocal interdependence between the legal order of the EC and those of its Member States.

In my presentation, I think, there are further notes which would not fit into the "European Symphony". One is the assumption of a right to leave the Community if it "runs wild" in the field of human rights. Another is the restrictive interpretation of the EEC Treaty concerning the status of directives. The Commission of the EC, before the Court of Justice of the European Communities, has taken a different approach. Then there may be more elements in my contribution which may not add to the harmony of an "European Symphony".

As Mr. *Lukashuk* indicated, an interesting issue will remain — the definition of the legal structure of the Community. Of course, it is possible to define the Community Treaties as treaties under public international law, or to define the Community an "economic federation". But both definitions are rather defective and do not describe the reality of the Community. The notion "Community Law" will indicate that there are many legal characteristics which are distinct from general public international law. Mr. *Oppermann* has referred to these various distinctions.

Even the notion "economic federation" seems to be defective. The notion "federation", at least in legal theory, has a connotation which comes close to the notion "federal State". The Community is not a federal State. It lacks the power to define its own territory and to define the citizenship of the individuals. Above all, the Community has not the power to define its competences.

Even the notion "economic" federation seems to be misleading. The activity of the Community is transgressing the economic sector and is, by necessity, involving common measures in other sensitive areas, such as the foreign policy of the Member States. A number of questions in

* *Editors'* note: The contribution was made in German and translated subsequently by the participant.

the field of cultural policy cannot be separated from the operation of the Common Market.

Another difference is the "transformation" of Community Law. It is correct to state that the Member States of the Community have, by giving their consent to the Founding Treaties, anticipated a general transformation of any future law of the Community. But apart from this anticipated transformation, Community Law is directly applicable in the Member States without any interference of the national legislator. There are only two exceptions. Any treaty amending the Founding Treaties will have to be transformed. And in the case of Community directives, the Member States have the choice of form and methods in which they are going to achieve the general aims of the directives. Consequently, the Court of Justice of the European Communities has to decide exclusively on the application and interpretation of Community Law. The Court follows its own rules of interpretation, neither national rules, nor rules under public international law are applicable. These are some elements which may indicate that one may not speak of "transformation" of Community Law.

Mr. *Simma* has mentioned the possibility to take recourse to the instruments of retorsion and reprisal under general public international law if the Community begins to operate outside its powers. I hesitate to adhere to this general statement. The Community Treaties have to be respected. They offer a broad range of means to overcome difficulties and to settle disputes which concern the limits of the Community's competences. In addition, one should discuss the possibility of applying general principles of Community Law which may give specific answers to the question how to overcome major difficulties within the Community.

I would like to add a number of questions to the parallel report of Mr. *Usenko*. What happens if a member State of the COMECON has failed to fulfil its obligations under the common Treaty? What are the mechanisms to control the fulfilment of obligations? Is there any procedure which guarantees a uniform interpretation and application of the common rules? Are member States allowed to depart unilaterally from the commonly agreed rules? But I am afraid, Mr. *Chairman*, that at this stage of the discussion, you will not allow these or even further questions. Thank you.

*Usenko:**

There is a mechanism of control. I certainly could give a brief answer to all your questions.

---

* *Editors'* note: The contribution was made in German and has been translated subsequently.

*Randelzhofer, Chairman:**

Also many thanks to you, Mr. *Hilf*. It appears that it is good if one has been in Brussels, but yet to look at things from a certain distance, one then comes to convincing results. I may express my thanks to both speakers as well as to all participants in the discussion and now, I can return my office to the Heads of Delegations.

Wolfrum:

I will not venture to summarize the discussions we have had over the days. I believe that we found much more common ground in discussing the impact of public international law on municipal law than we anticipated. This is definitely true for the first day, when we dealt with customary law and the relevance of resolutions and declarations, especially of the United Nations. I will leave it to every participant to judge the result of the seminar. You may judge it right now, or you may wait until you hold the publication in your hands.

Before I close and give the floor to Mr. *Tunkin*, let me say — also on behalf of Mr. *Bernhardt*, and the Institute — thank you to all the speakers and to all those, who have taken part in the discussions. Let me equally thank the members of the Institute for all their help and engagement. Thank you very much for coming and for your very constructive participation.

Tunkin:

Dear colleagues, in the name of the Soviet participants at this Colloquy, I would like to thank first of all the organizers of the Colloquy, Mr. *Wolfrum* and Mr. *Bernhardt*, and their staff — for an excellent organization and for an excellent hospitality accorded to us. I would also like to thank all the rapporteurs for their scholarly presentation of the various subjects we had on our agenda. Thank you and we will wait for you in Moscow in due time.

---

* *Editors'* note: The contribution was made in German and translated subsequently.

Annex

Treaties and Municipal Law: With Special Reference to Treaties on Private International Law

By R. A. Müllerson*

Every legal norm is a part of a larger legal entity: institution of law, branch of law, *etc.* Together these entities constitute a legal system. But one may wonder, whether these legal systems are not, in their turn, parts of a still larger legal entity and consequently whether all municipal legal systems and international law are not parts of one whole system, as was suggested by *Hans Kelsen*. Also, the rules of international law may be obligatory for a certain State and the municipal law of this State would thus merely be a component of one and the same legal system, as considered by other representatives of monistic doctrine.

In order to answer this question it is necessary to clarify what factors determine the formation and existence of independent legal systems. As *Kelsen* himself has rightly pointed out:

> In order to answer the question whether international and national law are different and mutually independent legal orders, or from one universal normative system, in order to reach a decision between pluralism and monism, we have to consider the general problem of what makes a norm belong to a definite legal order, what is the reason that several norms form one and the same normative system.[1]

A legal system always functions within the framework of a particular society, regulates social relations within this society. The interrelation between a municipal legal system and the State is manifested, firstly, by the fact that all legal rules, institutions, and branches express the will of the dominating classes of that society. Thus, the existence of separate municipal legal systems is the consequence of the existence of independent States. Every municipal legal order is a sub-system of society organized as a State.

Interactions between States form an international structure, within which international law functions.[2] One of the peculiarities of the inter-

---

* Doctor of Law, Head of the Department of General Problems of International Law, Institute of State and Law of the Academy of Sciences of the USSR.

[1] *Hans Kelsen*, General Theory of Law and State, New York 1961, 366.

[2] *Grigory Tunkin*, International Law in the International System, in: Recueil des Cours (1975/IV), 1—218 (59).

national system consists of the fact that it is not the result of the merging of independent, sovereign States. The international system is the result of interactions between States as integral sovereign entities. That is, why (1) States as elements of the international system do not dissolve in it; (2) the internal structures and processes maintain their independence with reference to the international system, and as such they are outside of it; (3) they form an environment of the international system and interact with it through the State as a whole. According to *Grigory Tunkin:* "it is of paramount importance to keep constantly in mind that the main components of the international system — States — exist above all outside this system. This fact makes the relations between the international system and its environment quite specific"[3].

Therefore international law, like municipal legal systems, has its specific sphere of functioning. International law constitutes a part and parcel of the international system, as its sources lie in the international system (interacting States not only form the international system, but also co-ordinate their wills creating thereby international law) and it operates within the framework of this social system.

The fact that every legal system is performing within a definite social system causes that specific hierarchical ties appear only between different parts of that legal system. Validity of rules of a given legal order is determined only by dispositions of this legal system. Thus, an international treaty concluded in violation of rules of municipal law is found invalid, according to the rules of international law, but not of those of municipal law (for example, for the State Parties to the Vienna Convention on the Law of Treaties of 1969 such a rule is enshrined in Article 46 of that Convention). The validity of rules of municipal law, moreover, does not directly depend on their conformity with the rules of municipal law of another State nor on rules of international law. Certainly, municipal law of some States recognizes stipulations according to which domestic rules are not applied if they contradict to the rules of international law on the subject. But again, their invalidity is determined by such rules of municipal law which specify that rules of municipal law contradicting international law are invalid. Hence, every municipal legal order as well as international law are independent legal systems, because they are regulative sub-systems of different social systems (different societies organized as States, or the international system, which in turn is the product of interaction of such societies).

So far we have analysed only one of the aspects of the relationship between international and municipal legal systems which may be called a static one. Such analysis reveals that all of them are different, inde-

[3] *Op. cit.*, 60.

pendent legal systems functioning within different larger social systems. But these larger systems are not isolated from each other, their independence is relative. They interact, and this interaction calls into being an interaction between corresponding legal systems.

It is necessary to give more detailed pictures illustrating our thesis that an interaction between international law and municipal law is a result of an interaction between the international system and internal social systems of States. From this conclusion three more reasons will be given for the interaction of international law and municipal legal systems.

A State as an element of the international system functions within this system as a whole, but it can act only through its organs and officials whose competence and activities are regulated by municipal law rules. So, the Law on Procedures for Conclusion, Execution, and Denunciation of International Treaties of the USSR of 1978 (Article 21) stipulates that "Ministries, State Committees, and Governmental Agencies of the USSR, Councils of Ministers of Union Republics, and other State organs charged with questions regulated in the treaties concluded by the USSR ensure the implementation of obligations assumed by the USSR". Hence every international treaty in force for the Soviet Union as a whole, after its coming into force on an international level, will become obligatory for specific State organs. If we, so to say, consider a rule of international law as a signal adressed to a State as a whole, this signal is always received by specified State organs and officials whose obligation to receive such signals is determined by rules of municipal law or by internal practice of the State.

The same situation appears when a rule of international law is being created. States being subjects of international law are also its creators. Municipal law, fixing the State structure and establishing competences of State organs, determines their rights and obligations in the matter of conclusion of international treaties. So it is the constitution of a State that stipulates what organ of the State is competent to ratify treaties, the necessity for an approval by Parliament, *etc.*

Therefore, the first reason for an interaction between international law and municipal law can be formulated as follws: As in international law a State is considered an integral entity, without any reference to its complicated internal structures and processes, municipal law — determining these structures and regulating these processes — ensures the functioning of a State as an element of the international system, and in that way it ensures the functioning of international law.

There is another reason causing the necessity for an interaction between international law and municipal law. Very often international law contains rules not aimed at the regulation of relations between

States, but that of relations between individuals or juridical persons which are not subjects of international law. On the other hand, municipal law provides rules regulating activities of a State in its international relations, and actual implementation of such rules is effectuated in the domain of international law. So, Article (Art.) 29 of the Soviet Constitution of 1977 embodies principles of Soviet foreign policy. These principles are obligatory for State organs of the Soviet Union representing the USSR in international relations. As activities of such organs are carried out within the international system, there is an obvious interaction between these constitutional principles of foreign policy and principles of international law.

Then one may wonder why international law, functioning within the international system, contains rules aimed at the regulation of social relations remaining outside of the international system.

Firstly, it happens, because sometimes internal social relations, their condition or trends of development, influence inter-state relations to such a degree that States find it necessary to conclude international agreements limiting their capability to regulate such relations individually. For example, one of the principal reasons why States co-operate in the field of protection of human rights is the fact that flagrant violations of human rights inside a country are, as a rule, accompanied by aggressive foreign policy. Measures taken for environmental protection in one State can often produce their desired effect only when accompanied by analogous measures in other countries. This provides a necessity for an inter-state co-operation in the field of environmental protection, not merely within the frontiers of the so-called international territories, *e. g.* on the high seas, but also within State boundaries. Here, too, an interaction between international and municipal law is inevitable.

Secondly, some rules of international law are aimed at the regulation of relations with the participation of individuals or juridical persons, because such relations often cross over State boundaries. They are international by their nature. But they are not incorporated into the international inter-state system. In our opinion, social relations going beyond State boundaries while not being strictly inter-state may be defined as trans-national relations, *i. e.*, relations passing State boundaries "when at least one actor is not agent of a government or an intergovernmental organization"[4].

There are various types of relations between individuals or juridical persons from various States, relations between a State and foreign citizens, or a firm, *etc.* From the juridical point of view, it is, that in

[4] *Robert O. Keohane / Joseph S. Nye* (eds.), Preface, Transnational Relations and World Politics, Cambridge, Mass. 1972, XII.

some of these relations a State participates in its authoritative capacity. This kind of trans-national relations is regulated by municipal law of the State, such relations being characterized as constitutional, administrative, procedural, and as other legal relations usually referred to as public law relations in most western States.

The second important group of trans-national relations are relations between individuals or juridical persons from different countries arising in connection with property or corresponding personal relations, *i. e.* trans-national relations of non-authoritative nature. If a State is a party to such relations it acts not in its authoritative capacity.

*

Traditionally, trans-national relations of a non-authoritative nature are regulated by norms of different municipal legal systems. But, as they do not fall within an exclusive jurisdiction of a State, as they do not have their "proper" legal system, a problem of conflict of laws emerges. Under the "proper" legal system in that case I mean that the source of validity and origin of norms, on the one hand, and social relations which are regulated by them, on the other, are the parts of the one and the same larger social system. For example, through interacting with each other, States form an international (inter-state) system. Here, by means of co-ordination of their wills they create norms of international law. Hence, sources of validity and origin of norms of a given municipal legal system, on the one hand, and social relations, which they regulate, on the other, are parts of one and the same society organized as a State. The social nature of legal norms corresponds to the character of relations regulated by them. Socialist norms govern socialist economic, political, *etc.*, relations; bourgeois norms govern bourgeois social relations. The character of relations within the contemporary international system corresponds to the general democratic nature of norms of contemporary general international law.

Substantive legal norms do not regulate trans-national relations of a non-authoritative nature directly, they are applied only when a conflict of laws rule indicates them. *Pierre Mayer* writes:

> Even in the case when an internal law of the country of the court contains a substantive rule specifically created to regulate international relations (international relations of a non-authoritative nature) it is applied only if a conflict of laws rule indicates it.[5]

Recently States have begun more and more frequently to conclude international treaties not to regulate relations between its creators, *i. e.* between States themselves. For example, they create norms which directly establish rights of and duties for different organs of inter-

---

[5] *Pierre Mayer*, Droit international privé, Paris 1977, 16.

national organizations, or international civil servants. By means of co-ordination of wills, States also can regulate and do regulate relations to which international non-governmental organizations or international private organizations are parties to. They can as well through co-ordination of their wills create rules, directed at the regulation of international relations of non-authoritative nature. For example, the Agreement on International Passenger Communication, concluded between Socialist countries of Europe, in its Art. 2 says: "This Agreement is obligatory for railways, passengers of sea-going steamship lines, senders and recipients of goods"[6]. There are a lot of treaties of that kind. An author from West Germany, *Ferenc Majoros*, writes: "there are hundreds of multi-lateral treaties, which contain only norms of private international law. There are also many such rules in treaties of political and economic character. There are thousands of bi-lateral treaties on private law"[7].

Treaties on private international law (it would be more correct to speak of norms of private international law in international treaties, because such treaties may contain not only norms of private international law) are complex by their nature. According to their source of origin and validity, they belong to norms of public international law. *Majoros* is right, stating that "international treaties on private international law are part of public international law"[8]. The method of their conclusion is no different from that of international treaties on disarmament or treaties of alliance. Furthermore, they come under the effect of the Articles of the Vienna Convention on the Law of Treaties of 1969 concerning the conclusion, validity, termination, and suspension of treaties. But as to their content and destinators, they differ from other norms of international law. They are specially designed to regulate international relations of a non-authoritative nature. This fact determines their specific character as norms of private law. They form the norms of private international law, which have crystallized in the boiler of inter-state relations, but which are designed to regulate relations between private persons. They are inter-state (public) by origin and by the method of creation. But in regulating relations of a non-authoritative nature, they are private by the objective of regulation.

That is, why one can say that, like municipal legal rules regulate relations crossing over State boundaries, there are norms of international law which function outside the international system, *i. e.* regulate

---

[6] Multilateral Economic Co-operation of Socialist States (in Russian), Moscow 1972, 449.

[7] *Ferenc Majoros*, Les conventions internationales en matière de droit privé, abrégé théorique et traité pratique, I, Paris 1976, 67.

[8] *Op. cit.*, 85.

international relations of non-authoritative nature. Such a situation is due to the fact, as I have already mentioned, that, unlike inter-state relations or relations within a State, these relations have not their "proper" law. In a sense we can call it a "borrowed" regulation.

*

There are authors considering private international law only as part of municipal legal system, who hold that private law norms in international treaties become a part of private international law only after their transformation into norms of municipal law.[9]

This opinion seems to me somewhat artificial. Such norms are specially designed to regulate international relations of non-authoritative nature. Their transformation into a municipal legal system would distort their content, their meaning. And a problem of conflict of laws would arise: because norms of different national legal systems, though transformed from one and the same treaty, would begin to conflict with each other.

Furthermore, the practice of the USSR and especially of such countries as France, Belgium, The Netherlands, and many other States demonstrates that courts and arbitration tribunals very often decide cases by applying norms of international law. The civil law chamber of the Moscow City Court, for instance in its judgment of November 26th, 1977, stipulated that, "according to section I of Art. 23 of the Agreement on International Communications", a railway is liable. There are hundreds of judgments of Soviet courts where treaties on private international law have been applied. The analysis of an application of international treaties by French courts shows, that courts apply, as a rule, treaties on private international law.[10] The practice of Belgian courts is analogous.[11]

But is it possible, in this case, to speak of the direct, immediate, application of rules of international law to the regulation of international relations of a non-authoritative nature? I think, it is not. The parties of international relations of non-authoritative nature are subjects of different municipal legal systems, *i. e.* citizens or juridical persons of different States. It is for the States, by means of their legal norms, to decide what rules should regulate the behaviour of their citizens or juridical persons. They can, of course, stipulate that in certain cases the

---

[9] For example, *Lasar' Adolfovič Lunz*, Course of Private International Law, General Part (in Russian), Moscow 1963, 66.

[10] *See*, for example, *Jean-François Lachaume*, Jurisprudence française relative au droit international (Année 1979), in: Annuaire Français de droit International 26 (1980), 809—869 (819).

[11] *See*, for example, *Joe Verhoeven*, Jurisprudence Belge relative au Droit international, in: Revue Belge de Droit International 16 (1981/1982), 265—329 (277—281).

behaviour of those addressees is regulated by rules of international law, or even by norms of municipal law of a foreign State. And States rather often do so. For example, Art. 55 of the Constitution of France says: "Treaties and agreements ratified and approved, have legal force superior to that of internal laws form the moment of their publication, provided, that every treaty or agreement is applied by the other party". Art. 129 of the Basic Principles of Civil Legislation of the USSR also promulgates that in the case of controversy between rules of an international treaty and international legislation the former will prevail: We can find in municipal legal systems a lot of norms which refer to the rules of international law, *i. e.* rules of *renvoi*. These rules sanction an application of norms of international law for the regulation of relations between individuals or juridical persons. That is, why it is not correct to speak of immediate or direct regulation by norms of international law or international relations of non-authoritative nature. International law does regulate these relations, but does so through the instruments of municipal law.

But on the other hand, it is not possible to say, that because of State sovereignty, (1) only internal legal norms of a given State can function within a sphere of jurisdiction of that State and (2) those rules only regulate the behaviour of its citizens and juridical persons. Such a statement, to my mind, would even be tantamount to a restriction of the sovereignty of a State. Every State is sovereign as to provide for an application of norms of international law concerning its citizens or juridical persons.

*

Not only norms of international law directed at the regulation of international relations of a non-authoritative nature, but also municipal law rules — when the question is that of regulating this group of social relations — do not function directly. A court or an arbitration tribunal applies foreign substantive norms when there is the doctrine of *renvoi* in its rules on conflict of laws. Such institutions for settlement also apply internal legal norms of substantive character of their State only in the case, when there is *renvoi* in their conflict of laws rules. The latter rules and a norm referring to international law have much in common. They themselves do not regulate social relations, but indicate what norms should be applied. With the help of these norms, it becomes possible for a court of the State to apply "foreign" legal norms. And finally, both of them are typical for the regulation of international relations of non-authoritative nature.

Such an indirect method or method of *renvoi* is characteristic of the regulation of these social relations. That is why, in my opinion, it is not precise to say that in private international law there are two methods that should be applied: the method of conflict of laws and the method of direct regulation by substantive norms. We can rather speak of a conflict of laws method and *renvoi* to international law method. The dual character of international relations of a non-authoritative nature (on the one hand, they are international relations and do not fall under the exclusive jurisdiction of any State, on the other hand, parties of these relations are subject to municipal legal rules, submitted to the jurisdiction of different States) predetermines such an indirect method of regulation.

Consequently, international relations of a non-authoritative nature constitute a specific domain of legal regulation — though these relations do not form an integral system as inter-state relations or relations within a State do —, they do not have a single source of norms which regulate them. At the same time, here we can find a specific method of application of the norms which govern these relations — an indirect one, conflict of laws, or *renvoi* to the international law method.

As norms which regulate international relations of a non-authoritative nature are part and parcel of some municipal legal system, it is possible to say that every municipal legal system has its own private international law. Furthermore, the system of public international law also has its specific sub-system, *i. e.* private international law which contains rules specially designed for regulation of international relations of a non-authoritative nature. I think that the fact that *public* international law contains a part which is private, in the sense that it regulates relations of a non-authoritative nature, is not more surprising than the fact that *municipal* legal systems contain *private* international law rules, in the sense that they regulate a specific group of international relations.

For this reason, a homogeneous group of social relations is regulated by norms of different legal systems. That is, why these norms do not form an integral legal order as international or municipal legal systems do. But on the other hand, these norms are closely connected and have a single object of regulation, they are characterized by a specific method of regulation — the indirect one. Norms of different legal systems interact while regulating international relations of a non-authoritative nature by means of rules of conflict of laws or norms of *renvoi*. Such interaction is not an accidental one, but is necessary to regulate this group ot social relations. These norms of different legal orders have much in common, they use identical terms *etc.* Without their interaction, it is impossible to regulate these relations. Again these "blocks" interact by means of norms of conflict of laws or rules of *renvoi*.

Thus we can define private international law as a poly-systematic normative complex consisting of relatively independent "blocks"; that is to say, sets of norms, which do not form any integral system and remain parts of their respective legal order (the different municipal legal system and the system of public international law). At the same time, however, they interact when regulating international relations of a non-authoritative nature.

This we should bear in mind while defining a relationship between public and private international law. One part of private international law relates to public international law as a part relates to the whole. It is private international law as sub-system of public international law. These norms are "public" according to the method of their creation; they are "private" as to the legal relations which they regulate. The relationship between public international law and other parts of private international law constitutes a specific aspect of relationship between international law and different municipal legal systems. As the practice of different States indicates, it is exactly in the domain of the legal regulation of trans-national relations of non-authoritative character where the interaction between norms of international treaties and rules of municipal law is most intensive. When domestic courts or arbitration tribunals apply norms of international law, these are mainly norms of treaties on private international law. Therefore, international treaties which are concerned with the regulation of transnational relations of non-authoritative nature are widely applied by municipal courts and in arbitrations. It is not necessary to transform these treaty norms into municipal law.

Treaty rules, which regulate international relations of a non-authoritative nature, can function without coming into conflict with rules of municipal law regulating analogously internal relations of State parties. For example, spheres of functioning of a treaty regulating the delivery of goods between companies or enterprises from different socialist States, General Conditions of Delivery of Goods of the CMEA, and that of municipal legal acts (in the USSR there are two corresponding decrees), which regulate deliveries inside a country, do not coincide. Treaty norms coordinate deliveries crossing over State boundaries. Norms of internal acts regulate deliveries of goods inside the Soviet Union. Their relationship is a relationship of *lex specialis* and *lex generalis*. But this is not the case when one is concerned with treaties which are aimed at the regulation of internal relations of States, for example, in the domain of human rights.

Norms of treaty, developed for the protection of human rights in the case of a State sanctioning their application inside the country, and the norms of the constitution, or other municipal rules regulate the same social relations. This is why their simultaneous application is not possible.

In that case, to my mind, the integrety of the legal system of the State would be in question. Therefore, an enactment of new internal rules, an amendment in change or revocation of existing ones, is a more expedient way of implementation of treaties on human rights or other internal questions (for example, on environmental protection).

There is one more reason for such a conclusion. Norms of treaties on human rights, as a rule, are no concrete rules ready to apply for the regulation of these rights. They are rather frameworks within which States themselves have to regulate corresponding social relations by means of their internal rules. So, in the House of Lords of the Parliament of Great Britain a representative of the Government of the United Kingdom said about the 1951 Convention on Refugees and the corresponding 1967 Protocol: "the language of international agreements, which is designed to cover countries with widely differing legal and administrative systems, is rarely suitable for direct incorporation into United Kingdom law"[12].

That is, why stipulations of treaties on human rights in States declaring international treaties to be part of the law of the land, or even superseding it, are not, as a rule, applied as being self-executing. Hence, the most expedient way of implementation of treaties on human rights is an adoption of necessary internal rules, the amendment or replacement of existing ones.

[12] *Geoffrey Marston* (ed.), United Kingdom Materials on International Law, in: British Yearbook of International Law 49 (1978), 329—437 (336).

Documentation

I. Article 29 of the Constitution and other Provisions of the Union of Soviet Socialist Republics*

Constitution
of the Union of Soviet Socialist Republics (Extract)

Chapter 4. Foreign policy

...

Article 29.

Relations of the USSR with other States shall be built on the basis of observing the principles of mutual renunciation of sovereign equality; mutual renunciation of the use or threat of force; inviolability of frontiers; territorial integrity of States; peaceful settlement of disputes; non-interference in internal affairs; respect for human rights and basic freedoms; equality and the right of peoples to decide their own destiny; co-operation between States; good-faith fulfilment of obligations arising from generally recognized principles and norms of international law, and from international treaties concluded by the USSR.

...

Law on the Council of Ministers of the USSR (Extract)

...

II. Competence of the USSR Council of Ministers

...

Article 15. Basic powers of the USSR Council of Ministers in foreign policy and international relations

The USSR Council of Ministers shall:

(1) exercise general direction in the domain of relations of the USSR with foreign states and international organizations, in the domain of foreign trade and other types of foreign economic activity on the basis of the State monopoly, and in the domain of scientific-technical and cultural co-operation of the USSR with foreign countries; ensure the implementation of measures for the expansion of international co-operation of the USSR and increasing the efficiency of foreign economic and scientific-technical links;

---

* *Adopted* with permission from: *William E. Butler* (comp., transl.), Collected Legislation of the Union of Soviet Socialist Republics and the Constituent Union Republics, Union of Soviet Socialist Republics, vol. 1, Constitution of the Union of Soviet Socialist Republics, (Oceana Publications, Inc.), Dobbs Ferry, New York 1985, 11; *op. cit.*, Law on the USSR Council of Ministers, 12, 13; *op. cit.*, Fundamental Principles of Civil Legislation of the USSR and Union Republics, 61, 62.

(2) organize and direct activity connected with the participation of the USSR in socialist economic integration and the international socialist division of labor; take measures toward ensuring the co-ordination of State plans of the USSR with State plans of member countries of the Council of Mutual Economic Assistance and to carry out production specialization and co-operation, and to work out and realize long-term special programs of co-operation with member countries of the Council of Mutual Economic Assistance;

(3) effectuate within the limits of its powers the representation of the USSR in foreign States, and also in international organizations;

(4) take measures to ensure the fulfilment of international treaties of the USSR; decide questions concerning the adoption of recommendations of the Council of Mutual Economic Assistance, and ensure the effectuation of recommendations adopted;

(5) confirm and denounce inter-governmental international treaties of the USSR.

. . .

Fundamental Principles of Civil Legislation of the USSR and Union Republics (Extract)

. . .

Section VIII. Legal capacity of foreign citizens and stateless persons; application of Civil Law of foreign States and international treaties

. . .

Article 129. International Treaties

If other rules have been established by an international treaty of the USSR than those which are contained in Soviet civil legislation, the rules of the international treaty shall be applied.

The same procedure shall apply with respect to the civil legislation of a Union Republic if other rules have been established in an international treaty of a Union Republic, containing other rules than those provided for by the civil legislation of this Union Republic.

II. Articles of the Basic Law of the Federal Republic of Germany*

Basic Law
of the Federal Republic of Germany (Extracts)

. . .

II. The Federation and the 'Länder'

. . .

Article 24. Entry into a collective security system

(1) The Federation may by legislation transfer sovereign powers to intergovernmental institutions.

(2) For the maintenance of peace, the Federation may enter a system of mutual collective security; in doing so it will consent to such limitations upon its rights of sovereignty as will bring about and secure a peaceful and lasting order in Europe and among the nations of the world.

(3) For the settlement of disputes between States, the Federation will accede to agreements concerning international arbitration of a general, comprehensive, and obligatory nature.

Article 25. International law as an integral part of Federal law

The general rules of public international law shall be an integral part of Federal law. They shall take precedence over the laws and shall directly create rights and duties for the inhabitants of the Federal territory.

. . .

Article 31. Priority of Federal law

Federal law shall override the law of the *Länder*.

Article 32. Foreign relations

(1) Relations with foreign States shall be conducted by the Federation.

(2) Before the conclusion of a treaty affecting the special circumstances of a *Land*, that *Land* must be consulted in sufficient time.

(3) In so far as the *Länder* have power to legislate, they may, with the consent of the Federal Government, conclude treaties with foreign States.

. . .

III. The Federal President

. . .

Article 59. Authority to represent the Federation in international relations

(1) The Federal President shall represent the Federation in its international relations. He shall conclude treaties with foreign States on behalf of the Federation. He shall accredit and receive envoys.

(2) Treaties which regulate the political relations of the Federation or relate to matters of Federal legislation shall require the consent or participation, in

---

* *Adopted* with permission from: *Albert P. Blaustein / Gisbert H. Flanz* (eds.), Constitutions of the World, vol. VI, Federal Republic of Germany, (Oceana Publications, Inc.), Dobbs Ferry, New York 1986, 50—52, 60, 67—70, 77, 78, 88.

the form of a Federal law, of the bodies competent in any specific case for such Federal legislation. As regards administrative agreements, the provisions concerning the Federal administration shall apply *mutatis mutandis.*

. . .

VII. The Legislation of the Federation

. . .

Article 77. Procedure concerning adopted bills—objection of the Bundesrat

(1) Bills intended to become Federal laws shall require adoption by the *Bundestag.* Upon their adoption they shall, without delay, be transmitted to the *Bundesrat* by the President of the *Bundestag.*

(2) The *Bundesrat* may, within three weeks of the receipt of the adopted bill, demand that a committee for joint consideration of bills, composed of members of the *Bundestag* and members of the *Bundesrat,* be convened. The composition and the procedure of this committee shall be regulated by rules of procedure to be adopted by the *Bundestag* and requiring the consent of the *Bundesrat.* The members of the *Bundesrat* on this committee shall not be bound by instructions. If the consent of the *Bundesrat* is required for a bill to become a law, the convening of this committee may also be demanded by the *Bundestag* or the Federal Government. Should the committee propose any amendment to the adopted bill, the *Bundestag* must again vote on the bill.

(3) In so far as the consent of the *Bundesrat* is not required for a bill to become a law, the *Bundesrat* may, when the proceedings under paragraph 2 of this Article are completed, enter an objection within two weeks against a bill adopted by the *Bundestag.* This period shall begin, in the case of the last sentence of paragraph 2 of this Article, on the receipt of the bill as readopted by the *Bundestag,* and in all other cases on the receipt of a communication from the chairman of the committee provided for in paragraph 2 of this Article, to the effect that the committee's proceedings have been concluded.

(4) If the objection was adopted with the majority of the votes of the *Bundesrat,* it can be rejected by a decision of the majority of the members of the *Bundestag.* If the *Bundesrat* adopted the objection with a majority of at least two thirds of its votes, its rejection by the *Bundestag* shall require a majority of two thirds, including at least the majority of the members of the *Bundestag.*

. . .

Article 79. Amendment of the Basic Law

(1) This Basic Law can be amended only by laws which expressly amend or supplement the text thereof. In respect of international treaties the subject of which is a peace settlement, the preparation of a peace settlement, or the abolition of an occupation regime, or which are designed to serve the defence of the Federal Republic, it shall be sufficient, for the purpose of clarifying that the provisions of this Basic Law do not preclude the conclusion and entry into force of such treaties, to effect a supplementation of the text of this Basic Law confined to such clarification.

(2) Any such law shall require the affirmative vote of two thirds of the members of the *Bundestag* and two thirds of the votes of the *Bundesrat.*

(3) Amendments of this Basic Law affecting the division of the Federation into *Länder*, the participation on principle of the *Länder* in legislation, or the basic principles laid down in Articles 1 and 20, shall be inadmissible.

Article 80. Issue of ordinances having force of law

(1) The Federal Government, a Federal Minister or the *Länder* governments may be authorized by a law to issue ordinances having the force of law (*Rechtsverordnungen*). The content, purpose, and scope of the authorization so conferred must be set forth in such law. This legal basis must be stated in the ordinance. If a law provides that such authorization may be delegated, such delegation shall require another ordinance having the force of law.

(2) The consent of the *Bundesrat* shall be required, unless otherwise provided by Federal legislation, for ordinances having the force of law issued by the Federal Government or a Federal Minister concerning basic rules for the use of facilities of the Federal railroads and of postal and telecommunication services, or charges therefore, or concerning the construction and operation of railroads, as well as for ordinances having the force of law issued pursuant to Federal laws that require the consent of the *Bundesrat* or that are executed by the *Länder* as agents of the Federation or as matters of their own concern.

. . .

VIII. The Execution of Federal Laws and the Federal Administration

Article 83. Execution of Federal laws by the Länder

The *Länder* shall execute Federal laws as matters of their own concern in so far as this Basic Law does not otherwise provide or permit.

Article 84. Administration of the Länder *and Federal Government supervision*

(1) Where the *Länder* execute Federal laws as matters of their own concern, they shall provide for the establishment of the requisite authorities and the regulation of administrative procedures in so far as Federal laws consented to by the *Bundesrat* do not otherwise provide.

(2) The Federal Government may, with the consent of the *Bundesrat*, issue pertinent general administrative rules.

(3) The Federal Government shall exercise supervision to ensure that the *Länder* execute the Federal laws in accordance with applicable law. For this purpose the Federal Government may send commissioners to the highest *Land* authorities and with their consent or, if such consent is refused, with the consent of the *Bundesrat*, also to subordinate authorities.

(4) Should any shortcomings which the Federal Government has found to exist in the execution of Federal laws in the *Länder* not be corrected, the *Bundesrat* shall decide, on the application of the Federal Government or the *Land* concerned, whether such *Land* has violated applicable law. The decision of the *Bundesrat* may be challenged in the *Bundesverfassungsgericht*.

(5) With a view to the execution of Federal laws, the Federal Government may be authorized by a Federal law requiring the consent of the *Bundesrat* to

issue individual instructions for particular cases. They shall be addressed to the highest *Land* authorities unless the Federal Government considers the matter urgent.

Article 85. Execution by the Länder *as agents of the Federation*

(1) Where the *Länder* execute Federal laws as agents of the Federation, the establishment of the requisite authorities shall remain the concern of the *Länder* except in so far as Federal laws consented to by the *Bundesrat* otherwise provide.

(2) The Federal Government may, with the consent of the *Bundesrat*, issue pertinent general administrative rules. It may regulate the uniform training of civil servants (*Beamte*) and other salaried public employees (*Angestellte*). The heads of authorities at the intermediate level shall be appointed with its agreement.

(3) The *Land* authorities shall be subject to the instructions of the appropriate highest Federal authorities. Such instructions shall be addressed to the highest *Land* authorities unless the Federal Government considers the matter urgent. Execution of the instructions shall be ensured by the highest *Land* authorities.

(4) Federal supervision shall extend to conformity with law and appropriateness of execution. The Federal Government may, for this purpose, require the submission of reports and documents and send commissioners to all authorities.

. . .

IX. The Administration of Justice

. . .

Article 100. Compatibility of statutory law with the Basic Law

(1) If a court considers unconstitutional a law the validity of which is relevant to its decision, the proceedings shall be stayed, and a decision shall be obtained from the *Land* court competent for constitutional disputes if the constitution of a *Land* is held to be violated, or from the *Bundesverfassungsgericht* if this Basic Law is held to be violated. This shall also apply if this Basic Law is held to be violated by *Land* law or if a *Land* law is held to be incompatible with a Federal law.

(2) If, in the course of litigation, doubt exists whether a rule of public international law is an integral part of Federal law and whether such rule directly creates rights and duties for the individual (Article 25), the court shall obtain a decision from the *Bundesverfassungsgericht*.

(3) If the constitutional court of a Land, in interpreting this Basic Law, intends to deviate from a decision of the *Bundesverfassungsgericht* or of the constitutional court of another *Land*, it must obtain a decision from the *Bundesverfassungsgericht*.

. . .

X a. State of Defence

. . .

Article 115 lit. l. Termination of state of defence; repealing of extraordinary laws; conclusion of peace

(1) The *Bundestag*, with the consent of the *Bundesrat*, may at any time repeal laws enacted by the Joint Committee. The *Bundesrat* may request the *Bundestag* to make a decision in any such matter. Any measures taken by the Joint Committee or the Federal Government to avert a danger shall be revoked if the *Bundestag* and the *Bundesrat* so decide.

(2) The *Bundestag*, with the consent of the *Bundesrat*, may at any time declare the state of defence terminated by a decision to be promulgated by the Federal President. The *Bundesrat* may request the *Bundestag* to make a decision in any such matter. The state of defence must be declared terminated without delay when the prerequisites for the determination thereof no longer exist.

(3) The conclusion of peace shall be the subject of a Federal law.

. . .

III. Provisions of the Council for Mutual Economic Assistance*

Charter of the Council for Mutual Economic Assistance (Extracts)

. . .

Article II
Membership

1. The initial members of the Council of Mutual Economic Assistance shall be the countries which have signed and ratified the present Charter.

2. Admission to membership in the Council shall be open to other countries which share the purposes and principles of the Council and have manifested their consent to assume the obligations contained in the present Charter.

New members shall be admitted by decision of a session of the Council on the basis of official requests of countries concerning their admission to membership in the Council.

3. Each member country of the Council may withdraw from the Council, having notified the depositary of the present Charter thereof. Such notification shall enter into force six months after its receipt by the depositary. Upon receiving such notification, the depositary shall inform the member countries of the Council thereof.

4. The member countries of the Council agree:

(a) to ensure fulfilment of the recommendations of organs of the Council adopted by them;

---

* *Reprinted* with permission from: *William E. Butler* (ed., transl.), A Source Book on Socialist International Organizations, (Sijthoff & Noordhoff), Alphen aan den Rijn, The Netherlands 1978, 125—127, 155, 187, 188.

(b) to render to the Council and its officials the neccessary assistance in the fulfilment of the functions provided by the present Charter;

(c) to grant to the Council the materials and information needed to carry out the tasks entrusted to it;

(d) to inform the Council about the fulfilment of the recommendations of the organs of the Council adopted by them.

. . .

Article IV

Recommendations and Decisions

1. Recommendations shall be adopted on questions of economic and scientific-technical co-operation. Recommendations shall be communicated to member countries of the Council for consideration.

The implementation by member countries of the Council of recommendations adopted by them shall be carried out by decisions of the governments or competent agencies of these countries in conformity with their legislation.

2. Decisions shall be adopted on organizational and procedural questions. Decisions shall enter into force unless provided otherwise in the decisions themselves or follows from the character of the decisions, from the date on which the protocol of the session of the respective Council organ is signed.

3. All recommendations and decisions of the Council shall be adopted only with the consent of the interested member countries of the Council, each country having the right to declare its interest in any question being considered in the Council.

Recommendations and decisions shall not extend to countries which have declared their non-interest in a particular question. However, each of these countries may subsequently accede to the recommendations and decisions adopted by the remaining member countries of the Council.

. . .

Rules of Procedure
for the Session of the Council for Mutual Economic Assistance (Extracts)

. . .

IX. Recommendations and Decisions

Rule 25

Recommendations shall be adopted by the session on questions of economic, scientific, and technical co-operation. Recommendations shall be communicated to member countries of the Council for consideration.

The implementation by countries of recommendations of the Session adopted by them shall be by decisions of governments or other competent agencies of those countries in accordance with their legislation.

Within 60 days of the date of signing the protocol of the session, a member country of the Council shall notify the Secretary of the Council of the results of the consideration of recommendations of the Session by the government or other competent agencies of the country. The Secretary of the Council shall notify the other member countries of the Council thereof without delay.

. . .

Statute on the Secretariat of the Council for Mutual Economic Assistance (Extract)

. . .

I. Functions and Powers

1. The Secretariat of the Council shall:

(a) prepare materials or assist in the preparation of materials for sessions of Council organs in accordance with the work plans of these organs relating to questions of economic, scientific, and technical co-operation and the development of socialist economic integration of Council member countries;

(b) draw up economic surveys and carry out economic research relating to materials of Council member countries; prepare and publish informational, reference, and other materials relating to questions of economic, scientific, and technical co-operation of Council member countries, and also prepare other surveys and research;

(c) prepare proposals on particular questions of Council work for their consideration in respective Council organs;

(d) organize the preparation and assist the holding of sessions of Council organs and meetings held within the framework of the Council.

For these purposes, the Secretariat of the Council shall:

prepare draft work plans of Council organs and draft agendas for sessions of these organs in accordance with their rules of procedure;

undertake necessary measures to ensure the timely preparation and distribution of materials to sessions of Council organs, as well as to meetings held within the framework of the Council;

ensure the fulfilment of the functions of secretariats of Council organs;

carry out other functions arising from the rules of procedure of Council organs;

(e) further the exchange of information and materials between Council member countries concerning economic agreements concluded between and with third countries;

(f) work out or further the working out of draft multilateral agreements relating to questions of economic, scientific, and technical co-operation in accordance with recommendations and decisions of Council organs;

(g) organize and keep a record of recommendations and decisions of Council organs, as well as a record of their fulfilment; summarize the information of Council member countries on the course of the fulfilment of recommendations of Council organs which they have adopted and prepare appropriate proposals for their consideration;

(h) exercise supervision over the timely fulfilment by Council organs of decisions of the Session of the Council and the Executive Committee of the Council; . . .

. . .

IV. Provisions of the European Communities

*Treaty Establishing the European Economic Community (Extracts)**

Part one. Principles

. . .

Article 2. The Community shall have as its task, by establishing a common market and progressively approximating the economic policies of Member States, to promote throughout the Community a harmonious development of economic activities, a continuous and balanced expansion, an increase in stability, an accelerated raising of the standard of living and closer relations between the States belonging to it.

. . .

Article 5. Member States shall take all appropriate measures, whether general or particular, to ensure fulfilment of the obligations arising out of this Treaty or resulting from action taken by the institutions of the Community. They shall facilitate the achievement of the Community's tasks.

They shall abstain from any measure which could jeopardise the attainment of the objectives of this Treaty.

Article 6. 1. Member States shall, in close co-operation with the institutions of the Community, co-ordinate their respective economic policies to the extent necessary to attain the objectives of this Treaty.

2. The institutions of the Community shall take care not to prejudice the internal and external financial stability of the Member States.

. . .

Article 8. 1. The common market shall be progressively established during a transitional period of twelve years.

This transitional period shall be divided into three stages of four years each; the length of each stage may be altered in accordance with the provisions set out below.

2. To each stage there shall be assigned a set of actions to be initiated and carried through concurrently.

3. Transition from the first to the second stage shall be conditional upon a finding that the objectives specifically laid down in this Treaty for the first stage have in fact been attained in substance and that, subject to the exceptions and procedures provided for in this Treaty, the obligations have been fulfilled.

This finding shall be made at the end of the fourth year by the Council, acting unanimously on a report from the Commission. A Member State may not, however, prevent unanimity by relying upon the non-fulfilment of its own obligations. Failing unanimity, the first stage shall automatically be extended for one year.

---

* As amended; *adopted* with permission from: *Bernard Rudden / Derrick Wyatt* (eds.), Basic Community Laws, (Clarendon Press), Oxford 1980, 20—99 (21—23, 31, 50, 51, 56, 57, 75—80, 92, 93, 95, 96).

At the end of the fifth year, the Council shall make its finding under the same conditions. Failing unanimity, the first stage shall automatically be extended for a further year.

At the end of the sixth year, the Council shall make its finding, acting by a qualified majority on a report from the Commission.

4. Within one month of the last-mentioned vote any Member State which voted with the minority or, if the required majority was not obtained, any Member State shall be entitled to call upon the Council to appoint an arbitration board whose decision shall be binding upon all Member States and upon the institutions of the Community. The arbitration board shall consist of three members appointed by the Council acting unanimously on a proposal from the Commission.

If the Council has not appointed the members of the arbitration board within one month of being called upon to do so, they shall be appointed by the Court of Justice within a further period of one month.

The arbitration board shall elect its own Chairman.

The board shall make its award within six months of the date of the Council vote referred to in the last subparagraph of paragraph 3.

5. The second and third stages may not be extended or curtailed except by a decision of the Council, acting unanimously on a proposal from the Commission.

6. Nothing in the preceding paragraphs shall cause the transitional period to last more than fifteen years after the entry into force of this Treaty.

7. Save for the exceptions or derogations provided for in this Treaty, the expiry of the transitional period shall constitute the latest date by which all the rules laid down must enter into force and all the measures required for establishing the common market must be implemented.

Article 8 A.* The Community shall adopt measures with the aim of progressively establishing the internal market over a period expiring on 31 December 1992, in accordance with the provisions of this Article and of Articles 8 D, 8 C, 28, 57 (2), 59, 70 (1), 83, 99, 100 A and 100 B and without prejudice to the other provisions of this Treaty.

The internal market shall comprise an area without internal frontiers in which the free movement of goods, persons, services and capital is ensured in accordance with the provisions of this Treaty.

Article 8 B.* The Commission shall report to the Council before 31 December 1988 and again before 31 December 1990 on the progress made towards achieving the internal market within the time limit fixed in Article 8 A.

The Council, acting by a qualified majority on a proposal from the Commission, shall determine the guidelines and conditions necessary to ensure balanced progress in all the sectors concerned.

Article 8 C.* When drawing up its proposals with a view to achieving the

* Amended by Articles 13—15 of the Single European Act, Final Act of the Conference of the Representatives of the European Communities' Member States, 17 and 28 February 1986; *reproduced* with permission from: International Legal Materials 25 (1986), 506—518 (510, 511).

objectives set out in Article 8 A, the Commission shall take into account the extent of the effort that certain economies showing differences in development will have to sustain during the period of establishment of the internal market and it may propose appropriate provisions.

If these provisions take the form of derogations, they must be of a temporary nature and must cause the least possible disturbance to the functioning of the common market.

. . .

Part two. Foundations of the Community

Title I. Free Movement of Goods

. . .

Chapter 2. Elimination of Quantitative Restrictions Between Member States

Article 30. Quantitative restrictions on imports and all measures having equivalent effect shall, without prejudice to the following provisions, be prohibited between Member States.

. . .

Part three. Policy of the Community

Title I. Common Rules

Chapter 1. Rules on Competition

Section 1. Rules Applying to Undertakings

Article 85. 1. The following shall be prohibited as incompatible with the common market: all agreements between undertakings, decisions by associations of undertakings and concerted practices which may affect trade between Member States and which have as their object or effect the prevention, restriction or distortion of competition within the common market, and in particular those which:

(a) directly or indirectly fix purchase or selling prices or any other trading conditions;

(b) limit or control production, markets, technical development, or investment;

(c) share markets or sources of supply;

(d) apply dissimilar conditions to equivalent transactions with other trading parties, thereby placing them at a competitive disadvantage;

(e) make the conclusion of contracts subject to acceptance by the other parties of supplementary obligations which, by their nature or according to commercial usage, have no connection with the subject of such contracts.

2. Any agreements or decisions prohibited pursuant to this Article shall be automatically void.

3. The provisions of paragraph 1 may, however, be declared inapplicable in the case of:

— any agreement or category of agreements between undertakings;
— any decision or category of decisions by associations of undertakings;
— any concerted practice or category of concerted practices;

which contributes to improving the production or distribution of goods or to promoting technical or economic progress, while allowing consumers a fair share of the resulting benefit, and which does not:

(a) impose on the undertakings concerned restrictions which are not indispensable to the attainment of these objectives;

(b) afford such undertakings the possibility of eliminating competition in respect of a substantial part of the products in question.

Article 86. Any abuse by one or more undertakings of a dominant position within the common market or in a substantial part of it shall be prohibited as incompatible with the common market in so far as it may affect trade between Member States. Such abuse may, in particular, consist in:

(a) directly or indirectly imposing unfair purchase or selling prices or unfair trading conditions;

(b) limiting production, markets or technical development to the prejudice of consumers;

(c) applying dissimilar conditions to equivalent transactions with other trading parties, thereby placing them at a competitive disadvantage;

(d) making the conclusion of contracts subject to acceptance by the other parties of supplementary obligations which, by their nature or according to commercial usage, have no connection with the subject of such contracts.

. . .

Chapter 3. Approximation of Laws

Article 100. The Council shall, acting unanimously on a proposal from the Commission, issue directives for the approximation of such provisions laid down by law, regulation or administrative action in Member States as directly affect the establishment or functioning of the common market.

The Assembly and the Economic and Social Committee shall be consulted in the case of directives whose implementation would, in one or more Member States, involve the amendment of legislation.

. . .

Title II. Economic Policy

Chapter 1. Conjunctural Policy

Article 103. 1. Member States shall regard their conjunctural policies as a matter of common concern. They shall consult each other and the Commission on the measures to be taken in the light of the prevailing circumstances.

2. Without prejudice to any other procedures provided for in this Treaty, the Council may, acting unanimously on a proposal from the Commission, decide upon the measures appropriate to the situation.

3. Acting by a qualified majority on a proposal from the Commission, the Council shall, where required, issue any directives needed to give effect to the measures decided upon under paragraph 2.

4. The procedures provided for in this Article shall also apply if any difficulty should arise in the supply of certain products.

. . .

Part five. Institutions of the Community

Title I. Provisions Governing the Institutions

Chapter 1. The Institutions

. . .

Section 4. The Court of Justice

Article 164. The Court of Justice shall ensure that in the interpretation and application of this Treaty the law is observed.

. . .

Article 169. If the Commission considers that a Member State has failed to fulfil an obligation under this Treaty, it shall deliver a reasoned opinion on the matter after giving the State concerned the opportunity to submit its observations.

If the State concerned does not comply with the opinion within the period laid down by the Commission the latter may bring the matter before the Court of Justice.

. . .

Article 171. If the Court of Justice finds that a Member State has failed to fulfil an obligation under this Treaty, the State shall be required to take the necessary measures to comply with the judgment of the Court of Justice.

Article 172. Regulations made by the Council pursuant to the provisions of this Treaty may give the Court of Justice unlimited jurisdiction in regard to the penalties provided for in such regulations.

. . .

Article 173. The Court of Justice shall review the legality of acts of the Council and the Commission other than recommendations or opinions. It shall for this purpose have jurisdiction in actions brought by a Member State, the Council or the Commission on grounds of lack of competence, infringement of an essential procedural requirement, infringement of this Treaty or of any rule of law relating to its application, or misuse of powers.

Any natural or legal person may, under the same conditions, institute proceedings against a decision addressed to that person or against a decision which, although in the form of a regulation or a decision addressed to another person, is of direct and individual concern to the former.

The proceedings provided for in this Article shall be instituted within two months of the publication of the measure, or of its notification to the plaintiff, or, in the absence thereof, of the day on which it came to the knowledge of the latter, as the case may be.

. . .

Article 177. The Court of Justice shall have jurisdiction to give preliminary rulings concerning:

(a) the interpretation of this Treaty;

(b) the validity and interpretation of acts of the institutions of the Community;

(c) the interpretation of the statutes of bodies established by an act of the Council, where those statutes so provide.

Where such a question is raised before any court or tribunal of a Member State, that court or tribunal may, if it considers that a decision on the question is necessary to enable it to give judgment, request the Court of Justice to give a ruling thereon.

Where any such question is raised in a case pending before a court or tribunal of a Member State, against whose decisions there is no judicial remedy under national law, that court or tribunal shall bring the matter before the Court of Justice.

. . .

Chapter 2. Provisions Common to Several Institutions

. . .

Article 189.* In order to carry out their task the Council and the Commission shall, in accordance with the provisions of this Treaty, make regulations, issue directives, take decisions, make recommendations or deliver opinions.

A regulation shall have general application. It shall be binding in its entirety and directly applicable in all Member States.

A directive shall be binding, as to the result to be achieved, upon each Member State to which it is addressed, but shall leave to the national authorities the choice of form and methods.

A decision shall be binding in its entirety upon those to whom it is addressed.

Recommendations and opinions shall have no binding force.

. . .

Article 192. Decisions of the Council or of the Commission which impose a pecuniary obligation on persons other than States shall be enforceable.

Enforcement shall be governed by the rules of civil procedure in force in the State in the territory of which it is carried out. The order for its enforcement shall be appended to the decision, without other formality than verification of the authenticity of the decision, by the national authority which the Government of each Member State shall designate for this purpose and shall make known to the Commission and to the Court of Justice.

When these formalities have been completed on application by the party concerned, the latter may proceed to enforcement in accordance with the national law, by bringing the matter directly before the competent authority.

Enforcement may be suspended only by a decision of the Court of Justice. However, the courts of the country concerned shall have jurisdiction over complaints that enforcement is being carried out in an irregular manner.

. . .

Part six. General and Final Provisions

. . .

Article 220. Member States shall, so far as is necessary, enter into negotiations with each other with a view to securing for the benefit of their nationals:

* Article 161 of the Euratom Treaty is equivalent with this Article.

— the protection of persons and the enjoyment and protection of rights under the same conditions as those accorded by each State to its own nationals;

— the abolition of double taxation within the Community;

— the mutual recognition of companies or firms within the meaning of the second paragraph of Art. 58, the retention of legal personality in the event of transfer of their seat from one country to another, and the possibility of mergers between companies or firms governed by the laws of different countries;

— the simplification of formalities governing the reciprocal recognition and enforcement of judgments of courts or tribunals and of arbitration awards.

. . .

Article 228. 1. Where this Treaty provides for the conclusion of agreements between the Community and one or more States or an international organisation, such agreements shall be negotiated by the Commission. Subject to the powers vested in the Commission in this field, such agreements shall be concluded by the Council, after consulting the Assembly where required by this Treaty.

The Council, the Commission or a Member State may obtain beforehand the opinion of the Court of Justice as to whether an agreement envisaged is compatible with the provisions of this Treaty. Where the opinion of the Court of Justice is adverse, the agreement may enter into force only in accordance with Art. 236.

2. Agreements concluded under these conditions shall be binding on the institutions of the Community and on Member States.

. . .

Article 235. If action by the Community should prove necessary to attain, in the course of the operation of the common-market, one of the objectives of the Community and this Treaty has not provided the necessary powers, the Council shall, acting unanimously on a proposal from the Commission and after consulting the Assembly, take the appropriate measures.

. . .

*Single European Act (Extract)**

. . .

Title III

Provisions on European Co-operation in the Sphere of Foreign Policy

Article 30. European Co-operation in the sphere of foreign policy shall be governed by the following provisions:

1. The High Contracting Parties, being members of the European Communities, shall endeavour jointly to formulate and implement a European foreign policy.

* Final Act of the Conference of the Representatives of the European Communities' Member States, 17 and 28 February 1986; *reproduced* with permission from: International Legal Materials 25 (1986), 506—518 (517, 518).

2. (a) The High Contracting Parties undertake to inform and consult each other on any foreign policy matters of general interest so as to ensure that their combined influence is exercised as effectively as possible through co-ordination, the convergence of their positions and the implementation of joint action.

(b) Consulations shall take place before the High Contracting Parties decide on their final position.

(c) In adopting its positions and in its national measures each High Contracting Party shall take full account of the positions of the other partners and shall give due consideration to the desirability of adopting and implementing common European positions.

In order to increase their capacity for joint action in the foreign policy field, the High Contracting Parties shall ensure that common principles and objectives are gradually developed and defined.

The determination of common positions shall constitute a point of reference for the policies of the High Contracting Parties.

(d) The High Contracting Parties shall endeavour to avoid any action or position which impairs their effectiveness as a cohesive force in international relations or within international organizations.

3. (a) The Ministers for Foreign Affairs and a member of the Commission shall meet at least four times a year within the framework of European Political Co-operation. They may also discuss foreign policy matters within the framework of Political Co-operation on the occasion of meetings of the Council of the European Communities.

(b) The Commission shall be fully associated with the proceedings of Political Co-operation.

(c) In order to ensure the swift adoption of common positions and the implementation of joint action, the High Contracting Parties shall, as far as possible, refrain from impeding the formation of a consensus and the joint action which this could produce.

4. The High Contracting Parties shall ensure that the European Parliament is closely associated with European Political Co-operation. To that end the Presidency shall regularly inform the European Parliament of the foreign policy issues which are being examined within the framework of Political Co-operation and shall ensure that the views of the European Parliament are duly taken into consideration.

5. The external policies of the European Community and the policies agreed in European Political Co-operation must be consistent.

The Presidency and the Commission, each within its own sphere of competence, shall have special responsibility for ensuring that such consistency is sought and maintained.

6. (a) The High Contracting Parties consider that closer co-operation on questions of European security would contribute in an essential way to the development of a European identity in external policy matters. They are ready to co-ordinate their positions more closely on the political and economic aspects of security.

(b) The High Contracting Parties are determined to maintain the techno- logical and industrial conditions necessary for their security. They shall work to that end both at national level and, where appropriate, within the framework of the competent institutions and bodies.

(c) Nothing in this Title shall impede closer co-operation in the field of security between certain of the High Contracting Parties within the framework of the Western European Union or the Atlantic Alliance.

7. (a) In international institutions and at international conferences which they attend, the High Contracting Parties shall endeavour to adopt common positions on the subjects covered by this Title.

(b) In international institutions and at international conferences in which not all the High Contracting Parties participate, those who do participate shall take full account of positions agreed in European Political Co-operation.

8. The High Contracting Parties shall organize a political dialogue with third countries and regional groupings whenever they deem it necessary.

9. The High Contracting Parties and the Commission, through mutual assist- ance and information, shall intensify co-operation between their representatives accredited to third countries and to international organizations.

10. (a) The Presidency of European Political Co-operation shall be held by the High Contracting Party which holds the Presidency of the Council of the European Communities.

(b) The Presidency shall be responsible for initiating action and co-ordinating and representing the positions of the Member States in relations with third countries in respect of European Political Co-operation activities. It shall also be responsible for the management of Political Co-operation and in particular for drawing up the timetable of meetings and for convening and organizing meetings.

(c) The Political Directors shall meet regularly in the Political Committee in order to give the necessary impetus, maintain the continuity of European Political Co-operation and prepare Ministers' discussions.

(d) The Political Committee or, if necessary, a ministerial meeting shall convene within forty-eight hours at the request of at least three Member States.

(e) The European Correspondents' Group shall be responsible, under the direction of the Political Committee, for monitoring the implementation of European Political Co-operation and for studying general organizational pro- blems.

(f) Working groups shall meet as directed by the Political Committee.

(g) A Secretariat based in Brussels shall assist the Presidency in preparing and implementing the activities of European Political Co-operation and in administrative matters. It shall carry out its duties under the authority of the Presidency.

11. As regards privileges and immunities, the members of the European Political Co-operation Secretariat shall be treated in the same way as members

of the diplomatic missions of the High Contracting Parties based in the same place as the Secretariat.

12. Five years after the entry into force of this Act the High Contracting Parties shall examine whether any revision of Title III is required.

List of Participants

Bernhardt, Rudolf — Prof. Dr., Director at the Max-Planck-Institute of Foreign Public Law and International Law, Berliner Str. 48, 6900 Heidelberg 1

Bothe, Michael — Prof. Dr., Institute of Public Law, Faculty of Law, Johann-Wolfgang-Goethe-University, Senckenberganlage 31, 6000 Frankfurt / a. M. 1

Danilenko, Gennady M. — Dr., Senior Researcher, Institute of State and Law of the Academy of Sciences, 10, ul. Frunze, 119841 Moscow

Delbrück, Jost — Prof. Dr., LL.M. (Indiana), Rector of the Christian-Albrechts-University and Director at the Institute of International Law at the University of Kiel, Olshausenstr. 40/60, 2300 Kiel 1

Hilf, Meinhard — Prof. Dr., Chair of Public, European and Public International Law, Faculty of Law, University of Bielefeld, Postfach 8640, 4800 Bielefeld 1

Klein, Eckart — Prof. Dr., Faculty of Law and Economics, Johannes-Gutenberg-University Mainz, Postfach 3980, 6500 Mainz

Korbut, Ludmila V. — Mrs., Scientific Secretary of the Soviet Association of International Law, 10, ul. Frunze, 119841 Moscow

Kunig, Philip — Prof. Dr., Faculty of Law, University of Heidelberg, Friedrich-Ebert-Anlage 6—10, 6900 Heidelberg 1

Lukashuk, Igor I. — Prof. Dr., Leading Researcher at the Institute of State and Law of the Academy of Sciences, 10, ul. Frunze, 119841, Moscow

Mosler, Hermann — Prof. Dr. Dr. h.c., Former Judge of the International Court of Justice, Mühltalstr. 117 a, 6900 Heidelberg

Oppermann, Thomas	Prof. Dr. Dr. h.c., Faculty of Law, Eberhard-Karls-University Tübingen, Wilhelmstr. 5, 7400 Tübingen
Randelzhofer, Albrecht	Prof. Dr., Institute of International and Foreign Law and Comparative Law, Free University of Berlin, Van't-Hoff-Str. 8, 1000 Berlin (West) 33
Rudolf, Walter	Prof. Dr., Under-Secretary of State of the Ministry of Justice of the Land Rheinland-Pfalz, Mainz, and Faculty of Law and Economics, Johannes-Gutenberg-University Mainz, Postfach 3980, 6500 Mainz
Schweisfurth, Theodor	Prof. Dr., Max-Planck-Institute of Foreign Public Law and International Law, Berliner Str. 48, 6900 Heidelberg
Shinkaretskaya, Galina G.	Mrs., Senior Researcher, Institute of State and Law of the Academy of Sciences, 10, ul. Frunze, 119841 Moscow
Simma, Bruno	Prof. Dr., Institute of International Public Law of the Ludwig-Maximilians-University München, Professor-Huber-Platz 2, 8000 München 22
Starushenko, Gleb B.	Prof. Dr., Deputy Director, Institute for Africa of the Academy of Sciences, 30/1 Alexey Tolstoy Str., Moscow, K-1, 103001
Tunkin, Grigory I.	Prof. Dr. Dr. h. c., Chair of International Law, Faculty of Law, Moscow State University, Corresponding Member of the Academy of Sciences, President, Soviet Association of International Law, 10, ul. Frunze, 119841 Moscow
Usenko, Eugeny T.	Prof. Dr., Chief of Division, Institute of State and Law of the Academy of Sciences, 10, ul. Frunze, 119841 Moscow
Wolfrum, Rüdiger	Prof. Dr., Director at the Institute of International Law at the University of Kiel, Olshausenstr. 40/60, 2300 Kiel 1

MIX
Papier aus verantwortungsvollen Quellen
Paper from responsible sources
FSC® C105338

Printed by Libri Plureos GmbH
in Hamburg, Germany